Siam Mapped

Siam Mapped

A History of the
Geo-Body of a Nation

Thongchai Winichakul

University of Hawaii Press / Honolulu

94 95 96 97 98 99 5 4 3 2 1

Library of Congress Cataloging-in-Publication Data
Thongchai Winichakul.
Siam mapped: a history of the geo-body of a nation / Thongchai
Winichakul.
p.   cm.
Includes bibliographical references and index.
ISBN 0–8248–1337–5
1.   Thailand—Historical geography.
DS563.9.T47   1994
911.593—dc20   93–34494
CIP

Design by Kenneth Miyamoto

Contents

Illustrations

Preface

IN THIS LAST DECADE of the twentieth century the world, pushed by the European Community, is moving toward a new kind of community. Multinational corporations, not a single government, increasingly predominate; markets and production are becoming global; the monetary system and the flow of information and capital know no boundary. Asia, the Pacific world, and America are trying to catch up with the European move. The world seems to be preparing to go beyond the legacy of nineteenth-century Europe: nations and nationalism will sooner or later be obsolete. At the same time, however, the collapse of the socialist bloc has unleashed the power of nationalism—indeed a rather old ethnic nationalism, which has proved more powerful than Marx or Lenin would have thought. New "old" nations are emerging again. Nationhood is strongly desired even as it becomes obsolete.

This book originated in such a context. A nation touches everyone's life. It has a government, an economy, a social and cultural condition, all of which affect individuals. Indeed, nationhood has a powerful grip that can hold together a community whose members may never know each other. So powerful is it that lives can be sacrificed for it. It has inspired generations to strive for innovative and constructive achievements. In fact, nationhood is desired even among the radicals in many countries who may be no less loyal to their country than their adversaries.

Yet the destructive effect of nationalism has been enormous. Indeed, its destructiveness makes us more aware of the arbitrariness and artificiality of a nation. At this conjuncture in which economic transnationalism and political nationalism coexist, the study of nationalism and nationhood can take a new direction. We are no longer overwhelmed by its pervasiveness and its pretentions. Such a consciousness has created a distance in the relationship between individuals and their nation, for we can now examine nationhood from a vantage point which is supposedly beyond the world of nationhood. A nation can be viewed from afar as a cultural construct of a particular historical context, a construct which embodies both virtue and evil. Such a position is not real, yet it is not unreal; it is a discourse, a possibility of enunciating in a new way, a possibility created as we are approaching the end of the twentieth century.

Taking Siam, the former name of Thailand, as its case, this book examines how nationhood has been arbitrarily and artificially created by a very well known science—namely, geography and its prime technology of knowing, mapping—through various moments of confrontation and displacement of discourses. Even the most concrete identification of a nation, such as its territory, and its related values and practices, all of which I term the "geo-body," was discursively created. The introduction addresses the issue of the significance of nationhood in an unusual way: by questioning the identity of the Thai nation through the eyes of one of its own nationals, a supposedly "inside" view instead of an Orientalist one, as Edward Said might call it. It sets up main questions and aims of the study with its basic concept and methods.

Chapter 1 then explores several indigenous conceptions of space, both the cosmographic or religious notions and the profane or worldly ones. It establishes that premodern societies never lacked the knowledge and technology to conceive space. Chapter 2 lays out the modality in which the transition of geographical knowledge could take place. By studying the early Siamese textbooks on geography, this chapter looks at the displacement of knowledge through a semiological operation. Then a great moment of transition is explained in similar terms.

Chapters 3, 4, and 5 study the displacement of the geographical knowledge in three major conceptual and practical arenas: boundary, territorial sovereignty, and margin. In these arenas, modern geography pushed out the indigenous conceptions and asserted itself as a new legitimate "true" knowledge in different ways involving diverse issues on every frontier of Siam. In all cases, the semio-political operations were never simply intellectual or academic. The displacements always took place in diplomatic and political practices, in wars and interstate relations, even in papers of correspondence as well as on the earth's surface. Chapter 6 describes how mapping has played a decisive role in the creation of a new kind of Siam. Operating in tandem with military force, mapping both anticipated and executed what Siam should be. The geo-body of a nation emerged.

Chapters 7 and 8 discuss how the discourse of the geo-body has shaped knowledge of Siam in a particular way that serves its own existence. Focusing on history, the discussion shows how the new geo-body has shaped the way the past of Siam is viewed and known. In fact, the moment of the emergence of the geo-body itself has played a key role in the creation of a new plot of Thai history which has dominated Thai historical consciousness throughout the twentieth century and will certainly do so for years to come.

The hegemony of modern geography, mapping, and the geo-body of a nation is far stronger than perhaps we are prepared to realize. It reproduces itself to subsume us under its regime. This is true not only of the Thai people; it extends to many other cases in this mapped world.

Thai Language Conventions

THIS BOOK adheres to the phonetic transcription for most Thai words, but without tonal marks. This practice follows the "General System of Phonetic Transcription of Thai Characters into Roman" devised by the Royal Institute, Bangkok, in 1954. Moreover, because of the constraints of typesetting, the superscript and subscript marks of certain vowels and consonants are not shown.

Exceptions are those names which have been transcribed by various other systems or perhaps no system at all. In the case of a name which is widely known or which can be checked, the owner's transcription has been adhered to. Otherwise, the spelling follows the system of romanization mentioned above. The English names of certain Thai kings, princes, and nobles, as they are known among historians (Mongkut, Chulalongkorn, Vajiravudh) have been adopted rather than the official lengthy titles. Likewise I refer to Damrong, Phichit, Prachak, Wachirayan, Thiphakorawong, and so on rather than their full titles and names. In most cases, however, their ranks such as Prince, Phraya, Chao Phraya, and their longer titles are given in the first reference to each.

Finally, as in conventional usage, Thai people are referred to by their first names while Westerners are referred to by their surnames. In the bibliography, Thai names are entered according to first names.

Acknowledgments

THE EFFORT undertaken here is inspired by, and dedicated to, the friends who lost their lives, who were physically and mentally injured, and the thousands whose lives have been affected by the massacre on Wednesday morning of 6 October 1976 at Thammasat University in Bangkok. This effort is of little value compared to their sacrifice.

Throughout the years in Sydney, my learning process, from improving my poor English to the study of new ideas and the adventure into this research, was under the guidance and care of my great teacher, Craig J. Reynolds. Undoubtedly, he is one of the best: a teacher who not only masters the field and embraces new theoretical concepts in humanities and social science, but also dedicates himself to developing every one of his students. Without him, this book would never have been written.

Special gratitude goes to Charnvit Kasetsiri, Kanchanee La-ongsri, Supaporn Jaranpat-Shigetomi, and Chaiwat Satha-anan, my teachers and colleagues at Thammasat University who, in different ways, helped me through the turbulent college years and into the academic world. The comments and encouragement of Ben Anderson of Cornell University have been especially significant: though we have met only a few times, his inspiration, directly and otherwise, has been vital for me in recent years. The comments of David Chandler of Monash University and Anthony Day of Sydney University have been valuable as well.

I would like to thank Sujit Wongdes and Singkom Borisutdhi for their help in obtaining good illustrations of the Tamnan Map and the Coastal Map. Grateful acknowledgment is given to the magazine *Sinlapawatthanatham* [Art and Culture] for permission to reprint figures 2 and 4 from its resource; to the National Library, Bangkok, for permission to reprint figure 3; to the Royal Survey Department, Ministry of Defense, Thailand, for permission to reprint figure 5; to the British Library for permission and duplication of figures 9 and 10, and to Andrew Turton who worked with the library until the duplication was finished. I am also grateful to Thaiwatthanaphanit Co. for permission to reprint figures 13–19 from the geographical atlas it publishes. My special thanks to Conrad Taylor for permission to reprint figure 20. Thanks also to Pamela Kelley of the University of Hawaii Press who worked hard on this manuscript and kept pushing me to finish it despite so many problems on my part. I wish I could mention all the people who are part of this book in many ways. Their encouragement, their care, and their assistance will always be remembered.

Finally, although I do not like to follow convention, I must admit that without the care, hard work, and sacrifice of my wife, Somrudee, I might not have been able to finish this book.

I do not know whether or not this book will contribute in some way to making this a better world. My hope is humble: that someday all the irrational rationality will be exposed so that people may become more tolerant and considerate.

Introduction
The Presence of Nationhood

AFTER DENMARK DEFEATED Scotland in the first round of the World Cup soccer tournament in 1986, it was reported that 97 percent of Denmark's population of five million had tuned in to the telecast of the match. A TV announcer commented on the remaining 3 percent: "Only the Swedes and the traitors must not have been watching."[1] The humor of this comment is revealing. It is a comic reference to the significance of nationhood in modern times. Yet its tragic aspects are countless. As the world approaches the twenty-first century, we witness the breakup of socialist Eastern Europe into serious ethnic and nationalist conflicts among the would-be states. Indeed, all over the planet there is conflict among people who identify themselves as part of a particular nation against another. The comment about the audience of the soccer match makes sense because the international competition evident in the statement implies the wider context of hostilities, rivalries, and antagonism among nations in other spheres. The comment was intelligible because it played with the normative perception of the nature of a nation and its relations to modern individuals.

The Two-Way Identification of Nationhood

On the one hand, it is generally supposed that a nation is a collective body to which individuals must belong. It is further presumed that a nation is an entity whose atoms or parts—its nationals—possess a similar nature. A nation has essential traits commonly imbued in its members, who, moreover, have the same national interest. Patriotism, loyalty, and other affiliations in terms of ideas, sentiments, and practices appear to be natural relationships. On the other hand, it is always supposed that a nation exists in the global community of nations. That is to say, there are other nations who have other

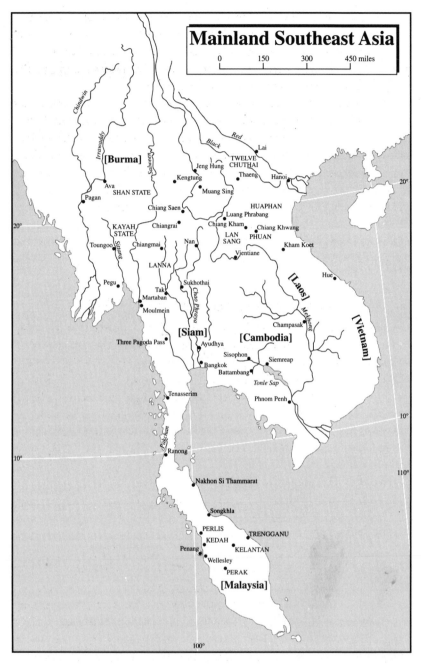

Mainland Southeast Asia before Modern Boundaries

essences and interests dissimilar to ours, competing with us, or even antagonistic to us. The discourse of a modern nation usually presupposes this two-way identification: positively by some common nature, identity, or interests; negatively by the differences with other nations. Our modern civilization is to a great extent based on these identities and differences.

How does the identity of a nation and its opposition to others—that is, the two-way identification of a nation—come about? Or how is it made? How can modern human beings talk, know, or act in relation to the nation? Indeed, how has the knowledge of a nation been constructed in our civilization? The answer to these questions should not be framed as just another study about the rise of a nation-state or nation building. Rather, this will be a study of the discourse of nationhood. This study concerns the case of what has been known as Siam or Thailand. But its significance goes far beyond the case study. It applies to many other modern nations which have appeared on the globe during the last two centuries.

The Positive and Negative Identification of Thainess

In Thailand today there is a widespread assumption that there is such a thing as a common Thai nature or identity: *khwampenthai* (Thainess). It is believed to have existed for a long time, and all Thai are supposed to be well aware of its virtue. The essence of Thainess has been well preserved up to the present time despite the fact that Siam has been transformed greatly toward modernization in the past hundred years. Like other nationalist discourse, it presumes that the great leaders (in this case monarchs) selectively adopted only good things from the West for the country while preserving the traditional values at their best. Although a skeptic might doubt the validity of such a view, the notion prevails even among scholars.

One of the most quoted illustrations of this selective modernization based on Thainess was the reaffirmation of Buddhism as the state religion vis-à-vis the adoption of Western science and technology throughout the period of modernization. Another famous proof was the instruction by certain prominent Siamese kings regarding the extent to which Western knowledge should be adopted: it must be based on its suitability to Siam, they argued, not on the models or standards of its origins. But it is hard to determine exactly what constituted the needs, appropriateness, goodness, usefulness, or right things. The "right" things have never been clearly defined; indeed, it would be impossible to do so. Thus various interpretations of Thainess are advanced from time to time. This has been happening since the last century.

What was not "good"? King Chulalongkorn (r. 1868–1910) declared in

1885 that the concepts of political party and parliamentary system were not appropriate to the Siamese political tradition.[2] On another occasion he even suggested that the Chinese attempt to form a political party in Siam was contrary to the interest of Siam and must be opposed whenever possible.[3] King Vajiravudh (r. 1910–1925) banned the first text on economics in Thai because it was not suitable to Thai society. Apart from the monarch, he argued, Thai people were all equal under him. Thus economics might cause disunity or disruption because it concerns social strata of rich and poor. Instead, he proposed his own economic philosophy based on a Buddhist precept that one should be satisfied with what one has. Not only was economics forbidden to be written about, but in 1927 legislation against the teaching of economics was passed.[4]

Exactly which things should be preserved is vague because the definition of Thainess has been discursively defined and claimed by the authorities of diverse ideological camps. It is well known among scholars of Thailand that the monarchical institution and Buddhism are the most important elements of the nation. King Vajiravudh proposed that the monarchy was most important to nationhood. Prince Damrong Rajanubhap (hereafter Damrong), a great historian and administrator, once suggested that the three moral pillars of Thai people were the love of national independence, tolerance, and compromise or assimilation.[5] The Phibun government during World War II (1938–1945) initiated many ambitious attempts to civilize Thai culture.[6] Many commissions were established to stipulate what Thai culture should be and to supervise its dissemination. A number of detailed practices—from private affairs to public ones, from domestic matters to social ones—were prescribed for people to follow.[7] Ironically, traditional clothing and the traditional practice of chewing the betel nut were prohibited, while trousers, skirts, and kissing before going out to work in the morning were prescribed. Some of these new elements of Thai culture did not survive beyond the life of the government, but others have continued to the present day.

There are many other views about Thainess, and the definitions never end. Thailand is a nation, though not the only one, which concerns itself with the preservation and promotion of the national culture as if it might suddenly disappear. Therefore a government body has always existed for this purpose, though its name and its tasks vary from time to time. One of the present entities is the Commission for National Identity, which has had to define Thainess in order to clarify its tasks for planning, coordination, and consultation on the security of the institutions of the nation, religion, and monarchy. The commission has concluded that the nation is composed of eight elements: territory, population, independence and sovereignty, government and administration, religion, monarchy, culture, and dignity. The commission, however, has expressed its concern that, "as we shall see, the meaning of the term 'national identity' is quite broad, covering all aspects of the nation to the extent that it may cause some confusion and unclear understanding. Even the eight elements as defined are not agreed upon by everyone" (in the commission).[8] In fact, in a small booklet of twenty-six pages, *Ekkalak khong chat* (National Identity), three eminent persons have given various interpretations of the elements of Thai identity. The elements are not in contradiction to each other. Indeed, they all count, and readers are expected to accept all of them.[9] The number of traits and institutions regarded as Thai seems unlimited. Redundancy is necessary and useful.

Although Thainess is never clearly defined, it is supposed that every Thai knows it is there. One of the most prominent statesmen and scholars in modern Thailand, Kukrit Pramoj, confessed that he was not quite sure what identity means. Yet he was confident that it was imbued in him: "The identity belonging to the people of a nation . . . is ascribed to oneself at birth. Thainess for the most part arises together with Thai people. Being a Thai means having such and such feelings, having a certain character. No one can change these things."[10] If the domain of what is Thainess is hard to define clearly, the domain of what is not Thai—that is, un-Thai—is identified from time to time. Simultaneously, this identification helps us to define the domain of Thainess from the outside. As Edmund Leach has pointed out in the case of Upper Burma, ethnic peoples define themselves in terms of the differences among ethnic groups, rather than in accordance with a set of shared characteristics of a tribe which is merely a sociological fiction.[11] This is what I call "negative identification."

Quite often, reference to otherness is made by identifying it as belonging to another nation. But the referent nation or ethnicity is usually ill defined. In Thai, for example, *farang* is a well-known adjective and noun referring to Western people without any specification of nationality, culture, ethnicity, language, or whatever. *Khaek* is another term which covers the peoples and countries of the Malay peninsula, the East Indies, South Asia, and the Middle East without any distinction. *Khaek* also denotes Muslim, but by no means exclusively so. That is to say, a reference is sometimes made regardless of whether or not a certain characteristic really belongs to any particular nation or ethnic group, because the aim of the discourse is to identify the un-Thainess rather than to define the characteristic of any particular people. Once the un-Thainess can be identified, its opposite, Thainess, is apparent.

Examples of negative identification are not hard to find in everyday life. In a conversation between the Thai ambassador in Canberra and Thai students in mid-February 1987 about Asian people in Australia, the ambassador instructed the students "not to behave like the Vietnamese." It is not clear whether he meant the Vietnamese in Australia, the communist Vietnamese in Vietnam, or both. Probably he did not care what his term specifically referred to. In this case, the term "Vietnam" represented a sort of otherness or un-Thainess one should avoid, regardless of whether or not the Vietnamese actually behave in such a way.

Un-Thainess is sometimes not a matter of nation or ethnicity. A reporter said that he once teased a Thai about being a communist, but the Thai did not find the remark funny and quickly replied: "I am not a communist. I am a Thai."[12] This is how the Thai state officially views communism as well. In a nutshell, the rationality of the anticommunist act (1952), whose model was the un-American activities legislation, was that communism is un-Thai in its ideas and as a way of life.[13] Twenty or thirty years ago, during the Cold War, a poster about the threat of communism was widely distributed to all primary schools. In the picture, a tiny map of Thailand stood under the threat of a huge red demon originating from the mass of the Asian mainland to the north. Here communism and other nations were combined as a demonic otherness. (A similar but more recent poster will be discussed extensively later in the book.)

The radical movement during 1973–1976 was from time to time accused of collaborating with the enemy. The enemy in this case seemed to be communism plus other nations. Student leaders were alleged to be Vietnamese descendants, since Vietnam after 1975 had become a symbol of the worst otherness in the official Thai view. In the massacre of students on 6 October 1976, when thousands of demonstrators were attacked by police and right-wing paramilitary groups, some were lynched because the wild mob had been indoctrinated to think that the victims were Vietnamese. Vietnam, communism, and radicals in this context function in a similar way to the Swedes and traitors for the TV announcer. The existence of otherness, un-Thainess, is as necessary as the positive definition of Thainess. Perhaps we can say that the former is indispensable to the latter.

Thai Studies

Despite the unclear identification or constitution of Thainess, the notion is obvious enough in the minds of Thai people. It is a "thing" on earth, and in history, which possesses particular features, all of which are distinct from others. For many Thai scholars, a study of the thing is what Thai people profoundly know better than anyone else.

Thai people, scholars or not, have always been warned not to *tamkon farang* ("tag along behind the Westerners"). For them, Thainess, Thailand, Thai people, Thai studies, or whatever Thai, is something the *farang* can approach but never reach with the utmost intimacy that Thai people can. This Thainess is what Thai people belong to and are part of. In another sense, it is what belongs to them and is a common part of their lives. The sense of identity as a part of each other enables Thai scholars to presume a privileged status in the field of Thai studies because "Thai" is not just an area of study but an intrinsic part of them. By contrast, *farang* scholars have to overcome an enormous distance between the writing self and the subject written about.

Sometimes the distance is explicitly and concretely measured, even along Thailand's borders. A leading political scientist on foreign policy once took issue with foreign scholars on the Cambodian question, saying that those foreign scholars were remote from what was happening in Cambodia and along the borders, unlike Thai (people? scholars? soldiers?) who directly experience the effects. Therefore, he said, "I am sorry for the fact that some [Thai scholars] are convinced by the reasons given by those foreigners who look at the problem more superficially than Thai."[14]

Edward Said has argued that the discourses on the countries and peoples outside Europe, particularly "the Oriental," have been a part of the European's power relations that constitute the presence of "the Other" in order to confirm the identification and, more often than not, the superiority of the European metropolis itself, rather than being the documentation of what "the Oriental" actually is.[15] Nonetheless, the awareness of Eurocentrism and its prejudice against others has been common among Western scholars for quite some time. As a correction, apology, or cure for what the Orientalists had done before, this guilty conscience has pushed Western scholars in the opposite direction—that is, to recognize indigenous perspective. A recent study on Southeast Asia declares that the work was done with "styles of research which do less injustice to the peoples with whom . . . we work."[16] But this opposite direction sometimes goes too far. Unlike the cases of other colonial countries, the fact that there was no struggle between colonial and anticolonial scholarship in Thai studies has sometimes led to uncritical intellectual cooperation by pro-indigenous Western scholars who have tended to accept the established views of the Siamese elite as *the* legitimate discourse about Thailand.[17] If the intellectual enterprise is constituted by power relations as Said suggests, in this context being indigenous becomes a privilege, at least for many indigenous scholars.

While Orientalism has been inscribed basically as the Other of Western civilization, the Thai of Thai people is the field of "We" or one's own self.

The spoken, studied, or imagined reality is not a "counter-part" but a self, a social and collective one. For this reason, a national community and its numerous aspects—nationalism, patriotism, identity, culture, history, image, worldview, and so on—are not merely the objects of scientific study. They are aspects, physically and spiritually, of We-self for studies as well as for empathy, loyalty, partiality, and obsession.

In the guise of scientific method and academic format (especially footnotes, quotations, and bibliography), studies of Thai by Thai people have been located deep within the paradigmatic discourse of We-self. This provides them with certain viewpoints, sentiments, and values as well as constraints, taboos, alibis, and plausibility. The field of We-self also has its own political economy and its own questions dissimilar to the field of Thai study by foreigners. Thailand as seen and studied by Thai academics may not be the same as that of non-Thai academics.[18] As part of the discourse of We-self, a study seems to attain a natural authority and becomes the inside view on what is good or bad for Thai, what is Thai or not. One famous subject which claims this inside view as an incomparable advantage is the ethnographic study of ideas or worldview. As one study claims:

> [This book] would . . . try to achieve some of the benefits of the new trend derived from the emic or "inside view" approach to ethnography by looking at the Thai world view through the eyes of Thais. Though many writers in this volume studied in the West, one expects that they are basically Thai in their thinking and behavior. The writings in this volume then should reflect the cognition and perception of Thai and not Western people.[19]

The notion of "Thai"—worldview, people, eyes, thinking, behavior, cognition, and perception—in this statement seems to be homogeneous and demands no further clarification because it is embodied in the writing subjects, or authors. This kind of research has become abundant recently, mostly carried out by centers of ethnographic studies in each region and by historians. Consequently, we have worldviews of northern, northeastern, and southern Thai and worldviews of Thai people in the Sukhothai, Ayudhya, and the early Bangkok periods.[20] The methodology is virtually the same— that is, the cataloging of source materials according to the researchers' predetermined notion of what constitutes a Thai worldview. The writers then paraphrase from their sources—folk tales, songs, proverbs, games—and offer the results as an analysis of Thai worldviews.[21] None of them ever questions whether the results are Thai worldviews or the outcome of the writers' taxonomies which are specified at the beginning of each research as a methodology. Probably it is assumed that both are the same thing. Again the source of the Thai worldview is a writing subject. The materials are merely the substantiation of the Thai-worldview subject. This criticism is not a rejection of the particularity of a society. But the discourse of We-self is not only an exaggeration of such particularity—hence an overemphasis of the significance of familiarity—but also a claim by certain people and texts to have privilege, rights, or power over the field of Thai studies or Thainess because of their ascriptive relationship, or having been *insiders.* An indigenous view is a good antidote to the power relations of the Orientalist discourse. But the discourse of Thainess has its own sphere of power relations as well. In the context of global power relations, it may represent the periphery's resistance to the metropolis. But in the context of power relations within Thai society, it is a claim to legitimacy of, more often than not, the official or hegemonic discourse operating in its own particular cosmos over the subordinated or marginal ones. As has been the case in the postcolonial era, an anti-Western discourse may belong to an oppressor, not the oppressed, to reaffirm its grip over its own sphere of power. Since the definition of Thainess has never been (and never will be) clear, therefore, the domain of what is Thainess and the power relations arising from it constitute an arena over which different interpretations from various positions struggle to gain hegemony.

Struggles for Interpretation

Since the late 1970s, the network of army-owned radio stations, which comprises two-thirds of the radio stations in Thailand, has broadcast two programs daily at 6:45 A.M. and 6:00 P.M. to call for order and unity and to stimulate nationalism and the awareness of national security amid the communist threats from within and without. Its topics range from political commentary on social issues, including attacks on the civilian and elected governments from time to time, to letters and obituaries. But the themes are clear: what is right and wrong for Thai people, how they should behave, and how to think on every issue. It attempts to impose social and intellectual discipline, an overt brainwashing program which penetrates into every house and every bus two times a day. Quite often the legitimation given to such a standard view is no more than "according to Thai . . . [culture, values, tradition, history]."[22] Positively, the commentaries often quote history, the king's speeches, and the words of the incumbent army commander as authority for particular aspects of Thainess. Negatively, they usually refer to what is happening in other countries, especially in Indochina, as examples of evil, degradation, and the values Thai must avoid. To speak more precisely, the evil and degradation are often alleged to be whatever is happening in those countries: the Other. Apart from mobilizing popular support behind the army, the broadcast is clearly part of the official industry to produce a standard of Thainess.[23]

While these attempts at standardization aim for inarguable interpretations of Thainess, there are other contending interpretations. In all cases, however, they challenge the official view only in order to propose yet another standard of Thainess. To dissolve the notion of Thainess altogether is perhaps unthinkable. Even the Communist Party of Thailand (CPT), the most radical opposition to the Thai establishment in recent history, achieved its successful ideological propagation in the late 1970s partly because of its strong nationalist sentiment, which was on the threshold of anti-Westernism. An obvious sign of this tendency was the somewhat puritanical character of its cultural programs calling for traditional, populist culture while attacking the influx of decadent Western culture and the hypocrisy of the state, which could not prevent the deterioration of Thai culture. A student leader who joined the party in the jungle and finally departed from it once remarked that, "considering traditional values, the Communist Party inherits the Thai legacy more than observers recognize."[24] So far, Thai critics of the CPT have been silent on this point. But is it because they have not recognized this conservative characteristic of the CPT or is it an identical tendency commonly held by those critics as well?

Another contending interpretation of Thainess which is more recent and still influential is an intellectual tendency that attracts many people by its conservative radicalism. Basically it attacks the failure of modern Thai society in the light of Buddhist Thai tradition, arguing that modernity, capitalism, and consumerism have uprooted Thai people from the fundamentals of Thai civilization—hence the degradation of modern culture and the deterioration of morality and Buddhism in Thai society as a whole. In turn, it calls for a return to Thainess, the roots or fundamental values of Thai civilization, and the reassertion of Thai intellect, all of which are based on Buddhism.[25] These people also oppose militarism and the establishment, since militarism is responsible for the degradation of Thai society and is in no way comparable to the monarchical leadership of the past.[26]

Some people of this current persuasion, moreover, propagate the idea that Thainess is deeply rooted in the ways of life and the intellect of the people, particularly the peasantry. Thainess and Thai intellect in this view are located in the countryside and originate from the opposite end of the elitist pole.[27] Like the elitist Thainess, however, its opposition is Western culture. A book of poetry by a prime propagator of this view claims:

[These verses] go beyond the preponderance of the ways of thinking which follow Western philosophy. . . . [This] leads to the perception of rural villages and development projects in a lively and realistic fashion. . . . [The verses are written by] an artist and thinker who uses Thai intellect to challenge the Western one . . . in an age when many artists are losing their Thai identity and are moving toward new identities that are pouring in from other lands.[28]

For the military, despite the constant threat from the left, Thainess is in good health. For the Buddhist radicals, it is in crisis because of the preponderance of Western culture; therefore, it must be urgently restored as the only alternative for the future.[29] As one Buddhist radical observed: "The present generation of Thai people has departed from Thainess, feeling alienated and losing pride in their own nation, because the elites of Thai society in the past hundred years, preoccupied with tagging along behind the *farang*, did not use their intellect in the quest for our identity."[30] Ironically, the concern about the deterioration of morals is shared by another recently influential Buddhist movement: the Thammakai (Dhammakaya), which is supported by some members of the royal family and military leaders and which the Buddhist radicals detest. This movement expresses its distrust of Western knowledge and culture and their effects on Buddhism.[31] This concern is not shared, however, by a well-known anticommunist monk, Kittiwuttho. He agrees that commercial greed and higher education have caused the decline of morals and spiritual faith in Western countries, but he is confident that in Thailand, where Buddhism is the guiding light, technology and science will further the Buddhist faith.[32]

The point is not which interpretation should be regarded as the correct and legitimate meaning of Thainess. Rather, while the alleged ascriptive and natural intimacy is believed to provide Thai people with familiarity or intuitive knowledge about Thainess, it does not guarantee an unambiguous notion of it. Nor are the struggles over this issue among Thai people less violent, oppressive, and hegemonic than the Orientalists' desire to inscribe the Oriental. Charges of communism, subversion, rebellion, and lèse-majesté are not uncommon.

These examples also point to the fact that no matter which interpretation becomes hegemonic, or what eclecticism is produced, the reign of Thainess would be unchanged. Although the interpretations sharply disagree with each other in many ways, they share a similar concern about Buddhism and the threat of Western culture to Thainess. Despite their political diversity, all struggling forces claim their legitimacy by adherence to Thainess. It is a paradigm of political ideas which no one dares to violate. If one is accused of violating this fundamental, one loses credibility and authority. This was a strategy the right wing used to counter the rise of the leftist movement in Thailand during 1973–1976, and it was partly the cause for the collapse of the CPT. Having learned firsthand that the CPT had slavishly followed Chinese models for the Thai revolution, and had even been under the direct influence of the CCP, the young radicals who joined it after 1976 became disillusioned.[33] To these young students, the authority of the CPT and the power of its discourse on class struggles and Thai society had virtually disappeared because of its foreign elements.

But Thainess, or Thai nationhood, which Thai people perceive as "Weself," the source, reference, and justification of legitimacy, criteria, standards, sentiments, inspiration, and antagonism, has never been seriously questioned. Where and how did it come into existence? Is it really natural for Thai people to claim an ascriptive relationship with it? If not, how then is Thainess made?

Siam as a Cultural Construct

Fundamentally, history is a prime database of what may be regarded as Thainess. Most interpretations of Thainess proudly claim to find support for their views in history. In this sense, history also becomes an authority of what is, and is not, Thainess. There is hardly any interpretation of Thainess which does not use history to authorize its validity. It can be said that the *oeuvre* of historical studies is the backbone of the scholastic and scientific discourse on Thai nationhood. For this reason, if anything is to be done for Thai studies, particularly by Thai people, it should not be another text to be incorporated in the existing *oeuvre*. It should, on the contrary, be a challenge: a counterhistory.

A conventional historical study about Thailand always presupposes the definite presence of a political or socioeconomic "thing," a kingdom or a state since time immemorial. Only by doing so can a historian talk about polity, economy, culture, or the development and transformation of the thing. The thing is given; the study only reaffirms it. This study, however, is a history of how Thai nationhood was created. It will examine an episode which is much celebrated by conventional historians as one which confirms the excellence of Thainess—namely, the making of the modern Siamese nation. But instead of discussing the process of nation building, it will show that Siam was a discursive construct. The Thai monarchs were merely the instrument of the new discourse. And Thainess was nothing but a construct of humble origin.

As with other nations outside Europe, history regards Siam's struggles against European imperialism in the nineteenth century as the advent of the modern nation. Unlike others, however, Siam was never formally colonized —a distinctive phenomenon Thai people are always proud of. Therefore, Siam has been regarded as a traditional state which transformed itself into a modern nation, thanks to the intelligence of the monarchs who responded wisely and timely to the threats of the European powers by modernizing the country in the right direction at the right time. Thus continuity, homogeneity, and the persistence of traditions, especially Thai Buddhism and Thai monarchy, have been the distinct characteristics, or even the unique features, of modern Siam. Despite some challenges, this established view of Thai history has occupied a firm place in Thai society, among scholars on Thailand, as well as among the circles of young radicals today.[34] Of course, it lends authority to militarism as well.

In Thailand, the established view was questioned by the Thai Marxist historiography of the 1950s and 1970s.[35] A number of alternative histories have been proposed, particularly in terms of class struggle and socioeconomic change. The advent of modern Siam in this view was the result of its entry into the global market, symbolically marked by the formal treaty with Britain in 1855. The direct counterargument about the role of the monarchy in building the nation-state emerged, as well, represented by the proposition that the actual start of the nation-state was not before the end of the absolute monarchy in 1932 and that Siam from the late nineteenth century to the first three decades of the twentieth century was an absolutist state.[36]

Alongside the domestic discourse on the Thai state, Western scholars raised similar questions. Siam is regarded as an indirect colonial country, both economically and politically, from the mid-nineteenth century through several dictatorial regimes after World War II.[37] The nation building and the role of the monarchy in the late nineteenth century were also critically questioned as anything but the beginning of a nation-state. Central to this argument is the fact that the Thai state has been unable to achieve modern national political integration of minorities of all sorts—ethnic, religious, or ideological—with the majority of Buddhist Thai under monarchical rule.[38] In the discourse of Western scholars, the notion of the "thing" known as the modern Thai nation has been recently defined in a heterogeneous way.[39]

These challenges attempt to counter the exaggerated credit given to the ability of the monarchs and the adaptability of traditional institutions. Instead, they contemplate the impersonal forces in history and even attempt to separate the seemingly nationalist monarchs from the birth of the present nation, emphasizing the inability of the Thai state, especially under the monarchical regimes, to become a true nation-state. This socioeconomic approach, however, must presuppose an archetype or a number of criteria constituting the notion of a nation-state and then compare Siam, a given socioeconomic entity, to that model. The task is to determine whether Siam was or was not a nation-state or to discover the nature of the state by applying the qualifications stipulated by scholars.

An orthodox king-and-battle history assumes a static old-fashioned definition of the Thai nation-state and applies it to the past. An alternative history proposes dynamism and process but only according to certain scholastic criteria found outside the history it describes. Indeed, scholars have tried throughout the history of the European nation-states to determine the true and natural constitution of a nation, that is, the truth or the identity of it. The entire history of a nation presumes the existence of such an entity or presupposes a definite qualification of it, as if its identity were already given.

This difficulty is not exclusive to the modern history of Southeast Asian nations. One of the major questions yet haunting the historians of early Southeast Asia concerns the formation of states. To be more specific, how one can talk about a state's formation without taking for granted what a state is—the criteria usually prescribed by social scientists, not by the early Southeast Asian peoples themselves. Thus historians sometimes doubt that the state qualifies as a state at all.[40]

Moving beyond the nation, Donald Emmerson has shown that even the identity of the thing called Southeast Asia had not been known as such before World War II. Colonial rulers identified the region in terms of dominions of various imperial powers. It was warfare, not scholarship, particularly the Japanese occupation, that abolished the colonial distinctions. In addition, "making wars means making maps." The National Geographic Society produced a map of Southeast Asia; the Allies established the Southeast Asia Command. After the war, consequently, the term "Southeast Asia" became known even though its definition has been a controversial issue.[41] Even as the former Soviet Union and Yugoslavia become separate nations called Russia, Lithuania, Latvia, Ukraine, Croatia, Bosnia, Serbia, and so on, who can say for sure whether Burma and Sri Lanka deserve to be unified nations or the separate states of Myanmar, Mon, Karen, Shan, Sri Lanka, Tamil Nadu, and others? What has been believed to be a nation's essence, a justifiable identity, could suddenly turn out to be fabrication.

Instead of searching for the true identity of a nation, Ben Anderson takes a nation as an imagined community.[42] A nation is not a given reality. Rather, it is the effect of imagining about it. Compared to the religious dominion and the dynastic realm, a nation is conceived as a new era, a new kind of community whose spatial parameters and temporal homogeneity have been formulated in various ways. This identification is possible only through mediation by certain means such as language. As a prime technology of imagining nationhood, a language works a nation out in different manners—for example, by a spoken vernacular, the written language, the printing press, a court's language, a state mechanism like education, or the unified language of a colonial rule. In short, a language enables a certain group of people to think of their community in an unprecedented, spatiotemporal definition. Nationhood is an imagined sphere with no given identity or essence; it is a cultural construct. We can know about it as long as we employ certain technologies to inscribe the possible sphere. In turn, such technologies create the knowledge of it, create a fact of it, and the entity comes into existence.

Anderson's pioneering work does open up a wide range of possible studies on nationhood. Yet it begs more critical questions as well. First of all, the languages mediating the imagined communities in Anderson's study are at the level known as parole to structural linguists—that is, the spoken, operational language of normal conversation. A language in a broader sense is any kind of mediator between human individuals and the external world. What are the other kinds of mediators—technologies, other kinds of languages, apart from a vernacular—and how do they operate in mediating and creating the imagined communities?

Second, Anderson seems too concerned with the imagination, the conceivability of a nation. It sounds as if a nation is produced out of one's head and is sustained only as long as the reproduction remains in one's head—hence an imagined community. One may still wonder how such a mediator formulates the social institutions and practices which perpetuate the operation and reproduction of the imagined community in actual human relations. The primacy given to consciousness over the operation in human practices is always prone to idealism. Hence the new imagined community seems to be created out of the frictionless propagation of new ideas—like inscribing a new language on a blank sheet of paper. If a nation is not the first or the only kind of imagined community, and if a new mediator does not operate in a vacuum, then a meeting, contention, combination, or conjuncture between the old and new mediators must have occurred.

Third, the identification of Anderson's imagined community is a positive one. His linguistic mediation creates a sphere of identity, configuring and defining the spatiotemporal axes of a field of commonness. Yet to figure out a sphere of commonness is to identify the difference between that sphere and the one beyond. An imagined identity always implies the absence of such an identity at the point beyond its boundary. In fact, ethnographers are familiar with how problematic an ethnic identification is. Basically, an ethnic identification is a dynamic mechanism defining or demarcating the sphere of "us" against "them." In many cases, the idea of who we are is possible only by identifying those characteristics which do not belong to us, rather than by considering positively any natural qualification of "us." Moreover, the differentiation is cultural, not based on any natural quality, and can be changed.[43] This is a truth for the identification of nationhood as well.

This book is not another study of nation building, state formation, or the origin of a nation. It is not a political or economic history of the transition from a premodern empire to a modern nation-state. It is a history of *identification* of nationhood: what constitutes the presence of Thai nationhood and how has an identity of it been created?

Subject and Method

Nationhood comprises many elements. Anderson's work emphasizes that the new temporal consciousness helps to formulate the sense of a new community in historical lineage (as distinct from previous imagined communities) and the sense of homogeneous time of the new community. This study will focus on another element of nationhood: the geo-body. It describes the operations of the technology of territoriality which created nationhood spatially. It emphasizes the displacement of spatial knowledge which has in effect produced social institutions and practices that created nationhood.

The choice was not made for any theoretical or historical reason. Rather, to challenge the metaphysical notion of Thainess or We-self, we should deal with the most concrete, seemingly natural, and stable feature of a nation in order to illustrate how even the most "natural" element constituting the presence of a nation has been culturally constructed by a certain kind of knowledge and technology. Yet this is done with full recognition that around the same time, the "revolution in time" was under way and not unrelated.[44]

A nation's territory is not simply a sizable piece of the earth's surface. It is a territoriality. According to a geography theorist, "Territoriality [is] the attempt by an individual or group to affect, influence or control people, phenomena, and relationships, by delimiting and asserting control over geographic area. . . . [It] is not an instinct or drive, but a rather complex strategy, . . . [and] the device through which people construct and maintain spatial organizations."[45] Territoriality involves three basic human behaviors: a form of classification by area, a form of communication by boundary, and an attempt at enforcing. Above all, as the basic geographic expression of influence and power, "territoriality is always socially or humanly constructed. . . . [B]ecause it is a product of social context, whatever is said about it . . . can have normative implications affixed to it and can lead back to a social context."[46] Likewise, the geo-body of a nation is a man-made territorial definition which creates effects—by classifying, communicating, and enforcement—on people, things, and relationships.

Geographically speaking, the geo-body of a nation occupies a certain portion of the earth's surface which is objectively identifiable. It appears to be concrete to the eyes as if its existence does not depend on any act of imagining. That, of course, is not the case. The geo-body of a nation is merely an effect of modern geographical discourse whose prime technology is a map. To a considerable extent, the knowledge about the Siamese nationhood has been created by our conception of Siam-on-the-map, emerging from maps and existing nowhere apart from the map.

The term "geo-body" is mine. But the definition of the term is neither strict nor conclusive. Readers will find that it is flexible enough to convey meanings concerning the territoriality of a nation. We all know how important the territoriality of a nation is. Unarguably it is the most concrete feature, the most solid foundation, literally and connotatively, of nationhood as a whole. There are innumerable concepts, practices, and institutions related to it or working within the provision and limitation of a nation's geo-body: the concept of integrity and sovereignty; border control, armed conflict, invasions, and wars; the territorial definition of national economy, products, industries, trade, tax, custom duties, education, administration, culture, and so on. But the term geo-body is used to signify that the object of this study is not merely space or territory. It is a component of the life of a nation. It is a source of pride, loyalty, love, passion, bias, hatred, reason, unreason. It also generates many other conceptions and practices about nationhood as it combines with other elements of nationhood.

Despite its concreteness, or perhaps because of it, there have been few studies on the history of a national territory. Most of them concern disputes over territories and boundary demarcations. Such studies always presuppose the existence of the territoriality of a nation in modern form. Accordingly, they merely legitimate or refute a claim and therefore merely entail a political history in a politico-technical sense. Only in the works by Edmund Leach on Burma have the effects of the arbitrariness and recent origin of boundaries been seriously considered.[47] Leach, however, merely exposes the limitations or inapplicability of a modern boundary to ethnic entities. He does not consider its positive role as a creator of a nationhood.

The lack of interest in the history of a nation's geo-body has led to many misleading historical interpretations which assume a modern concept of space in explaining the incidents in which the premodern discourse still prevailed. No study has been done on the relationships—either the transformation or shift or confrontation—between the premodern geographical discourse and the modern one. The absence of definite boundaries of the premodern realm of Siam is not taken seriously, as if it were due to some practical or technical reason.[48] Many historians have demarcated the boundary of a premodern nation retrospectively. Innumerable texts include anachronistic maps of historical space. In this respect, this study is not simply a record of how mapping has been implemented and boundaries settled by treaty. Rather, it emphasizes how the new geographical discourse displaced the indigenous one, generating conflict, confrontation, and misunderstanding. Central to the whole study is the question of how a map created the geo-body of a modern nation.

Geography is regarded here as a kind of mediator. It is not a given object "out there." It is a kind of knowledge, a conceptual abstraction of a supposedly objective reality, a systematic set of signs, a discourse. The strategy of this study is to analyze the premodern and modern discourses and then to detect the moments when the new and the old discourses collided. Those moments were in fact the politico-semiological operations in which the new discourse threatened and displaced the existing one. They occurred whenever the notions of geography, boundary, territorial sovereignty, and margin were in conflict. Those moments could appear in every sort of social activity: diplomatic relations, scientific observations, correspondences, travels, textbooks, warfare, and, of course, surveys and mapmaking. They could take place anywhere from the palace's study room to the jungle on a remote border. Those moments of collision can be determined by locating the events in which ambiguous meanings about space were signified, since the confronting discourses were playing upon the same field of terminology and practices. The relations between mapping and military force are emphasized here as the mutual operation of knowledge and power in executing the truth of geographical knowledge.

My use of the terms Siam, Siamese, Thailand, and Thai throughout the book follows a simple criterion: Siam and Siamese are used for the country and its people before the change of the country's name in 1941; Thailand and Thai are used for the post-1941 context. This is done with full acknowledgment of the controversy surrounding the name: changing the name of the country and its people was the political act of a chauvinist regime to promote the domination of the ethnic Thai and their culture over others. But even though the racial prejudice expressed in the name's etymology and in reality is far from dissolved, it is no longer the dominant signification of the term. Application of the term Thai is now wider than its limited racial denotation. For example, *khwampenthai* (Thainess) as discussed in this introductory chapter is not meant to denote characteristics of the ethnic Thai exclusively but of the country's nationals as a whole. On the other hand, the usage of the term Siam is more limited. Again, no one uses the term *khwampensayam* (Siamness) to signify the supposed common characteristics of all citizens of the nation. The new nomenclature has not been changed since its inception. But its application and its reference, the country and people, have changed. So the complications surrounding the issue will be left aside in this study.

Another term which is very misleading is "modern"—a vague and relative term which hardly signifies any specific historical character. Indeed, except as a proper noun, such as Modernism in the arts, it can mean too many things, depending on the noun after it and on the context. The modern period of Southeast Asia, for example, is not the same as that of Europe or that of the arts. In the context of the history of Siam, this adjective generally means westernized as opposed to traditional. But I wonder if the westernized Siam of the late nineteenth century is still considered modern. Its vagueness renders other terms in relation to it—such as "traditional," "premodern," and so on—ambiguous. In most situations, each of these terms is intelligible only in reference to the others.

Moreover, the term "modern" usually implies a state of advancement, betterment, progress, even goodness or virtue. That is to say, it claims superiority over its counterpart, the premodern and traditional. This claim, of course, is not necessarily true. Unfortunately, because of its relativity and vagueness, the term is flexible and encompassing and therefore applicable to any occasion. As a result, it is very useful in this respect.

Chapter One
Indigenous Space and Ancient Maps

MOST STUDIES ON premodern Thai ideas of space tend to focus on the Buddhist cosmography known as the Traiphum cosmography. The Traiphum, literally meaning three worlds, was an important doctrinal tradition within Theravada Buddhism. In Thai the best-known text of this tradition is *Traiphum Phra Ruang*.[1] It is believed to be a major treatise of the Sukhothai kingdom, a major Thai state in the upper Chao Phraya valley in the thirteenth century, though the actual date of the text is still in doubt.[2] The significance of this cosmography is evident. Even in the late eighteenth century, two prominent monarchs, King Taksin and Rama I of Bangkok, in order to restore the kingdom after the old one was destroyed by Burma in 1767, supervised the reconstruction of the Traiphum texts as one of their major tasks. The outcome was not the recopying of *Traiphum Phra Ruang;* rather, the new texts were constructed within, and added to, the same tradition. It is misleading, however, to assume that the Traiphum was the only indigenous spatial conception before the advent of modern geography.[3]

Sacred Topographies

In the Traiphum cosmography, beings are classified by their merit and designated to live in particular places according to their store of merit. The most evil beings are in the lowest section of hell; the more merit one makes, the higher the level where one resides. The store of merit can be accumulated or diminished by one's deeds and account for one's next birth. By this logic, one's present existence is the outcome of the previous one. Overall the thirty-one levels in the three worlds formed a qualitative classification of existence in which the human level was simply one. Space in the Traiphum was the

20

qualitative manifestation of imagined existence. Yet all of the surviving Traiphum texts give concrete descriptions of various worlds, particularly the human one, as well as accounts of the movements of the sun and moon and the seasonal changes.

While *Traiphum Phra Ruang* and other texts of the same genre are primarily about beings at each level of the three worlds and the truth of nirvana, with only a chapter or two about the cosmos, the planetary movements, and the figuration of the world, certain important texts in this genre such as *Lokkabanyat* and *Chakkawanthipani* are archetypes of cosmographic doctrines.[4] In *Chakkawanthipani,* regarded as the best of this cosmographical description, for example, the content focuses directly on the configuration of the earth and the cosmos: definitions of the earth and the cosmos; the size and detail of each part (mountains, great seas, and the like); the four continents of the human world; stories of the thirty-six cities and twenty-one country areas; descriptions of the world of deities and the underworld.[5] For the human world, there are four great continents in the four cardinal directions of the earth's central mountain, Mount Meru, and seven rings of oceans and mountains between the four continents and Mount Meru. Apart from the southern continent, Chomphuthawip, the other three continents are little known, or known only symbolically. Chomphuthawip is the land where the Buddha was born and all the known countries are located. Although the description of this world is given in numerical details, which in most cases are identical, varied depictions of the human world appear in different texts. The world can be imagined in various forms.

The studies of this Theravada Buddhist cosmography and its shift to the modern one in the late nineteenth century are well known to historians of Thailand.[6] It is not clear, however, what the relationship was between this cosmography and other geographical ideas. In fact, an interest in other ideas of space is rare. Reducing the varieties of indigenous conceptions of space to the Traiphum framework alone misleads us in two ways. On the one hand, the human world of the Traiphum cosmography is treated as if it were the native's view of the planet earth, a distorted or primitive one, contaminated by false belief or lack of knowledge.[7] It is doubtful, however, whether the symbolic representation—the maps of the Traiphum world—was in fact designed to represent the planet earth. The fact that the depictions of the earth are varied (for example, a square flat earth or a round one) does not indicate the development of local knowledge of the earth or the lack of it. More probably, it suggests that the materiality of the human world can be imagined in more than one way, whereas the spiritual meaning of the three worlds must be obeyed. The spiritual dimension is the "reality" of the

Traiphum space, and the most important knowledge needed to be transmitted correctly.

On the other hand, the indigenous conception of material space is ignored as if it were virtually nonexistent. Under the domination of the Traiphum cosmography, there were other indigenous conceptions of space, including the concept of the profane, material earth. The classic study of Robert Heine-Geldern on the relation of the microcosms to the macrocosms is the first to be considered. Studying the architectural forms of Southeast Asian palaces and religious buildings, he showed that the sovereign realm of a king, its center, and his sacred residential space were believed to be the microcosms. Palaces and religious buildings had to be designed according to the cosmographic order. Within the Buddhist, Hindu, or Islamic traditions alike, the architectural space was a kind of spatial arrangement metaphorically related to the cosmographies.[8] Yet the two kinds of space were not identical. The architectural space had its own set of rules, traditions, and patterns of change. In fact, the sacred space of the center is a subject well known to historians and anthropologists of Southeast Asian studies.[9]

Frank E. Reynolds once toured four temples in contemporary Thailand and discovered a journey into what he called a Buddhological space. He classified the Theravada Buddhist ideas into three strands: the Nipphanic philosophy, the Traiphum cosmology, and the Buddhological stories such as the life of the Buddha, the Jataka, the stories of relics, prophecies, and so forth. The three strands of ideas are interdependent, yet they are basically different approaches of Buddhism. They even interweave with local beliefs or other Indic ones. The mural paintings at the temples he visited tell the stories of the Buddha's life in connection with the locales of such temples.[10] The particular locality of the temples and the universal land of the Buddha in these paintings are tied together, apparently becoming a Buddhological geography which does not necessarily correspond to the terrestrial earth we know. The painting is similar to an indigenous genre of legend, known as Tamnan in Thai or Thamaing in Burmese, which connects the place and time of the Buddha to each locality. Like the Traiphum worlds, the truth-value of this Buddhological geography does not lie in the accuracy of its description of the earth's surface, but in its representation of spiritual reality transmitted through the story. Unlike the Traiphum depiction, however, the space it concerns is not the three-world cosmography but the religious space of Buddhology. The units of this space are conceivable in relation to local Buddhist stories, and the paintings are another kind of spatial representation.

Another kind of religious space is the topography of pilgrimage and fate. Charles Keyes has marked out the twelve shrines sacred to the people of

Lanna, now the northern provinces of Thailand. Each is believed to have power over each year in the twelve-year cycle; hence one's fate is under the power of the shrine of one's birth year, hence a duty to pay respect to one's shrine. Keyes pointed out that the twelve-year cycle was an archaic, pre-Indic cosmic order in the region which was later converted to a Buddhological one. So the twelve Buddhist shrines took over the places of local deities. All of them are believed to be related to the Buddha's life in one way or another, although some are of rather recent age. The shrine locations may change but the number must be twelve.[11] Moreover, the twelve sacred places together form a cosmic topography in which people make pilgrimages to worship, either to make merit or to secure a good fate. Remarkably, this topography covers parts of today's Burma, Laos, and northern Thailand and connects them to the origin in India. One of the shrines is in Dawadung (or Tavatimsa), a level of heaven, and a proxy temple has to be assigned for people's worship. Not only does the shrine network extend across national boundaries, but it also extends beyond the human world. It encompasses the imaginative space of heaven and Chomphuthawip, as well as the actual terrestrial space of Lanna, Burma, Laos, and India where the pilgrims make their visits. A map of pilgrimage, however, is nothing like a modern map of places and distances on the earth's surface. It is more like a memoir of travels in diagram form, showing places with connections of some kind (see Figure 1).[12]

The geography of pilgrimage was not the only pre-Indic cosmic order which provided a framework for conceptualizing space. H. L. Shorto and David Chandler have studied the spatial order of the realms of the Mon and Cambodian kingdoms which were conceived and arranged by pre-Indic cosmographies. They were not imaginative space like the Traiphum order, however, but the spatial organization of the terrestrial earth, a "territoriality" in Robert Sack's word. The Mon kingdom, an ancient realm along the southern coast of Burma today, was always divided into thirty-two *myo* (townships), not including the capital. No matter if the realm expanded or diminished, the number remained thirty-two. Stories of the origin of the thirty-two *myo* are varied. One account held that they were pagoda sites where the Buddha's tooth relics were enshrined. Hence the Mon realm was the true Buddhist kingdom according to the Buddha's prophecy. Another suggested that they were the seats of the prince-rulers who had white elephants, regarded as sacred objects of kingship. Shorto, however, found that in any case the order was the same as the one for the worship of the thirty-seven *nat*, the indigenous pre-Buddhist spirits such as local guardians, mountain spirits, or ancestor spirits, many of which were later converted to Buddhism or became relics.[13] In short, taking all the origin stories into account, the realm of the thirty-two townships was a holy space bound together by a system of thirty-two sacred objects, whether they were white elephants, the *nat*, the Buddha's relics, pagodas, or in most cases a combination of them, with the most superior one residing at the capital. This was the cosmic rule of the territorial organization of the Mon realm, as well as the Burmese realm which adopted the Mon tradition.

A realm was arranged according to a cosmic order, be it an Indic or pre-Indic scheme. A religious conceptual system rendered it sacred. The holy territoriality was marked by local shrines, many of which had celestial characteristics. Moreover, though the number here is not twelve as in the space of pilgrimage above, the rationale behind the numbers was similar.[14] The cosmographic ideas seem to be more closely related to the territorial arrangement of a kingdom, yet they were not the same kind of space.

Chandler studied toponyms in two old Khmer texts and found that the Cambodian realm was a sacralized topography of places looked after by local spirits *(mesa, nakta)* or places where sacred rituals were performed. Although Chandler did not discuss the cosmic order behind such a spatial arrangement, he emphasized another aspect of the list of toponyms: it was an indigenous map of the whole realm before the map of modern geography was introduced.[15]

In the case of Siam, the notion that the realm was conceived as a sacred topography is evident in the terms denoting a kingdom or a sovereign territory. Literally, the term *anachak* means the sphere over which the king's *chak* —a sunlike disk representing sovereignty—could orbit. Another term, *khopkhanthasima*, literally means the sphere bounded by sanctuary stones. *Sima* or *sema* is the stone boundary marker of consecrated space, normally in a temple, within which an ordination can be performed. It also refers to stones of similar shape on the top of a city's wall. Thus a realm was said to be a sacred domain under the power of the king's wheel or a consecrated territory as within a sanctuary's *sima*. Apart from that, there is also a text in Thai from the early Ayudhya period, at least the mid-fourteenth century, which is very similar to Chandler's Cambodian texts. Although there has not yet been a study of the sacred numbers or the federation of local spirits in the text, the idea that a town has its own guardian spirits is well known. In Bangkok today, the name of the guardian spirit, Phra Sayamthewathirat, is often cited in a blessing of the whole country.

Imaginary Spatial Depiction: Ancient Maps

The Traiphum map is a pictorial representation of the existence of all beings. The configuration of the three worlds is to us symbolic; that is, it is not a map of the worldly geography. The maps can be found not only in the manuscripts but also on the walls of a large number of Buddhist temples, in most cases in the sanctuary of the main Buddha image of each temple, signifying the Buddhist values of the cosmos. It should be noted here again that depictions of the Traiphum space may vary. The shape of Chomphuthawip can even be an oval or a triangle.[16] The differences reflect the various traditions or schools of painting rather than the development of knowledge about the earth.

But the Traiphum cosmography is only one among the famous subjects depicted on these temple walls. There are Buddhological themes as well, such as the story of the Buddha's life, the popular story of the Vessantara Jataka or the tenth great birth of the Buddha, and many other stories of relics, Buddha images, or various localities. In most cases, the cosmographic and Buddhological themes are on different walls of the same sanctuary.[17] There is also a manuscript which is so far the major source of pictures of these Buddhological stories. Dated from 1776, the manuscript has no title. But the one given to it later, *Samutphap traiphum chabap krung thonburi* (Pictorial Manuscript of the Traiphum: Thonburi Version), may mislead us into thinking that the pictures are all configurations of the Traiphum genre only. Though the pictures of the three worlds constitute the main part of the manuscript, in fact not only Buddhist narratives but different kinds of maps are also included.[18]

The manuscript is a huge strip of thick, locally made folded paper. It consists of the Traiphum cosmography, the life of the Buddha, various Great Jataka, and legends about Buddhism coming to "Suwannaphum," mainland Southeast Asia today. It begins with the picture of the Mahanakhon Nipphan (Great City of Nirvana)—the space of eternal salvation above and beyond the three worlds of all beings—which is followed by pictures of various deities ranked down to the four guardians of the universe. Then, in the longest section of the manuscript, is shown every quarter of hell down to the lowest sector. The description of the human world starts with the mythology of the Buddha's life, followed by many Jataka stories and pictures of mythological places and animals. The final section contains pictures of the Vessantara and other great births of the Buddha. Pictures of the Jataka and mythological stories are placed along a river symbol (〰️), which makes this part of the picture look like a map. Strikingly, a number of the pictures in this part, between the story of the Vessantara and other births, undoubtedly constitute a geographical map. The river symbol might not only signify a geographical relationship in our sense but other kinds of relationships such as genealogy or simply the sequence of the story as well.

If we look at the map closely (see Figure 2), panels (1) to (4) represent the story of the Buddha's life, beginning with many Buddhological cities and countries followed by a highlight of great moments before and after the enlightenment. As the manuscript is basically a pictorial text of various *phum* (space, land), these moments are marked by places: the heavenly city of the Buddha's father; the tree under which he was born; the place of enlightenment; the seven trees where he relaxed and reconsidered the truth he found; and many places he visited throughout his preaching career, including a mountain of giants and demons and a town of animals.

Following the river symbol into panel (5), the locality adjacent to the Buddhological places is obviously Lanna, or northern Thailand today. Along the top of panels (5), (6), and (7) are the Lao and Vietnamese regions, including Champa, an ancient kingdom defeated and lost to the Vietnamese in the sixteenth century. The bottoms of panels (7) and (8) are the Burmese and Mon regions including Pagan, Moulmein, Syriam, Thaton, and Tavoy. The focus of these pictures are the towns in Lanna and Siam including Ayudhya but not Bangkok. Panel (8) shows the deltas of many rivers and the whole peninsula from the Kra isthmus, which appears as a big island. Panels (9) and (10) depict the sea where two renowned Buddhist sages in Southeast Asia, Phra Phutthakhosachan and Phra Phutthathatta, were traveling to and from Ceylon, now Sri Lanka. Along the bottom of panels (8) to (10), a well-known episode from the *Ramayana* appears. Rama orders his monkey-commander to build a road across the sea to Longka, a town of demons which bears a similar name to Ceylon in the Thai language—Langka. Panel (11) is Sri Lanka with emphasis on the shrine of Buddha's relic. Some descriptions of places, travel times, and distances are also given. Panel (12) is a mythological creature, Anon Fish.

Michael Wright, in an article in a Thai magazine which is the only account of this map, regarded the whole set of pictures as an old geographical map from Ayudhya times (mid-fourteenth to mid-eighteenth centuries) that was, perhaps, uninfluenced by foreign maps.[19] While noting that the locations of many towns in Lanna and the central plain are generally correct, he was puzzled by two serious mistakes: the adjacency of the Buddha's places and Lanna without Burma in between and the locations of India and Sri Lanka at opposite ends of the map. He also noticed that Ayudhya, as the center of the kingdom, had no privileged status in this map. He did not say anything about the mythological road of Rama or the relevance of the story of the Buddha's life at the beginning of the map.

If one concedes that a map does not have to be a representation of the earth's surface, but can depict other relations of space, it is easier to understand this set of pictures. Placed right after the end of the Vessantara story, it is the story of the following birth as the Buddha. But to people in the region, the meaningful story of Buddhism apart from the Buddha's life is the prospering of Buddhism in Suwannaphum, that is, mainland Southeast Asia. The pictures establish the lineage of Buddhism in the region by claiming its origin directly from Chomphuthawip and the Buddha's time on the one hand, and its foundation by the two sages from the land of genuine Buddhism, Sri Lanka, on the other. All these relationships are configured in the form of related places. But while the space of Lanna, the Chao Phraya valley, the Burmese coastal towns, and Sri Lanka is based on a mapmaker's knowledge of these parts of the earth's surface, the space of the Buddha's life, the two prophets, and other mythical beings is completely imaginative. This set of pictures is not designed to be a true geography of the region as Wright expected. The artist deliberately put the map into a larger framework of description, juxtaposing details about Chomphuthawip, Suwannaphum, and Sri Lanka together in a single set of descriptions.

Thus the adjacency of Chomphuthawip and Lanna without Burma in between is in no way a mistake. For the artist and his audience, it correctly signifies the genesis of local Buddhism from its universal origin. There is no need for correction or explanation (such as that in olden days there might have been a special route between them) as Wright has provided.[20] The map of the mainland and Southeast Asia as a whole, with the east at the top and the west down at the bottom, is a single unit of a particular region where Buddhism has prospered. The space of this unit is not imaginative or cosmographical, so a topographical map is in use here and the river symbol stands for actual rivers. Sri Lanka is also concrete.[21] But the relationship between Sri Lanka and Suwannaphum is symbolized by the story of the two sages. The sea becomes symbolic enough to put some mythological stories in it. The positions of Chomphuthawip and Sri Lanka at opposite ends of the map, their distance from each other, and the incorrect directions in relation to Southeast Asia are not geographical mistakes. Nor do the positions of Lanna and Siam in the middle of the map signify their status as the center of the Traiphum world. All of them are correctly put in their right places according to this description about Buddhism in Suwannaphum, not according to the earth's surface.

In all, this set of pictures tells a story similar to those on the walls of temples. Some parts of this set are exactly the same pictures of Buddhological stories which can be found elsewhere—the mid-ocean meeting between the two Buddhist sages, for example, and the Buddha's great departure, the moment when he abandoned his worldly life.[22] A similar description about the connection between Lanna and the Buddha's lifetime can be found in many local Buddhist legends, or Tamnan. Some historians have taken it as an account of actual geography in order to work out the origins of the Tai people. But it has been argued more convincingly that it is an idealized geography, the "Tamnan geography."[23] So the whole set of pictures under discussion is a "Tamnan Map," a relation of space according to a Tamnan story, though a significant unit in the set is a map in our modern sense.

Our discussion so far has shown different kinds of indigenous conceptions of space and maps before the coming of modern geography. The prevalence of cosmography was beyond doubt, but various spatial conceptions existed together and produced complex knowledge, practices, and maps. Most of these spaces were conceptually sacralized by religious concepts and symbolism. In pilgrimage, for instance, "the faithful impart unquestioned truthfulness not only to the conceptions of ultimate reality and its symbols, but also to those dimensions of physical space which are associated with meaningful symbols and which are proper settings for valued religious actions."[24] Or we can say that space was conceived and made meaningful by systems of sacred entities. These entities mediated between space and human, creating particular kinds of imagined space. Consequently, the character of such space was determined by the relationships of sacred entities according to a belief—for instance, the hierarchical thirty-seven *nat* and the thirty-two *myo*, the twelve Buddhist shrines and the idea of pilgrimage, the Tamnan geography and its myth-ritual story. To understand the space and the map, one has to understand its concept (its grammar) and its symbolism (its morphemes).

Despite all these sacred topographies, the map of the profane earth's surface should not be regarded as nonexistent. The map of mainland Southeast Asia in the Tamnan Map is evidence. Chandler tells us that in the case of Cambodia there are many maps of small localities such as villages and travel routes, but there are only a few specimens of what he calls a national map. He attributes this to the Cambodian people's lack of interregional life and to the sporadic, isolated pattern of Cambodian villages.[25] In the case of Siam, however, the premodern maps of small localities and routes are rare, perhaps due to the lack of interest in this subject. (If this is true, perhaps plenty of them are yet to be discovered.) Figure 3 is a portion of a strip map of the eastern bank of Songkhla Lagoon, latitude 7–8 degrees north, on the Gulf of Siam. Dated between 1680 and 1699, the whole area is consecutively portrayed in terms of sixty-three temples.[26] As a study of it has noted, the landscape was read, that is, conceived and marked, by sacred sites which made the topography meaningful.[27] But the sacred shrines depicted here were not a symbolic representation of a belief system. They represented the existence of the localities in which they resided. The spatial unit in this map was not a cosmographic or imaginary world of any kind. It was a map of the profane earth's surface. It should be recalled that a route map or diagram similar to a treasure map was an early form of ancient map in every culture. This sort of diagram of a piece of the earth was certainly known to the indigenous people of Siam as well.

There is another fascinating map in the Thonburi version of the Traiphum pictorial manuscript: a coastal map from Korea to Arabia which was incorporated into the description of the human world in the Traiphum scheme (see Figure 4).[28] In this map, all the coasts are lined up along the bottom part of the map and all the seas are in the upper part. It begins with Korea and Japan situated in the sea, followed by the Chinese coast opposite Taiwan rightward to Canton (panel 1). Then the Vietnamese coast appears like a peninsula jutting into the sea with the mouth of the Mekhong River at its peak and the coast along the Gulf of Siam in a trough (panel 2). At the bottom of panel (3), Ayudhya appears as the biggest city in the gulf. The Malay peninsula, like the Vietnamese, juts upward (panel 4). At the bottom of this bay are the Mon and Burmese towns (panel 5). Apart from these identifications, none of the toponyms on the supposed Indian coasts (panels 5–6) can be identified with names we know, except one in the middle of the coast of panel (6) whose name is "Roam Noi" (Little Rome). In the seas, there are many islands with the same somewhat oval shape. Many of these islands can be identified, such as Japan, Taiwan, Sichang (in the Gulf of Siam), the Andamans, and Sri Lanka. In panel (1) and half of (2), the top of the map is the east. For the rest of the map, the top is the south; all the coasts northward are at the bottom, and the east is on the left and the west on the right.

Wright suggests that the Coastal Map follows the Chinese tradition. Terwiel argues that the seventeenth-century European map was "the chief source of inspiration for this map."[29] Wenk suggests that it is a Traiphum cosmographic chart, since it is part of the manuscript. Supporting Wenk's analysis, Terwiel considers it in that light but with hesitation:

> [It is] an example of the Thai capacity to absorb detailed new information and adjust it to fit in with Traiphum cosmographical ideas. . . . [It] is not a geographical work in the strict sense of the word: many coasts twist unrealistically in direction, the relative proportions of countries are wrong and there is no grid. Many islands have been placed in a blatantly false location. . . . The conclusion that the creators of the chart were more interested in cosmography than in geography is amply supported by such palpable divergence from reality. The chart may be regarded as an attempt to depict a large part of the coastline of the Traiphum's Southern continent, together with a selected assortment of its five hundred islands."[30]

It would be wrong, however, to assume that knowledge of the earth's surface was unknown until the Europeans came, or that the new information can be understood only through the Traiphum cosmographic ideas. It is also a mistake to dismiss indigenous knowledge on the basis that it is not accurate according to our scientific criteria. The Traiphum earth and the geographical earth are different, but related, kinds of space operating in different domains of human conception and practice. The incorporation of the Coastal Map into the description of the Traiphum space, like the map of mainland Southeast Asia in the Tamnan Map, makes it a single unit in the overall cosmographic narrative. Yet in itself it was actually a geographical map of the earth's surface, not a cosmographic one. Considering specifically this Coastal Map, it had many characteristics more similar to the Chinese tradition of coastal charts than to the European map. Although some information might have come from European sources, the basic pattern of this map seems to derive from the Chinese model.[31] The making of coastal charts was a tradition among the Chinese dating back to the early Christian era, a tradition which then gave way to European mapping through the influence of the Jesuits only around the sixteenth and seventeenth centuries. Among the charts left to us, some were "narrow-strip-maps in which the coast, or a long stretch of the coast, is represented as running in a horizontal direction from right to left irrespective of its true direction."[32] The basic directions were toward the land or outward to the sea, and the land was along the top or the bottom of the maps. The scale was uneven. Indeed, one might say there was no scaling method in the making of these maps.

The Chinese were among the earliest travelers in the Far East, Southeast Asia, and beyond. They provided information about places they had visited or heard about for later native maps. Maps of this region had been produced and names of places entered in their records since the early Christian era.[33] So it is not surprising that details about places along the South China Sea on the way to the Indian coasts were richer than for the Arab and European world. Nonetheless, it is difficult to say at this stage how strong the Chinese influence was on Siamese mapmaking or how far the Siamese had localized the Chinese tradition. To produce a map, the creator might have acquired information from various sources, including European ones, probably without having direct experience of the coasts. The names, distances, or even locations could even have come from hearsay and mythical stories about various places without the scientific criteria we use today.

The last map to be discussed here is the so-called Strategic Map of King Rama I (see Figure 5). It is said to be the oldest map in Thailand.[34] This statement is obviously wrong if we regard the indigenous charts discussed so far as maps as well. The Strategic Map is, however, free of all religious codings, thus illustrating the indigenous knowledge of the profane earth. It is a local map, and the earth's surface it covers is the former Lao region which is north-eastern Thailand today. This map has been studied by Victor Kennedy, who examines the one existing copy, a reproduction from the period of King Vajiravudh, Rama VI of Bangkok (r. 1910–1925). Investigating the details of the map, he concludes that it is the map for Siamese troops fighting in the war against Vientiane in 1827. But it is likely that the original of this map is itself a copy of an older one, with modifications made specifically for military purposes.[35]

The map shows travel routes from Bangkok to the northeast, mostly along the rivers but including mountains, rivers, fortresses, and towns along the way. The distance between two places was measured in terms of the time it took to travel from one point to another. In his attempt to evaluate its accuracy according to the modern map, Kennedy finds many shortcomings. Locations of many places are wrong. There is no scale. Distances are unreliable. Yet some of these anomalies are the clues to his findings—namely, that some areas are disproportionately enlarged with more details than others because they were important to the 1827 operation.

Despite the anomalies, the space of this map is made meaningful, and can be imagined, not in terms of sacred entities but in terms of places the travelers experienced along the routes on the earth's surface. It is obviously not a map of sacred topography nor a cosmographic plan. It is a map of a piece of the earth's surface similar to a modern map. But unlike a modern map, it does not yet show how such a piece of the earth's surface relates to, or is situated on, the globe. There is no reference to the larger earth's surface, such as latitude and longitude lines, or the relation of this territory to nearby kingdoms in terms of boundaries. Such a relationship was probably not a matter of concern for a local map, since the knowledge about the whole planet earth belonged to the cosmology. The isolation of a piece of the earth's surface from the entire globe might be compared to the isolation of the earth from the whole galaxy in our minds today. In other words, the classification of a local geography and the whole globe as separate categories in the indigenous knowledge about space is comparable to the separate classification in modern science today of geography and astronomy or astrophysics.

To return to the Tamnan Map and the Coastal Map in the light of this Strategic Map, what may be regarded as errors, "palpable divergence from reality" in Terwiel's eyes, and distortions might be due to indigenous methods of mapmaking and travel data. These maps were made without the scientific criteria and standards of reliability we use today. But the mapmakers might have had their own methods and standards. In the Tamnan Map, it seems that the river routes and the information about travel along them from north to south were the major data it recorded. The whole of mainland Southeast Asia was known mostly by towns and rivers or places along them. Hence the vast inland area between the Chao Phraya valley and the Mekhong River was almost nonexistent, whereas the narrow strips of land where the four rivers flow out to the Gulf of Siam were enlarged. Furthermore, traveling along each river, travelers might have had difficulty in distinguishing the different latitudinal positions of the Irrawaddy and Chao Phraya deltas. So they appeared on the same level, or the towns in the Irrawaddy delta seemed to be more southward than they should have been. Perhaps because of the perspective of river travelers, all of them were thought to be parallel. In the maps of mainland Southeast Asia made by Europeans before the mid-nineteenth century—when none of them had actually surveyed the inland areas and had to rely on the information of native people—all the major rivers from Burma to the Vietnamese coast also appear somewhat parallel.

Maritime travel along the coasts from China to India without cross-checking by land travel might have produced information which was affected by navigational factors, seasonal weather and wind, swells, and so forth. This information plus myths or hearsay might account for the crudity of a coastal map which could plot positions along the coasts and distances between them in terms of travel time fairly well but failed to obtain data about the land along the sea. Distortions or anomalies may be clues leading us to discern particular sources of information, purposes, or techniques of each indigenous map, as Kennedy did in the case of the Strategic Map. In contrast to the approach taken by many studies, these anomalies must be regarded positively as traces leading us to understand the methods or conceptions behind several features of the maps. We should not simply evaluate their scientific merit. Nor should these anomalies be regarded as evidence that such a map had nothing to do with the geography of the earth's surface, and thus belonged to the cosmographic scheme.

In comparing several kinds of indigenous map, one distinction between a depiction of imaginary space and a map of the material space emerges: the measurement of distance between places. Although there are many numerical values in the Traiphum and Buddhological maps, they are symbolic figures of various worlds, ideal places, descriptions of beings, or symbolic quantities of sacred objects. Many of them can be calculated by arithmatic formulas, such as the size of the earth and other levels or the sizes and distances between the seven rings of mountains and oceans.[36] Only in the maps of a piece of the earth's surface are the details of time-distance between many places mentioned. In the Strategic Map, for example, the distance in terms of travel time is marked by lines between two places and a few words, such as *wannung, songkhun* (a day, two nights), close to each line. This time-distance appears in the Tamnan Map as well, where the distances between many places on the big island, right of the Menam delta, are marked by words such as *thanghawan* (five-day distance). In the Coastal Map, there are also plenty of lines between places. The distance is measured in *yot* (*yochana* in Sanskrit), about 16 kilometers. It is also the unit of distance used in the Traiphum, but it is quite clear that the figures in these maps are distances measured by human experience, perhaps calculated from travel time as well.

The Coexistence of Different Concepts of Space

The Traiphum cosmography and other kinds of sacred topography could have been imagined in terms other than the geographical "reality" with which we are familiar. Their space is religious or imaginative to us—hence a space that does not necessarily correspond to the earth's surface. The reality, meaning, and message expressed through these spatial relations have nothing to do with our worldly geography. As a result, there might be an indefinite number of different depictions of the same message. For many centuries, the concept of the three worlds has inspired artists from modern schools as well as traditional ones.[37] The knowledge of local geography or certain parts of the earth's surface, on the other hand, was another kind of spatial conception. It is neither symbolic nor sacred.

We may say there were several discourses on space existing in the field of premodern geographical knowledge. Each of them operated in a certain domain of human affairs and everyday life. In other words, there were terrains of knowledge within which particular conceptions operated; beyond their limits, other kinds of knowledge came into force. The knowledge of certain villages and towns might have been operating at local levels. The space of the Strategic Map or the Coastal Map might have had an effect on commanders of troops and Chinese merchants. Yet such knowledge might have been called into operation only in a military exercise, in administrative works, or for maritime trade. But when people thought or talked about Siam, the kingdom of Vientiane, or China, another kind of spatial conception might have come to mind. And when they thought or talked about the earth or the world they lived in, the pictures of the Traiphum might have preoccupied their minds. Like many other concepts in human life today and yesterday, shifts from one kind of knowledge to another or from one domain of spatial conception to another are not uncommon.

In speaking of "Siam," therefore, various conceptions of Siam might be at work. A striking illustration of this occurred in the second quarter of the nineteenth century—the period in which the Siamese elite were introduced to Western geographical knowledge and maps, and in which there were signs of changes in the Siamese view of the world. Frederick A. Neale tells a fascinating story about a Siamese court discourse on the map of "Siam." One day, Neale reports, the Siamese king told the European visitors about a conflict between Siam and Burma regarding a boundary question. The king then showed a picture of the two kingdoms, said to have been drawn by his prime minister to illustrate the Siamese talent in geography and brilliance in painting. With the eyes and mind of a civilized Englishman, Neale gives a three-page description of the map and his feelings, an account which deserves a lengthy quote together with a picture from his book (see Figure 6):

> We were, however, very nearly outraging all propriety by bursting into fits of laughter, and very painful was the curb we were obliged to wear to restrain our merriment. The inclination to smile, too visibly depicted in our faces to be mistaken, was, happily, by His Majesty, construed into delight and admiration at the beautiful work of art set before us to dazzle our eyes with its excessive brilliancy of colour. The map was about three feet by two; in the center was a patch of red, about eighteen inches long by ten broad; above it was a patch of green, about ten inches long by three wide. On the whole space occupied by the red was pasted a singular looking figure, cut out of silver paper, with a pitch-fork in one hand and an orange in the other: there was a crown on the head, and spurs on the heels, and the legs, which were of miserably thin dimensions, met sympathetically at the knees, and this cadaverous looking creature was meant to represent the bloated piece of humanity seated before us, indicating that so vast were his strength and power that it extended from one end of his dominions to the other. In the little patch of green, a small Indian-ink figure, consisting of a little dot for the head, a large dot for the body, and four scratches of the pen to represent the legs and arms, was intended for the wretched Tharawaddy, the then King of Burmah. A legion of little imps, in very many different attitudes, were dancing about his dominions, and these hieroglyphics were to show to the uninitiated in what a troubled and disturbed state the Burmese empire was, and what an insignificant personage, in his own dominions, was the Burman king. Betwixt the green and the red, there was a broad black stripe, an indisputable boundary line; and on the red side of the black stripe, a little curved thin line drawn with ink, to indicate the territory laid claim to by the Birmans but disputed by the Siamese; the rest of the map was all blue, and on this blue, which was the ocean, all round the red or Siamese territory vilely painted ships were represented sailing to and fro, some with the masts towards the land, the others evidently bottom up, at least their

masts pointed in the wrong direction. The poor Burmese had not even so much as a boat to display. Having, of course, acquiesced in all that His Majesty said, and given utterance to exclamations of surprise in mute show, like so many ballet dancers, the old king seemed to be quite pleased and delighted, and ordering the map to be carried away indulged in a confidential chuckle for a few seconds.[38]

Probably this description of the event was colored, and Neale's picture showed the draftsman's ignorance of Siamese painting. But from the information given, we can imagine what the map looked like. If we replace the Siamese creature in the big square with the figure of a *thewada,* a heavenly deity in traditional Thai art, who must have a pointed crown, the *chada* or *mongkut,* and replace the long fork and orange with a short three-pronged sword, the *tri,* and a conch, the *sang,* respectively, the figure in the domain of Siam would be a heavenly deity. Hence Siam was the celestial domain. In contrast, Burma was the domain of demons, whose typical representation is similar to what Neale described. The court must not be misrepresented as knowing nothing of geography apart from the Traiphum space. Different conceptions of space were at work in different situations or for different purposes. In this case, the discourse on the existence of the two kingdoms was represented in the cosmographic fashion. To one's great surprise, however, the boundary question could be expressed in this nongeographic map.

In studies on the change of the Siamese worldview in the late nineteenth century, two conclusions are usually presented. First, the transition was rather a smooth process of westernization, thanks to the enlightened Siamese elite and, to a lesser extent, the contribution of hardworking missionaries. Confrontations with the indigenous knowledge are rarely mentioned and never serious. Second, since most studies tend to overemphasize the importance of the Traiphum cosmography while ignoring other spatial conceptions, it seems that the transformation was a shift from the Traiphum concept to modern geography. Moreover, there is no study on the shift of geographical knowledge per se. The changes of worldview are always subsumed within the context of the introduction of Western science in general.

The coming of modern geography and astronomy confronted not only the Traiphum cosmos, though that was one of the most turbulent arenas. It also found counterparts in the indigenous conceptions of local geography, boundaries, land plots, statehood, and more. Perhaps confrontations occurred in every arena of matching conception and practice: in the boundary marking, for example, and in the concept of a realm which was the basis of indigenous interstate relations.

Space itself has no meaning if human beings have not encountered and mediated it by certain concepts and mediators. In this case, sacred entities, religious ideas, and Traiphum worldviews supplied conceptual tools and signs and generated certain practices. Modern geography was not simply new data added to existing conceptions. It was another *kind* of knowledge of space with its own classificatory systems, concepts, and mediating signs. The question is this: what dramatic effects ensue when people stop imagining space in terms of orderly relations of sacred entities and start conceiving it with a whole new set of signs and rules?

To speak of a political-geographical unit such as a nation, the indigenous conceptions involved discourses of the realm on earth, local geography, sovereignty, and boundary, rather than the Traiphum cosmography. It was in such domains that modern geography—with its rules and its prime technology of spatial conception, the modern map—confronted its indigenous counterparts. The outcome of the confrontation was a totally new way of thinking and perceiving space, and the emergence of a new kind of territoriality of Siam.

Chapter Two
The Coming of a New Geography

by the early [am]

AROUND THE SAME TIME that the Siamese court presented foreign visitors with the picture of Siam as a celestial domain, the knowledge that Siam was one among many countries on earth was widespread. Contacts with the Europeans and other neighbors had been growing rapidly through trade.[1] By the early nineteenth century, names of the European and Asian countries were mentioned in an official inscription and a well-known work of literature.[2]

Two Earths, Same Space: The Advent of Modern Earth

We know more about the Siamese and their interest in Western astronomy and geography from the 1830s onward. It was a famous topic in most missionary memoirs, although their contributions to the modernization in Siam may be overrated. John Taylor Jones, one of the earliest missionaries in Siam, who arrived in 1833 with copies of the map of the world, tells about a monk who asked for an English map.[3] Jones, with two other well-known missionaries in Siam at the time, Bradley and House, also tells us that in some scientific experiments they organized for members of the Siamese elite, they showed their audiences a globe, a model of the solar system, and planetary movements.[4] Among the Siamese elite, Mongkut, who later became King Rama IV (r. 1851–1868), was said to have abandoned the Traiphum cosmology before 1836. He had a globe, a chart calculating the coming eclipse, and maps in his room, and he once asked these missionaries innumerable questions about the earth.[5] Bradley tells us that Mongkut was impressed by a book, *Almanac and Astronomy,* written in 1843 by the missionary Jesse Caswell to counter the Siamese belief in the Traiphum. It spread among Mongkut's disciples very quickly.[6]

In an evening conversation among Mongkut and his men in the mid-

1840s, a high-ranking nobleman told Mongkut that he eventually accepted the idea that the earth was spherical after reading Caswell's book. But Mongkut claimed that he himself had already held such a view fifteen years before—that is, before the appearance of the American missionaries in Siam. Another nobleman, however, rejected the idea and said he would never be convinced.[7] These exchanges show us at least two things. First, the question of the earth's shape had been receiving considerable attention from intellectuals: the issue was still lively and unsettled. Second, Mongkut was so firm in his belief in a spherical earth that he claimed to have abandoned the idea of a flat earth long ago in the remoteness of his past. His claim, even an exaggerated one, implied how outdated the traditional conviction was and how modern he himself had been. The stubborn believer in a flat earth, who appears in the same scene, attests to the resilience of the traditional conception of the earth. These stories indicate that certain sections of the Siamese elite already had a passing familiarity with Western geographical knowledge. They welcomed the new knowledge and were anxious to acquire it. Yet there is no doubt that the missionaries also encountered firm believers in the Traiphum cosmography.

Mongkut's interest in astronomy and modern geography began in the early years of his monkhood, especially because of his love for calculations of planetary movements. His understanding of the earth, compared to his contemporaries, seems pretty advanced. He once showed how important the scientific earth was in his view when he wrote a letter in reply to Bradley's explanation of the Creator and the Bible's role in civilization. He charged that the Bible was full of mistakes about the earth and nature, particularly the belief in the six-day Creation. If the Bible is the origin of civilization, he challenged, why does it not say anything at all about how to measure latitude and longitude?[8] Perhaps his love of calculating coordinates on the earth's surface was at times extravagant. Even before he became king, he wrote a letter to one of his American friends; the letter was written from "a place of sea surface 13°26′N. latitude and 101°3′E. longitude in the Gulf of Siam, 18th November Anbo [*sic*] Christi, 1849."[9]

When he became king he urged his royal relatives to have a European-style education. Modern geography and astronomy were among the lessons given by the missionaries.[10] Perhaps the status of geography in his mind can be summed up by his own verdict in a letter to Sir John Bowring, a prominent British diplomat of that time, talking about the account of an Ayudhyan envoy to France in the late seventeenth century. He commented that the account was unconvincing since it was "opposed to geographical knowledge which is the true facts about the earth."[11] Geography and astronomy appeared to be the first among the Western sciences he mentioned when he talked about the truth or wonderful science from the West.[12]

To be sure, Mongkut's case is significant because he was a leading figure whose attitudes toward the new sciences and geography were shared by others. But the disbelief in modern geography was not easily given up. Even the Siamese interpreter in the mission to Queen Victoria's court in 1857, who was fluent in English and familiar with Western ideas, asked in his poetical account of his journey:

> Why the sun does set in the sea?
> Also at dawn, it does rise up from the sea.
> Or is it true, as the English think,
> That the shape of the earth is like an orange?
> And does the sun, standing still, never move?
> Amusingly, the earth itself rotates,
> Even the three worlds are so huge.
> How dull I am not to understand how it can be.[13]

The Traiphum's earth had been too deeply entrenched to be abandoned. As one historian has observed, the shift occurred at a glacial pace. Indeed, that conception has survived in certain circles of social life, in traditionally rooted cultural life, such as the Buddhist order, rituals, religious festivals, and in what was later identified as popular culture, even to the present time.[14] A close scrutiny of the circumstances in which the shift took place will lead us to the forces which affected the establishment of modern geography. As it turns out, it was not a gradual, smooth diffusion of knowledge at all.

The quest for modern geography and other Western sciences took place in the same period as the Buddhist reform in the mid-nineteenth century, which resulted in the birth of a new sect in Siamese Theravada Buddhism. Both the reform and the quest for modern science were led by the same people— Mongkut and his disciples—from the early 1820s when he was a monk. In fact we can say that these were two trends of the same political and intellectual movement which questioned the purity and validity of the *sangha,* the Buddhist order, as it was practiced in Siam at the time.

Like other Buddhist reformations, the true Buddhism and *sangha* could be found in orthodoxy—the Pali Tripitaka, not the commentaries or exegeses— and the strict discipline of the *sangha* was believed to have been laid down since the Buddha's time. In the spirit of Mongkut's movement, nonetheless, true Buddhism was supposed to refrain from worldly matters and confine itself to spiritual and moral affairs. They believed that those alleged Buddhist doctrines which were concerned with cosmography were in fact contaminated by other false beliefs such as Brahmanism. Thus they distinguished worldly matters and spiritual affairs from each other, though they were related. They believed that Buddhism was the truth of the latter whereas Western science was the truth of the former. Thus they openly welcomed Western science more than any other group in Siam—so much so, in fact, that missionaries regarded this Buddhist orthodoxy movement as the progressive faction in Siam.[15]

This so-called progressive faction eventually came to power in 1851, and from that moment Siam changed dramatically toward modernization. The fact that the Siamese propagators of Western science now also had political power in their hands has already been regarded as a major reason for the smooth transition toward modernization and rapid diffusion of Western knowledge. Moreover, it is usually argued that the imperialist advances in Burma and China had alarmed Siam into urgent acquisition of the more influential and superior Western knowledge. The Mongkut factor and the imperialist victory meant that from now on not only did Western knowledge expand on its own merit but it was also backed by extra-epistemological power which gained it a stronghold in the society and made it all the more influential.

But the impact of Mongkut's religious movement, his royal authority, and the showdown with the Western powers did not automatically decide the outcome of confrontation between Western cosmography and the indigenous one. The two beliefs continued to struggle overtly throughout the reign in various ways. In 1866, for example, Bradley published a series of articles about the earth. It was still a lively and interesting subject for his readers, and his articles represented the only detailed explanation about the earth at the time. Starting from observable verifications of the sphericity of the earth, he also gave his readers a general topographical account: its size, surface composition, the names and locations of oceans and lands, the atmospheric zones, and so forth.[16] (Bradley's newspaper stopped printing that year, unfortunately, when Eskimos were the subject.) Bradley tended to use the new knowledge as a spearhead to penetrate traditional belief, targeting the faith in Buddhism in particular. A letter from Mongkut joined Bradley's attempt to destabilize the traditional view of the cosmos. But Mongkut also challenged the Bible in the same letter on the same ground.[17]

Only a year later, in 1867, one of the highest-ranking nobles in Siam, Chaophraya Thiphakorawong (hereafter Thiphakorawong), published a book titled *Kitchanukit*, a polemic against the traditional cosmography as well as Christianity.[18] Following the epistemological tendency of Mongkut's movement, the book was typical in its concept of the distinction between the worldly and the religious domains, whose truth can be found in Western science and Buddhism respectively.[19] He reaffirmed the truthfulness of Buddhism and argued against any contrary doctrines, especially criticism from the missionaries.[20] But in doing so, he had to deprive Buddhism of any relevance to the truth of the natural world: he had to make it the champion of morals and ethics alone.

In the first two-fifths of the book he gave his instruction on modern geography and astronomy as aspects of the true knowledge of the natural world. The question of the earth's shape became a focal point of confrontation in the text where the truth of the indigenous knowledge, especially Buddhist cosmology, was attestable in the light of the Western scheme.[21] He described the earth as a planet in the solar system with so firm a conviction of its sphericity that he could explain its origin on the one hand and polemically question those who believed in a flat earth on the other. In arguing how we can know that the earth is not flat, he cited observable phenomena and the story of Columbus's discovery of the New World, both of which could be found in Bradley's newspaper.[22] In doing this, he was aware that the Traiphum cosmography had become the target of his attack and that the authority of the Buddha could be cast in doubt since he was said to know every truth with infallibility. Not only could Thiphakorawong manage to avoid becoming a heretic, but by his argument he could go so far as to say: "One who thinks that the earth is flat is a follower of those who believe in God the Creator. For one who believes that the earth is spherical is following the Buddha's words about what is natural."[23]

His method of escape from the dilemma became typical for the modern Buddhist Thai whose faith in Buddhism is unshaken while objective knowledge of Western science is equally upheld. Apart from segregating the two domains of life, Thiphakorawong confirmed that the Buddha knew the truth of the earth, but the Buddha was also aware that what he knew was in conflict with people's belief. If the Buddha had raised this question, Thiphakorawong explained, people would have been obsessed with this topic and neglected the path to salvation. That is to say, it was a futile topic, meaningless to preach, worthless to challenge. He blamed old gurus of later generations for incorporating this subject into the Buddhist corpus while the best they could do was rely on those Brahmanic doctrines and some Pali exegeses which were ignorant of the truth.[24] It is clear that Thiphakorawong had no hesitation in accusing traditional doctrines of being contaminated by Brahmanism while promoting geography of the new kind with the approval of true Buddhism.

Modern geography appears to be a new knowledge for dealing with any question about space. This was not without difficulty. The author must explain, for example, a story in the Buddha's life about his trip to give a sermon to his mother in Dawadung, a level of heaven according to the Traiphum cosmos. Thiphakorawong concedes that it might be true. But that was not contradictory to the true geographical knowledge since, for him, Dawadung might be on another spherical planetary body far away.[25] The apparent conflict between the truth of the Buddha's life story and modern science is resolved fantastically and, to him, consistently.

Kitchanukit is a comprehensive testimony of the Siamese response to the influence of Western cosmographic concepts. In a sense, this epistemological strategy was a resolution to reconcile the conflicting sets of knowledge, regardless of any logical inconsistency in the hybrid. At the same time it was a thrust against the dominant indigenous cosmology. As Thiphakorawong stated in the introduction of his book, he wanted it to be read among the younger generation, replacing the "useless" books in circulation.[26]

With power in its hands, nonetheless, the ideological movement which tried to reconcile indigenous and Western knowledge had to struggle harder against the indigenous beliefs on the one hand and Christianity on the other. Mongkut himself had struggled throughout his life for his ideological hybrid which favored the Western sciences but at the same time championed Buddhism. In fact, the incident which ultimately cost him his life, the observation of the 1868 full eclipse at Wako, was a painful, disruptive moment of the confrontation of knowledge. It was indeed an event symbolic of epistemological struggle in many respects. The seemingly peaceful coexistence of the two knowledges of space was in fact a war of position, to use a Gramscian term, eventually to acquire hegemony.

Breakthrough: Astronomy via Astrology

In addition to his love for the calculation of coordinates on the earth's surface, Mongkut loved calculating planetary movements. He had developed his expertise primarily from the indigenous astrology which he had certainly learned in his monastic years. Mongkut—leader of the progressive faction, of the new Buddhist movement, and of westernization in Siam—was in fact an ardent student of traditional astrology. At the same time, however, he also developed his acquaintance with Western astronomy and mathematics from texts in English.[27]

As one renowned astrologer in Thailand today remarks, Mongkut's contributions to astrology were enormous. He replaced the horoscope of Bangkok, which was inscribed on a gold plate and buried under the shrine of the city pillar, when he found that it would have caused disaster in his reign because it conflicted with his own horoscope.[28] He often demonstrated his expertise in astrology in his royal proclamations. One of his contributions to Thai astrology was his calculation of the new Thai calendar. He even charged that the court astrologers never reexamined the accuracy of their calculations and in fact never questioned or even understood their astrological treatise. Hence the official calendar was messy: the Buddhist holy days in the calendar were seriously miscalculated and the times for auspicious moments were incorrect. His arguments in this case were undoubtedly the best illustration of his mastery of astrology.[29]

Apart from that, at every Thai new year's day in mid-April, called Songkran, the court would make an official announcement informing the public of the auspicious times for that year. The proclamation also inaugurated the coming year by announcing the exact time and duration of each of the twelve constellations of the zodiac, details of coming eclipses, important celestial phenomena, good days for auspicious occasions, bad days to be avoided, and so on.[30] Throughout his reign, Mongkut wrote this annual announcement and did the calculations himself. Sometimes he made comments on astrological knowledge, as in his contention about how to forecast the amount of rainfall for the coming year. Previously this had been done by the court astrologers in terms of the number of the *naga* which would provide rain and the predicted amount of rainfall in various parts of the Traiphum cosmos such as the heavenly forest, the seven rings of mountains and oceans, the human continent, and so forth. Mongkut disregarded these practices as unreliable.[31]

In the astrology Mongkut practiced, his interest was confined to the calculations of planetary movements, not the fortune-telling aspect of traditional astrology. He questioned the official calendar because he found inaccuracies in the calculation of the solar and lunar orbits. The Songkran announcement each year was full of details of the position of the earth in reference to the positions of stars in each constellation, the times the earth moved in and out of each constellation, the waxing and waning of the moon, and the forecast of eclipses. He also enjoyed observing the activities of other celestial phenomena such as comets, sunspots, and other planetary orbits.

Nonetheless, he never denounced fortune-telling. He simply divorced it from the science of celestial calculation. In his view, the celestial phenomena had no effect on human affairs. This idea was certainly different from the notions entertained by his contemporary astrologers. Twice in 1858 and 1861 when comets came, he warned against rumors of epidemics, disasters, wars, or bad omens. The same comet, he argued, had been seen in Europe before and thus was not a specific omen for Bangkok; moreover, human beings could calculate the coming of a comet in advance.[32] He made it clear when the moon and Saturn were aligned in 1868 and the sun and Mercury were aligned in 1861—phenomena regarded as bad omens in the astrological view —that sometimes those bodies orbited to the same point and therefore one must be hidden from our sight. They were natural phenomena:[33] "The celestial phenomena can be observed and calculated in advance. So, whatever strangeness may be seen in the sky should not be taken as any reason for fright. The causes [of such strange phenomena] have already been ascertained."[34] Moreover, the earth in his view was nothing but a planet like other stars. The earth's surface was full of countries, and Siam was merely one of them. In his forecast of eclipses, he sometimes announced that they would be seen in the human world but not in Siam; sometimes he gave precise positions on earth in terms of the coordinates that offered the best view of eclipses. His earth was obviously a global planet in the solar system.

This new cosmology was a departure from indigenous astrology. His royal authority might have precluded any danger of attack and provided a stronghold for his intellectual thrust, but it in no way toppled the establishment. On several occasions, when he argued with Bradley, in the latter's newspaper, about science and religion, he repudiated his fellow elite—senior monks, the patriarch, even his cousin, the previous king, for their ignorance regarding the earth and the sky. Even senior Burmese monks did not escape his attack for their cosmologic worldview.[35] It is not clear, however, how the astrologers at that time reacted to the challenge of the new worldview from within. In any case, Mongkut continued his struggle with confidence and an antagonistic attitude toward the court astrologers—most of whom were, ironically, like him, ex-monks who had learned their expertise in monasteries. The struggle was, by all means, serious to the end of his life.

Once, in a forecast of a lunar eclipse, he emphasized that it was calculated by the king, not the astrologers.[36] The reason for this emphasis was given on another occasion. When there were no details of eclipses in the Songkran announcement of 1866, he wrote: "There is a lot of work to do, and no time for calculation, but if we let the astrologers do it, it would be crude and unreliable."[37] Sometimes he labeled his adversaries as *hon sumsam*, that is, careless astrologers.[38] Some monks and ex-monks who did the calendrical calculation were scornfully called *then*, sham monks. He went further by classifying *then* into three types: *ngomthen*, those who were interested in nothing but eating and sleeping; *rayamthen*, those who were busy with women or other improper affairs; and *laithen*, ignorant monks who knew little of anything but curried favor with others. It was the last category who became the calendar officials of the court.[39] Mongkut used these terms whenever he attacked the practices of astrologers and monks, including their superficial knowledge of time measurement.[40]

The observation of the full solar eclipse at Wako in 1868 was the climax of his struggle. The forecast of the event was announced on Songkran that year without any detail because Mongkut had not had enough time for calculation. In August an official announcement was made. He calculated the exact time of the eclipse in the Thai system of time measurement *(mong, baht)* and the precise duration of the full eclipse, which was one *baht* or, as he said, "six minutes mechanic clock."[41] But the full eclipse would be seen only along a certain belt on the earth, which happened to cross the Kra isthmus at "longitude 99 *ongsa,* 40 *lipda,* 20 *philipda,* calculated from Greenwich, that is, only 49 *lipda* and 40 *philip.* west of Bangkok [and] latitude *khipthuwi* 11 *ongsa,* 41 *lipda,* and 40 *philip.* north, which is 2 *ongsa,* 3 *lipda,* 29 *philip.* south of Bangkok."[42] The units of measurement were the Thai versions of degrees, minutes, and seconds respectively. But the method of measuring in terms of coordinates on the earth's surface was undoubtedly Western. One study on this issue suggests that in his calculation Mongkut consulted an unorthodox doctrine—the *Saram,* one of the two Mon treatises for planetary calculation known in Siam—as well as Western texts.[43]

Damrong tells us that according to astrological knowledge prevailing in Siam, there could be a full lunar eclipse but there had never been a full solar eclipse and it was probably impossible. Therefore, most astrologers at that time did not believe Mongkut's forecast because of its unorthodoxy.[44] Damrong's retrospective explanation is exaggerated. A full solar eclipse is not incompatible with Thai astrology; it is mentioned at least once in the traditional astrological record.[45] Nonetheless, the most important implication of Damrong's recollection is that there was subtle contention between Mongkut and his court astrologers. Probably their forecast of the eclipse was greatly different owing to the fact that while Mongkut preferred the *Saram* and Western methods, most court astrologers consulted the other text.[46] The result of calculation by the latter was an eclipse but definitely not a total one —and, besides, there was no such thing as a belt on earth. It is not hard to imagine his isolation and the pressure created upon him as he took the risk of putting his royal credibility into the confrontation. It was much more than an intellectual exercise, and his opponents were not just astrological persons but a kind of establishment. Since he had forecast the eclipse, he was obsessed by the calculation in every precise detail to prove his knowledge and the king's credibility.

Confident in his wisdom, Mongkut organized an observation of this full eclipse and resolved to lead it himself, despite his age (sixty-four) and the hardship of traveling and residing in the jungle. For the sake of precision and in order to confirm his ability, moreover, he selected Wako, a wilderness in the middle of a disease-ridden rainforest, as the chosen place for observation because it was exactly the position pinpointed by the calculation.[47] Furthermore, he invited the high-ranking officials of European powers in the region to join the observation at Wako. The British and French accepted the invitation and brought with them a large entourage with many instruments for observation and scientific experiments. The Siamese party was large as well, and had many superfluous facilities for surviving the jungle and for entertaining the king and his royal guests. They prepared no instruments, for example, but brought ice from Bangkok. The Wako meeting became an international astronomical observation, perhaps the only one on such a majestic scale ever organized in this region. At its heart, symbolically, was the rendezvous of indigenous astrology and Western astronomy, as well as everything in the spectrum in between.

The fateful day, 18 August 1868, was an overcast day at Wako. Everyone was ready for the full eclipse, especially the Europeans who had already set their instruments. Unfortunately, the sun was hardly seen either by naked eye or by instruments. The weather almost upset the international event. But suddenly, just as the eclipse began, the sky cleared and the full eclipse was witnessed by everyone present. The full eclipse occurred in accord with Mongkut's forecast in every detail. Unlike his European guests, he had not prepared any scientific experiment: the full eclipse itself was a successful experiment. It was a magnificent recognition of his most important triumph.

His victory was not a total defeat for indigenous knowledge, however. His accomplishment owed as much to Western geographical and astronomical knowledge as to his own beloved expertise in native astrology. Only the new idea of celestial bodies and how to calculate them was proved to be superior. Even for Mongkut himself, the suddenly clearing sky was a miracle—a gift of deities who should therefore be partly credited for the success. Once the full eclipse began to recede, while the Europeans were still busy with their scientific experiments, Mongkut began making religious offerings in gratitude to those deities.[48]

When he returned to Bangkok, Mongkut found that the court astrologers, including the chief, Phra Horathibodi, and many high-ranking nobles who stayed in Bangkok, could not give proper answers to his questions about the eclipse as seen in Bangkok. He punished them severely, sending them to labor at the royal park for one day and sentencing them to prison for eight days.[49] Then he issued a letter about the full eclipse, attacking those who did not believe him. He condemned those who earned more money than the cost of offerings made to the deities but had not been interested in his calculation of the eclipse. He condemned them for their coarse, plebeian minds and stupid statements because of their negligence of his detailed prediction and their inattention to measurement and calculation by modern instruments. They left the servants responsible for timekeeping; they were careless toward detail and accepted the crude forecast of the court astrologers. Moreover, the way they watched the eclipse was vulgar—using hands to shade their bare eyes—and the clock they used was terribly unreliable: "Only temple people or old monks still used [that kind of clock]." He then scolded the astrologers who had been in the monkhood for many years for boasting of themselves while ignoring knowledge: "From now on, astrologers must stop their coarse, vulgar, plebeian behavior like that of temple people or ex-monks." Everyone involved in the event was ordered to make his own handwritten copy of this letter.[50]

To achieve such an accomplishment, unfortunately, Mongkut had worked so hard that his health deteriorated. The risk of choosing Wako as the observation site had produced success, but Mongkut and his son, Chulalongkorn, contracted malaria on the expedition. Chulalongkorn was in serious condition for a considerable period, but he survived. Mongkut did not. Mongkut won the struggle against the orthodox court astrologers and indigenous cosmology. But it was a tragic victory. He sacrificed himself for his cause.

Space in a New Mode: Modern Geography

Since we conceive the world via the mediation of a certain conception, different conceptions, in turn, affect our knowledge of the earth and related geographical practices. How different would the world be if a late-nineteenth-century Thai conceived it with modern geography? And how does this spatial discourse work in relating human beings to space? To answer the questions, we must examine modern geography as it was brought into that historical setting.

Thiphakorawong was unsuccessful in his efforts to have his book, *Kitchanukit,* read among schoolchildren. Nonetheless, modern geography was established in Siam very rapidly. Only eight years after Thiphakorawong's book, six years after Mongkut's fatal triumph, the first geography book in Thai was published in 1874. Based on an English text, *Phumanithet* was written by J. W. Van Dyke, an American missionary living in Siam between 1869 and 1886, with a dedication to King Chulalongkorn and best wishes for the future of Siam.[51] It was a book of "the world atlas" *(phaenthilok)* in Thai.

A white elephant stood in the middle of the front page above the publishing year given in Thai calendrical reckoning.

Phumanithet was used in only a limited number of schools, mainly in those run by the American missionaries. The book never received official recognition as a textbook. During the early years of the new educational system in Siam in the 1880s, geography was not a subject for all students except in the upper secondary levels of the English program offered in certain schools; the traditional doctrines of cosmology were still studied in most Thai schools. In 1887, following Chulalongkorn's criticism that the books then in use were worthless since they were full of stories of kings and battles *(chakchak wongwong)*, a new educational minister, Prince Damrong, initiated a reform of curriculum and all textbooks for Thai schools. In 1892 the new curriculum commenced; modern geography was now a subject at every level of the secondary schools.[52] A new generation of geography texts was urgently needed.

The new curriculum of 1892 stated that geography meant the study of the earth, solar system, planets, and natural phenomena. It also concerned the practice of drawing up plans for a house, a village, or a town and the use of maps.[53] Subsequent improvements of the curriculum in 1895 and 1898 required geography in almost every grade and more detailed and sophisticated treatments at the higher levels, such as the study of other countries and elementary techniques of mapmaking. Among the textbooks that proliferated under these initiatives was W. G. Johnson's *Phumisat sayam* (Geography of Siam), which later became a model for many other texts.[54]

These textbooks may tell us how modern geography was disseminated and conceived in those days. They are refined conceptual tools to equip students with new ideas of space, the new geography. These early texts were rather simple. They conveyed a very elementary knowledge of modern geography. When more sophisticated books were written, the earlier books were relegated to use by primary school children, if not discontinued altogether; one text became a reader for the study of Thai language, not of geography. Like the elementary grammar of a language, such a text is always simple, and necessarily so.

These textbooks indicate that by the early twentieth century the traditional belief in a flat earth was already marginalized. None of these books troubled to argue against such an idea. Nor was it mentioned. The only exception was the 1902 textbook by Phraya Thepphasatsathit which mentioned the idea that the earth was supported by the Anon Fish, a mythical creature. But here Thepphasatsathit made up a story of a rather dull boy talking with a local uneducated man.[55] In the same book, by contrast, when the teacher asked his pupils about the shape of the earth, all the children raised their hands, one answering, "like an orange."[56] For the author of this textbook, knowledge of the spherical earth was so common that every child should be able to answer such a simple question, although one of them might hesitate because of the opinions of an uneducated older man.

Certainly the world of the Traiphum cosmography had no place in these geographical texts. The earth of modern geography is a planet in the solar system and orbits around the sun. Its surface consists of a number of great continents and oceans. Above all, according to these texts, this earth is full of *prathet*, that is, countries or nations. The word *prathet* in the old usage simply meant a place or an area (district, region, town, even an area of the forest). It signified a piece of the earth's surface without any specific qualification of size, population, or power. Traces of this old meaning still appeared in most of the dictionaries of the Thai language compiled in the late nineteenth or early twentieth century.[57] But by that time, the meaning of *prathet* as a nation was also appearing in some of them.[58] The new specific definition of *prathet* came from the new geographical conception of the earth, as explained in Van Dyke's *Phumanithet* and Johnson's book.

According to Van Dyke, the earth's surface is divided into continents and oceans. A continent is composed of "governed (or occupied) territories" divided by boundaries and called kingdoms, empires, or republics. Each of these territories is a *prathet*. In a *prathet* there must be a capital and the supreme ruler, called a king, an emperor, or a president, and other parts governed by *chaomuang* (governors or provincial rulers) under the power of the capital.[59] With the exception of the first two chapters, the book devotes one chapter to each continent.[60] For each continent, selected nations *(prathet)* are described, starting with Prathetthai. The maps of each continent as well as Siam are shown at the beginning of the relevant chapters; notes on the scale and symbols used in the maps are provided on the last page of the book.

The use of the term "Prathetthai" throughout this book is worth noting since the Siamese called their country "Muang Thai," the country of the Thai, and the outside world called it "Siam" until the new name, "Thailand" in English and "Prathetthai" in Thai, was adopted in 1941. Likewise, other countries are identified in this book by putting their names after the word *prathet*. It appears that the term *prathet* was chosen to replace the term *muang*. *Muang* refers broadly to a community, a town, a city, even a country —that is, an occupied area under the exercise of a governing power but without specification of size, degree or kind of power, or administrative structure. While the meaning of *muang* has been flexible, the new knowledge took over a very broad unspecified term, *prathet,* ascribing to it a very specific meaning in the grammar of modern geography: a nation.

The new specific meaning of the word *prathet* was also hinted at by Johnson. In the earlier editions of his book, the names he uses for Siam are varied: Prathetsayam or Sayamprathet in the early pages, Krungsayam in the later pages.[61] The word for England is Krung-angkrit. The term *krung,* originally meaning a great city, had been used by Mongkut and his contemporaries to mean a kingdom, a usage that lasted for some time. But from the 1914 edition onward, most of the instances of *krung* in the earlier editions were replaced by the term *prathet,* with only a few exceptions in the final pages.

Johnson gave the definition of a *prathet* in the "introduction to geography" as parts of the earth's surface inhabited by different nationalities. The part of Asia where Thai people lived, for instance, was called Sayamprathet.[62] As a book of geography of Siam, here he defines the location by two kinds of statements. First, Siam is on the peninsula in the southeastern part of Asia; second, he lists the names of nations surrounding Siam.[63]

It appears that the most significant feature of modern geography as introduced to the children of Siam is a spherical earth filled with nations on its surface. Siam is one among them; it is certainly situated somewhere on earth. A *prathet* is a territory on the earth's surface which is empirically perceivable. It can be identified by at least two methods: first, by its definite place on earth in reference to the larger space of which it is part; second, by referring to the "boundary relation" to the governed space surrounding it. In the first method, sometimes the referential space is not a mere continent but the whole earth in terms of the coordinate specification preferred by Mongkut. Likewise, throughout the book *Phumanithet* Van Dyke could tell his readers about the existence of each nation only by referring to the part of the continent where such a nation stood and then by mentioning its neighboring territories. The empiricity of a nation such as Siam on the earth's surface was so real that one could say that its shape was like an old axe of the palace guard or a coconut-shell dipper. Modern geography has promised its believers the existence of Siam and all nations as if they were natural.

But if no one had ever seen a nation-filled earth with one's own eyes, and if the whole region of neighbors was never simultaneously observable, how could one understand these two methods? What made these statements sensible, apart from general knowledge of the spherical earth? Both methods have one thing in common. They require the knowledge of a map of the earth, or of a continent, or at least a specific part of the earth. In fact, Van Dyke in his *Phumanithet* has to provide his readers with maps of the round earth and a particular continent for each chapter. A brief explanation of what a map is and the basic reading technique is also given in the early pages of the book. He explicitly recommends that his readers use an atlas in reading his book for a better view of a nation's features. In the first edition of Johnson's book, there were two maps attached: the map of Asia (with sketchy details) and the "map of Siam's boundaries" with all the surrounding countries being mentioned.[64] We may wonder how one could understand where Siam was and what it looked like without having seen these maps and without having even an elementary knowledge of reading them. Without the general knowledge of a map, neither kind of statement is intelligible. It may be further doubted whether other kinds of communication in this mode of spatial perception could be possible without any knowledge of a map. But how can a map make statements intelligible in this kind of geography? To put it more simply, how does a map work? What is a map?

Space Encoded: The Modern Map

Another geography text of that first generation may help us answer the questions posed above. Thepphasatsathit's two volumes of *Geography* first appeared in 1902 and 1904 respectively.[65] Both of them may have been among the longest-serving texts for schoolchildren and the most frequently reprinted in the history of school curricula in Siam.[66] In the second volume, the first ten chapters are lessons on elementary knowledge about mapping—from how to determine the cardinal points to methods for reading and drawing a map. In this process, a student would learn step by step about a plan, a scale, a map, the relation between a plan and a map, and the relationship between them and the reality they represent.

According to the lessons, a plan is an "outline," in the very strict sense of the word, of a thing as if it were seen from above (chaps. 2–3). A plan is different from a picture because the latter can tell the viewer what a thing is as if it had been witnessed, whereas a plan can only indicate the configuration of the thing and its size or distances from other things in the same plan (chap. 4). A scale is a method to enlarge or reduce the size of a plan in proportion to the thing. These are all prerequisites for lessons on mapping and the map of Siam in chaps. 8–10. Since the original is written in the form of conversations between Uncle and two boys, I offer the following abridged version:

> Uncle asks, "What is a map?"
> "It's a picture," a boy quickly replies.
> "No," Uncle responds loudly, "a map is not a picture. If it were a picture, we must see a lot of houses, trees, and people in it. But here we can't."
> "A map is a plan, they're the same." He goes on explaining, "A map is a

plan of the earth's surface, be it of lands or waters. The map which shows the whole earth's surface is a plan of it."

Then Uncle points at the map of Siam and says, "This is the part of the earth where we live." He also explains that the colors on the map are not the earth's colors; they would see Siam very green if they could fly above it. They then look at the map of the Chao Phraya River and another one of Bangkok on which they enjoy pointing at the positions of important places.

The boys enjoy learning about the map very much. They also learn that a scale is always used in drawing a map, as well as many symbols which they have to remember.[67]

This simple lesson is striking because it tells comprehensively, though not in detail, how a map mediates between human thinking and space.

Since human beings experience the world and, apart from intuition or feelings, communicate to each other through signs in the complex play of innumerable sign systems in everyday life, a map is just another kind of sign. According to theories of cartographic communication, a map is a medium between spatial reality and human, of both cartographer and user, to help human beings perceive such space without the need of direct experience. The relationships between space, maps, and human perception—the fundamental trio of cartographic communication—are very complex. The diagram below constitutes a very basic and simplified explanation according to these theories.[68]

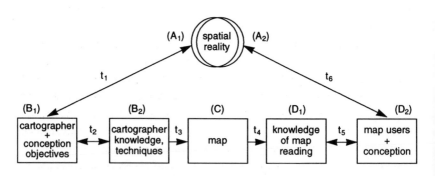

(A$_1$) cartographer's conception of reality
(A$_2$) map users' conception of reality
(B$_1$) cartographer subjectivity, especially his/her cognitive system, and objectives in particular projects
(B$_2$) cartographic knowledge, particularly techniques of transforming data into a map
(D$_1$) users' knowledge of how to read a map
(D$_2$) users' subjectivity, especially their cognitive system
t$_n$ the transformation or interpretation process

Source: Diagram based on A. Kolaeny's discussion in "Cartographic Information," pp. 47–49.

The cartographer observes or surveys the geographical terrain *(A)* with specific objectives for each kind of map. Then, by cartographic methods, he or she conceptualizes it *(B)*, transforms the data into a mapping form *(C)*, and the map is produced. The information transmitted by the map is perceived *(D)* and translated by the user's knowledge of mapping. The complexity, however, lies in each step of the diagram. The production of a map could be affected by many factors that would result in different outcomes—such as the cartographer's view, perception, particular objectives for each map, or different usage of symbols. All transformations from object to signs and from signs to the reader's conception involve an interpretive process.[69] Thepphasatsathit's lesson implies many of these theoretical steps without purporting to be a theoretical text. From all these theories and premises we can enhance our argument about the specific nature of a map and its mechanisms of representation.

First, like a picture, a map claims to be a representation of spatial reality in the form of two-dimensional graphics. As a kind of plan, it differs from a picture in its form of representing. According to Uncle, a picture records the content of the spatial object as if the viewer were witnessing it. Since the thing is viewed from just one point of view, its shape, its configuration seen in a picture, cannot correspond to the actual shape, but the viewer can recognize it from the content. A plan, on the contrary, documents the shape, the structural form, of a spatial object. For Uncle, a map is a kind of plan, viewing an object from above and preserving its form and structural relations of the contents only. That is to say, a map is the structural configuration of spatial objects.

Second, no matter how much a map may resemble the space it represents, it can do so only by transforming the complex three-dimensional material space into the mapping format. This transformation process requires at least three kinds of procedures. First, the method of generalization means the reduction, selection, combination, distortion, approximation, or exaggeration of the very details of space to make them data for each particular map. Second, the method of scaling means an enlargement or reduction of real measurements by certain ratios. Third, the symbolization means the use of symbols or other devices to represent certain things.[70] Thanks to geometry, the data are transformed by geometric calculation and represented mostly by geometric symbols. The result is an interpretive abstraction of the material space.

Third, despite this interpretive abstraction, a map claims to have a mimetic relationship with reality. A map is able to operate as long as one postulates that a map is the non-interfering medium between spatial reality and human perception—that reality is the source and the referent of the relationship. One of the important topics of cartographic communication is the degree of arbitrariness and mimesis in the devices used in a map, that is, the study of how particular marks, symbols, sizes, colors, or even positions of these devices can represent reality in different degrees of arbitrariness and mimesis.[71] Some even argue that a map has intrinsic connections with the external world of perceived reality whereas a diagram is merely an arbitrary device which has no such connection.[72] Without this assumption of an intrinsic connection with the external world, Uncle and the two boys could not have fun identifying public buildings and city sights on the map of Bangkok. As we shall see, however, this postulate is questionable.

Fourth, nonetheless, a map is communicable among producers and users, and conceivable in its relation to object, because in both the transformation process by cartographers and the reading process by users, the whole mechanism of a map—structure, symbols, scale, and so forth—is based on a common cartographic language. A map survives by conventions. Uncle must teach the boys the conventions. Schoolchildren in every society participating in this same global civilization of modern geography must learn the conventions. They must be put through this socializing process to keep the rules and conventions conventional. A map, a combination of symbols in the form of two-dimensional graphics, is given life by the rules and conventions provided only by the study of modern geography and the elementary techniques of mapping. Only by this global practice is the space represented by a map (if properly read) guaranteed to be unambiguous, though a few discrepancies are possible.

Finally, a map not only represents or abstracts spatial objects. Perhaps the most fascinating novelty of this technology is its predictive capacity. In fact, one of the most fundamental methods of mapmaking is mathematical projection. The globe is so huge; the human is so small; yet curiosity extends beyond the globe. Once the earth's surface was assumed as the ultimate reference of modern maps in the sixteenth century, the latitude-longitude grid for the entire planet was developed to establish a general matrix for measurement. Since then, the world has fascinated generations of humans by its unknown places yet to be discovered in order to fill in the blank squares established by the mathematical projection. A modern map can predict that something is certainly "there" at particular coordinates; the facts and knowledge will be "discovered" later by true believers of the modern map. Therefore, how could a nation resist being found if a nineteenth-century map had predicted it?

In short, a map is a code for a presumed spatial object in modern geography. As a sign, a map appropriates a spatial object by its own method of abstraction into a new sign system. A map encodes a space which, in turn, can be decoded to disclose knowledge of the supposed real space. It is a product of scientific method as well as of the social institutions of our modern time.

The kind of map considered here is totally different from the maps of premodern geography. The differences are due not only to techniques but also to different kinds of knowledge and the conceptions behind them. In the indigenous conception, for example, space is usually identified with certain aspects of the sacred or the religious. It is an intrinsic quality of space. Or to put it in another way: the religious subordinates the materiality of space, making the latter dependent on, or an expression of, religious value. By contrast, modern geography is a discipline which confines itself to the study of the material space on earth. Space on a modern map, at least space which human beings inhabit, is concrete and profane. Thus the premodern maps had no interest in the accuracy of measurements and required no scientific, empirical methods. A map merely illustrated the fact or truth that had been known already, either cosmography, moral teaching, or a traveling route. A modern map, on the contrary, dismisses the imaginary and sacred approaches to the profane world. It constitutes the new way of perceiving space and provides new methods of imagining space which prevent the "unreal" imagination and allow only legitimate space to survive after the decoding process.

In a premodern map, there was no inference that a spatial unit depicted was part of a spatial wholeness. There was no indication of the position of that unit on the earth's surface. But to draw a map of a nation always implies a global wholeness of which the spatial unit on the map is merely a part. The importance of the global plane of reference in its materiality adds one more distinction, perhaps the most important one. A premodern map was merely an illustration of another narration, be it a religious story or the description of a travel route. Some may not refer to any spatial reality at all. This kind of map was not indispensable. On the contrary, since the spatial reality a modern map of a nation purports to represent is never directly experienced in its totality—indeed, it is impossible to do so—a modern map is an indispensable mediator in perceiving and conceptualizing such macrospace in its totality, a function none of the premodern maps ever performed.

As a part of the globe, moreover, the map of a nation must be viewed against the earth's surface and the methods to indicate this are indispensable as well. All methods imply that each part of the globe, a nation, and its maps can be connected to form the whole globe through the patchwork of boundary lines. Indeed, boundary lines are so important for a map of a nation that the latter cannot exist without the former. A nation can be imagined without a word or other symbol or color on a map, but this is impossible if boundary lines, the symbol which forms the entity of a map of a nation, are excluded. Boundary lines are indispensable for a map of a nation to exist—or, to put it in another way, a map of a nation presupposes the existence of boundary lines. Logically this inevitably means that boundary lines must exist *before* a map, since a medium simply records and refers to an existing reality. But in this case the reality was a reversal of that logic. It is the concept of a nation in the modern geographical sense that requires the necessity of having boundary lines clearly demarcated. A map may not just function as a medium; it could well be the creator of the supposed reality.

A country represented by this code was entering a new kind of earth space which had another set of rules and conventions, another mode of relations. If a map is more than a recording or reflecting medium, the transformation may be more complex than anyone might expect. To put this problem into a historical framework, the imaginability of a nation in terms of a map involves a number of changes—both in concept and in the human practices concerning the domain and limits of a country. The most important precondition is the conception and practices of boundary lines which distinguish one unit of sovereign space from another. The boundary of a nation works in two ways at the same time. On the one hand, it sets a clear-cut limit on a sovereign unit; on the other hand, it imposes a sharp division between at least two units of space. In other words, it is the edge of one unit as well as a thing in between. Consequently, many conceptions and practices of interstate relations must be changed to conform with the new geography of a country. The indigenous concepts must be displaced.

Modality: Ambiguity and Displacement

A history of the geo-body of Siam is not a chronological description of boundary demarcations and the events which led to the making of Siam's map. Rather, the case of Mongkut and the relationship between astrology and astronomy, all highlighted by the Wako event, is a vivid example of how complex the displacement of geography was. It was a case in which different kinds of geographic knowledge coexisted, collided, and were finally displaced.

The Wako expedition highlighted the encounter of two sets of knowledge. Even its meaning to our time is ambiguous. Mongkut was praised as the Father of Thai Science and 18 August has now been officially declared National Science Day. The word "Thai science" means modern scientific knowledge in Thailand, not the indigenous Thai science, judging from the reasons given for Mongkut's elevation, such as his expertise in astronomy, his stand against superstition and astrologers, his interest in modern medical science and scientific innovations such as steamships and the printing press.[73] Not only are these terms unclear and subject to interpretation, but the reasons given do not quite account for what happened. Though it can be said that the Wako event and 18 August constituted the triumph of (Western) science, Mongkut's love of astrology and his belief in the assistance of the deities should not be discounted. Ironically, therefore, Mongkut has also been regarded by Thai astrologers as the "Father of Thai Astrology,"[74] meaning the indigenous astrology. Likewise, one cannot ignore the facts that the cosmological reference of his calculation came from Western astronomy and that Mongkut was hostile to traditional astrologers.

There is another appraisal of Mongkut and the Wako event which avoids deciding one way or the other between Western astronomy and native astrology. One can argue that the aim of the Wako event was in fact political-psychological. It proved that Siam equaled the West in terms of knowledge, and therefore the imperialists' claim that Siam was uncivilized and had to be colonized was unreasonable.[75] This idea assumes a patriotic unity of the court against imperialist aggression. It is beyond doubt a nationalistic retrospection. The adversaries in Mongkut's struggle were in fact traditional Thai astrologers, while the Europeans functioned as an international pressure group implicitly supporting Mongkut in his cause.

Nonetheless, the true meaning may be ambiguous rather than subject to a single interpretation. It would be a mistake to regard Mongkut's endeavor as the indigenous maneuver against the Western worldview or vice versa. It was an epistemological hybrid—regardless of whatever inconsistency, contradiction, or logical discomfort we may attribute to it. Each interpretation of the event has tried to prescribe a certain meaning—hence value—to it in order to claim Mongkut and his conviction as its predecessor. Rather, the ambiguity of the whole event and Mongkut's epistemological hybrid was in itself a critical phase of the shift of knowledge.

One of Mongkut's contemporary biographers wrote in the concluding paragraph of a famous account of Mongkut's life that

[Mongkut] understood astrology well, both in Siamese and European scripts. He could calculate the movements of the sun and all planets in great detail, predicting solar and lunar eclipses so precisely that no one could match him. He also knew *yiokrapfi* [geography] very well, measuring the sun and stars accurately. . . . He was unremittingly faithful to the Three Gems of Buddhism.[76]

Here was the first account of a Siamese king whose ability in a traditional "science" like astrology and his True Faith were mentioned on either side of a new ambitious discipline about the sun, stars, and certainly the earth though it was not mentioned, a discipline which was comprehensively called geography in the Thai tongue. The place of *yiokrapfi* in this paragraph was by no means accidental.

Astrology was a privileged science in a society which believed that human affairs are influenced or predetermined by celestial bodies. In astrology, the calculation of positions and movements of celestial bodies and the art of interpreting their influence are the two fundamental tasks. Astrologers became powerful "scientists" at every level of such a society, from the court to the village community, because they held the expertise to calculate celestial causes and predict the effects. The art of prediction may be, in our view, not objective or even superstitious, yet it is based on previous interpretations and the cumulative record of those phenomena believed to be influenced by celestial entities in certain positions. Furthermore, astrological calculation has mathematical rules in the framework of a cosmology developed through many generations. Perhaps the knowledge about celestial movements of astrology was no less mathematically objective than that of astronomy.

Astrology, accordingly, relies on the precision of its calculations, just as many modern sciences rely on mathematics. The more precise the calculation, the more accurate and reliable the astrological explanation. It appears that for the sake of precision of calculation, Western knowledge of celestial movements and the earth, as well as the scientific spirit of empirical observation, were, to some people like Mongkut and his followers, as attractive as many other sciences of worldly matters. These people replaced the indigenous knowledge with the new *yiokrapfi*. But in doing so, they did not aim at eradicating indigenous astrology. Rather, they were eager to obtain the most up-to-date knowledge to improve the calculations. *Yiokrapfi,* which in fact included astronomy as well, performed a task of indigenous astrology with more accuracy and hence more reliability. The two fundamentally incompatible kinds of knowledge were matched up and found to be functionally compatible. They could be placed side by side within the same paragraph of Mongkut's "life-text,"—biography.

It should be noted here that in the Thai astrological treatises of later times, the solar system and the astronomical universe served as the framework of celestial movements and calculation without disturbing the systematic methods of prediction. Up-to-date astronomical discoveries such as knowledge about the three furthest planets in the solar system are now regarded as a part of astrological knowledge and even help astrologers to improve or expand their method of horoscopic calculations. A renowned astrologer claims that Mongkut was his predecessor in this unorthodox approach.[77]

As a consequence of this conceptual and functional compatibility, the attempt to grasp modern geography was done only by assimilating it through existing concepts—and above all through the existing terminology—just as a new language is always learned through translation into one's mother tongue. Take physical geography as an example. The classification of physical geography in the first chapter of Van Dyke's book, in Johnson's "Geography of Siam," and in the first volume of Thepphasatsathit's book was very similar to the taxonomy of the Traiphum cosmology. This indigenous taxonomy provided the means by which modern geography could be understood. Despite different conceptual systems, the indigenous taxonomy also became the vocabulary of modern geography.

The word *phum,* generally meaning land or world, becomes the keyword for "geography" in Thai—*phumisat.* Moreover, the title of Van Dyke's book, *Phumanithet,* was in fact the title of a chapter in the classic cosmological doctrine, *Chakkawanthipani,* though in that case it was a chapter about the deities and the underworlds. Later, this word also appeared in documents with the same meaning as geography.[78] The Thai terms for continent, oceans, and other geographical units, including *prathet,* were also drawn from this storehouse of knowledge that paralleled the new nomenclature. For this reason, it is not surprising that most of the Thai terminology for modern geography, particularly about the cosmos and macrospace, is taken from the Traiphum taxonomy.

Not only did the two kinds of knowledge have similar subject matters, therefore, but they also shared the same terminology in comparable classifications. Thus, not only did they coexist, but they overlapped by sharing the same terminological domain. To put it in another way: the terminology—words—became the interface of two knowledges. Conversely, these terms in mutual usage had double meanings and different denotations according to the respective conceptual systems. The terminology, and perhaps the whole classificatory system, became a system of double signifiers. Hence the knowledge of space and its terminology became ambiguous. As a consequence, the new geography faced a twofold task: a defensive one, to unravel any confusion and to differentiate itself from the other; and an offensive one, to take advantage of the compatibility and the ambiguity of geographical discourse.

Consider the first task. Because the conceptual systems behind the same terminology and behind the comparable classification were not the same, a word could transmit different messages depending on the code in operation. The defensive or unraveling task meant that there had to be a certain signal to inform the audience of a new conceptual reference. The use of a modern map was an example of this signaling code, since it was a property exclusive to the new geography. For other signaling codes, Thiphakorawong's *Kitchanukit* is a splendid illustration of how both languages of space could play in the same field under different rules. The author was obviously conscious of the growing ambiguity of geographical knowledge as a whole, yet he understood the distinctions between the different languages. One of the most serious confrontations between the contending geographical languages lay, as we have seen, in the fundamental question of the concept of the earth. This issue came to demarcate the two sides. It seems that by beginning with statements of what the earth looked like, both Van Dyke and Johnson did more than just convey the correct idea to their readers. Indeed, they put up a sign at the entrance to their books. The statements about the spherical earth functioned as the signaling code—the "password" to communicate that the story inside belonged to that particular language. Later, among the books of that generation, it became a tradition to begin a geographical book with introductory statements about the earth, no matter what kind of geography they described —physical or political, of Siam or of other parts of the world. Even atlases of later times always started with maps of a round earth, similar to Johnson's introductory statements. It became a convention with its original function no longer performed; in other words, a tradition, not an active code.

The second task was more important. To say that the geographical discourse became ambiguous means the indigenous spatial discourse was no longer the only language which supplied the grammar, or monopolized the codes, for perceiving space. In addition to the powerful support from royal authority and the intellectual elite, modern geography now imposed itself as a contender—a contesting language which could share certain properties with the previous one—and asserted its authority over the field of signification.

In this condition of ambiguity, the existing knowledge of space was destabilized, while the alternative became a threat to change. Modern geography never passively coexisted; nor did it simply rely on political support, the nonepistemological force, to propose itself as an alternative. Even though translation into the indigenous terminology was done by human beings for the purpose of human apprehension, it was beyond human intention once the compatibility was established. Modern geography had the potential to drive itself to usurp those properties of the indigenous knowledge, asserting itself as a new channel of message transmission. It waited for human intervention only to settle ambiguity in one way or another. In short, modern geography took advantage of the overlapping domains to make the indigenous language unstable, or ambiguous, and then proposed itself as a new way of signifying those terms.

The displacement of knowledge was a process which by no means implied a gradual, smooth, continuous adjustment. It was a process in which critical moments erupted, determining the ambiguity in a particular way. It was more or less violent. The Wako event was one such critical moment. The ambiguity of retrospective evaluation of the Wako event was due to the ambiguous nature of Mongkut and his ideological tendency in whom and in which modern geography resided alongside the indigenous conceptions. Mongkut's attacks on astrologers and Thiphakorawong's book were also among such moments which brought the contending geographical ideas to disruptive confrontation.

To argue that the establishment of scientific ideas in Siam enjoyed a smooth-as-silk continuity is to imply there was no significant friction, let alone rupture, between conceptions and practices of the competing knowledge. That, however, was not the case. What did Mongkut's life mean if not a tragic victory in an epistemological battle? The explanation advanced here can serve as a model for other aspects of the displacement of geographical knowledge as well. They too resulted from various confrontations, ambiguities, and disruptive moments at different times, places, and paces. Our focus here is on the conceptions and practices of boundaries and territorial sovereignty. As we shall see, one of the most disruptive moments in the displacement of geographical knowledge is a well-known episode in Thai history. But it has traditionally been understood in another way: as an agonizing event for Thai of all strata because it ended with the so-called loss of territories to the European powers in the latter half of the nineteenth century.

Chapter Three
Boundary

SIAM AND BURMA had been arch-rivals since the sixteenth century. As both sides launched periodic attacks against each other, the towns between the two kingdoms, particularly those along the southern coast of Burma, which until then was known as the Mon region, became crucial for both sides. In fact the whole area between the two kingdoms consisted of vast rainforests and huge ranges of mountains from north to south along the entire frontier. Yet both sides regarded the Mon towns as rich sources of food and manpower for fighting, two of the most important factors in premodern warfare. From time to time, people and towns came under the control of one side to cultivate food for the troops while they were at the same time the targets of destruction from the other to prevent them from supplying the enemy.

Western Boundary on the Western Frontier

Our drama begins in the first half of the nineteenth century when the British waged the first war against Burma, then the kingdom of Ava, in 1824–1826. In 1825, the British envoy to the court of Siam, Captain Henry Burney, was assigned by the East India Company to negotiate with Siam on several issues, especially the affairs of the Malay states and the trade agreement between them. Despite what some historians have said about the Anglo-Ava war having frightened the Siamese court, the attitude of the court toward the British was described by Burney as cordial. It seems that the court cautiously welcomed any power which fought against the Burmese. Throughout his reports, Burney tells us that the Siamese court followed the course of the war intently and was eager to hear any information or rumors about the fighting. Having a common enemy, Siam and the British almost reached agreement on sending two regiments of Siamese troops to support the British. The agreement never came about, however, because of misunderstandings on both sides owing to different styles of warfare and because the war ended a few months later.

During the time Burney was in Bangkok in late 1825 and early 1826, the British had conquered the southern part of Burma, making it the British Tenasserim Province. Then the western frontier of Siam became a question.[1] Burney requested the court to depute a high-ranking official to negotiate the boundaries between their newly acquired territory and Siam. The Phrakhlang, who held a position equivalent to the minister of foreign affairs and trade, deflected the request by saying that both Tavoy and Mergui, two major ports in southern Burma, were in fact Siamese boundaries and Siam had been preparing to recover them from the Burmese. Now that they had fallen into British hands, however, for the sake of friendship between the two countries, whose common enemy was still in the north (Ava), Siam would no longer lay claim to them. "With more appearance of frankness and sincerity than . . . expected," Burney reported, the Phrakhlang also blessed the British occupation and "hoped a flourishing trade would be soon brought by the English to Bangkok through that channel."

As it appears, the answer did not quite respond to the question. So Burney repeated the request and suggested that the Phrakhlang himself should go to the frontiers. At this point, "the Minister rolled his large body round, stared at me, and seemed as much startled as if I had proposed to him to take a trip to Europe."[2] Burney explained this reaction by saying that the Siamese king (then Rama III) did not trust anybody from his court to conclude agreements with the British; therefore, the person deputed would not have authority and could not make any decision. D. G. E. Hall remarks that Burney's suggestion might have frightened the Phrakhlang because any negotiation with the British, apart from the one conducted in Bangkok, would jeopardize the independence of Siam.[3] Such was probably not the case. The Phrakhlang was frightened, but the question of independence was not the likely issue. It is more probable that under the territorial division of power of the Siamese regime at that time the southwestern part of the kingdom was under the authority of the Kalahom, another high-ranking noble. Thus any negotiation by the Phrakhlang over that domain meant a threat to the Kalahom's power. The Phrakhlang did not want to put himself at risk. Perhaps taking a trip to Europe would have been less frightening to him. In any case, the reply indicated that the boundary demarcation was not yet an issue for the court's concern.

On the following day the Phrakhlang carried a message from the Kalahom to Burney: the boundary question was not urgent since, at the time, it was not yet certain that the British would decisively defeat the Burmese and in fact be able to secure those towns.[4] For the Siamese court the boundary question depended on the outcome of the war. Had Burma struck back, it is more likely that the towns would have been sacked again rather than becoming the settlement of a boundary demarcation. For the Phrakhlang, friendship was a sufficient reason to put aside a question of such low priority as a claim to these ports; for the Kalahom, a boundary would not be necessary. Neither the Phrakhlang nor the Kalahom took the question as seriously as Burney did.

Despite the court's lack of interest, Burney repeatedly urged it to negotiate the boundaries. At last his efforts produced results. Astonishingly, the reply was simple and straightforward:

> With respect to what is said about the boundaries, the Country of Mergui, Tavoy, and Tenasserim, no boundaries could ever be established between the Siamese and the Burmese. But the English desire to have these fixed. Let them enquire from the old inhabitants residing on the frontiers of Mergui, Tavoy, and Tenasserim, what they know respecting the contiguous territories, and let what they point out be the boundaries between the English and Siamese possessions.[5]

If this reply was regarded as naive by later historians like Hall, it was considered absurd by Burney who realized that such a statement would be received with astonishment by British authorities.[6] But for a Siamese official on the negotiating team, nothing was strange in such a reply, since

> the boundaries between the Siamese and Burmese consisted of a tract of Mountains and forest, which is several miles wide and which could not be said to belong to either nation. Each had detachments on the look out to seize any person of the other party found straying within the tract.[7]

It is clear that a "boundary" as understood by the British on the one hand and their Siamese counterparts on the other was a similar thing but not the same. For the Siamese court, it was hard to imagine why the question of boundary should be so important; it should have been a matter for the local people, not those in Bangkok. As a result, in the draft of the treaty prepared by the Siamese there was nothing about boundary settlement, though there were many statements about the domains belonging to Siam and to the British, implying that for Siam the distinction was already clear without the British kind of boundary.[8] Eventually, however, Burney persuaded the court to reach broad agreement about the boundary demarcation, and he put it in the subsequent drafts and in the final 1826 treaty. Written in Siamese fashion, the unnecessarily long article merely noted that if either side doubted any boundary, it should depute some officials and people from the frontier posts to inquire and settle mutual boundaries in a friendly manner.[9] This meant that the existing boundary was not at issue and nothing needed be done. More than half a year in Bangkok was enough for Burney to learn that the best compromise he could manage in this matter was to put something about it in the treaty, even though it could be seen to be of minor utility for the British. In doing so, he conceded that he was speaking of the matter in the same language as the Siamese court.

Except for some minor incidents in 1829 in which local Siamese officers launched occasional raids into British territory,[10] until 1840 no issue was raised by either party. In 1840, when E. A. Blundell became the commissioner of Tenasserim Province, he raised the matter again because the unsettled boundaries were causing trouble. The problem was tin mining. The southernmost frontier of Tenasserim Province was traversed by the Pakchan River,[11] both sides of which were rich in tin and other minerals. When the Siamese local chief extended his authority by levying a share of revenue of the tin miners on both sides, the miners refused to be double taxed by the British as well while some Chinese tin miners requested British protection.[12] Blundell regarded the Pakchan River as the boundary on the ground that the oldest inhabitant said it was the furthest place Burmese troops had ever reached and made temporary camp. He then sent a letter to Bangkok saying that the Siamese local chief had made incursions into British territory. The court replied at the end of that year that no boundary had been fixed yet, implying that Blundell's claim was unacceptable.[13]

British authorities in India warned Blundell to be cautious, realizing from Burney's experience that for some unknown reason the Siamese court was not happy with its request on this matter. Even as late as 1842 the Bengal authorities were not convinced of any urgent necessity to formalize the boundaries.[14] Yet Blundell persistently urged Siam to depute officials to the river, though the local Siamese officials were uncooperative. Then in mid-1842, surprisingly, Siam agreed to indicate the boundary, although it did not agree to regard the Pakchan River as the boundary line.[15] The rainy season, however, prevented both sides from proceeding through the jungle to decide the matter.

Siam was urged again in 1844 to decide the problem, since a few minor incidents had already occurred along the borders. This time the new commissioner, Major Broadfoot, asked for the settlement of boundaries from Chiangmai down to the Pakchan River.[16] The court seemed annoyed but replied clearly that the reasons of the English and Siamese nations having an occasion to speak about the boundaries are . . . [that] . . . Siamese and the English nations being in the state of great friendship, and as Major Broadfoot . . . being desirous of continuing the existing friendship has written a letter regarding the settlement of the boundary in amicable terms, the authorities of . . . golden royal city [Bangkok] are also anxious to have the boundary decided. . . . Request that Major Broadfoot will . . . settle justly and fairly which is to be the boundary. The Chiefs of . . . golden royal city are desirous to agree.[17]

In other words, for the sake of friendship, what the British desired, so did Siam, provided it was fair.

In the letter cited above, dated 13 November 1844, the court showed its dissatisfaction with the British claim over the right bank of the Pakchan River. It argued that minor disputes along the borders occurred because British subjects and the people of Kra, the township exercising authority over the Pakchan River, lived too close to each other. This would "cause some bad feelings beteen [sic] the two great friendly nations," the letter said. The Siamese thus opposed the British proposal because the Pakchan River was just a few hundred meters from Kra.

What kind of boundary did the court prefer? Here is a suggestion:

Should the boundary line [be] fixed along the Pakchan River, this would be exceedingly close to Kra. On the other hand, should it be fixed at the limits within which the Siamese have been accustomed formerly to exercise jurisdiction, it would still be far from Mergui. There should be a just decision, so that the inhabitants of the two countries may live at some distance from one another.[18]

Perhaps the British did not properly understand this definition of a boundary, for they continued to reassert their proposal. The communication on this matter went on to cover the question of the boundary of Moulmein in the north of Tenasserim. Now the tone of the letters from the court in August 1845 and August 1846 turned sour. Ironically, the more annoyed the Siamese court became, the stronger its commitment to settle the matter. In the former letter the court put forward a long counterproposal defining the boundaries from Chiangmai down to Kra. Then the letter said:

Whatever place it is desirable to examine the Governor and under officers of that province will point out the extent of the Siamese boundary there. Let them speak uprightly and the matter can be decided. . . . Having come to a decision let there be a written agreement concerning every part of the boundary line, which shall be final. Thus there will be, in future, no trespassing on one another.[19]

In the letter of August 1846, the question of the boundary seemed to be very annoying. It referred to an incident in which a local Siamese officer was accused of another incursion into British territory, planting a flag and exercising his authority over people in that area. The British suspected the court's complicity in this action and questioned the sincerity of the court. The Siamese court investigated the case and concluded that the boundary must be settled urgently to prevent any further conflict.[20] Certainly the British were happy with this outcome. Although disagreement over certain boundaries like the one at the Pakchan River still remained, Siam was ready to recognize the importance of the boundary and committed itself to observing the demarcation. That is, Siam conceded to speak of the matter in the way that the British preferred.

The reason for the change of attitude—from an ignorant and innocently uncooperative one in the early years to a somewhat displeased but actively cooperative one—is still unclear. The British tried to analyze this welcome change. They attributed it to the effect of a battle which was then taking place for a Kayah (or Red Karen) town in the mountainous area on the border of Chiangmai and Ava. The British thought it was a battle between Burma and Siam, hence an international dispute. They logically put the two events—the changing policy of Siam and the battle—into a diplomatic-military rationale: Siam was concerned about the security of its tributaries in the north, so it was naturally desirous of meeting the wishes of the British to secure the southern and western parts of the country. The British themselves were alarmed by the Burmese campaign, but they stayed neutral. Communications among the British authorities between late 1844 and early 1846 were full of discussions, reports, and speculations about the effect of the war on the strained relations between Ava and Bangkok, since the British thought that the Burmese intended to test the Siamese frontiers. They also urgently informed the Siamese court of their neutrality on the issue.[21]

The British, however, exaggerated the issue according to their own rationale. Bangkok knew nothing about the Burmese attacks on the Kayah township until December 1845 when the battle was already over. Chiangmai merely reported that the Burmese had attacked a Red Karen township and failed. Even Chiangmai did not regard the battle as its affair because the Kayah town, as the report said, "belongs to no one."[22] That was all there was to it. So, unsurprisingly, in the reply from Bangkok regarding the British neutral stand, the court did not mention anything about the battle.[23]

The change in attitude toward the boundary question was in fact one among many changes taking place in the last decade of the reigning Siamese king, Rama III (r. 1824–1851). The relationship between Siam and the West had been very good until then, and from the account of Burney himself it is unlikely that this amicability had, as historians have suggested, deteriorated since the 1820s as a result of the Anglo-Ava war.[24] Siam under Rama III was remarkable for its record of diplomatic relations with the West, and the king was described by a contemporary British diplomatic officer as having been "fond of the English."[25] In the last decade of the reign, however, the court turned against the West. Although this change has not yet been adequately accounted for, several explanations have been given: the conflicts in trade relations, the impact of British operations in Burma and the 1840 Opium War in China, and the threat of an American merchant who was in conflict with the court and demanded that the British naval force support him.[26] These incidents, plus the court's cool reception of many diplomatic missions from Western countries, indicate that the honeymoon period was over.

It appears that for the sake of friendship in the early years of the reign, Siam was not interested in the settlement of a boundary as the British had repeatedly urged. Yet when relations turned sour and the Siamese were annoyed by increasingly aggressive British authorities in the 1840s, they became more committed to it. Again, there is a hint here that the conceptions and functions of boundaries held by both sides were not the same.

Clashes of Conceptions of Boundary

During 1834–1836 a British mission was sent to Chiangmai, the center of the Lanna kingdom, in the north of Thailand today. One of the tasks was to prepare for a negotiation of the boundary between Tenasserim Province and Lanna. The British saw the potential of the area's timber industry, but, studying local records, they found evidence of Burma's rights over the eastern side of the Salween River. Therefore, they prepared to propose the Salween as their boundary. The authorities in India approved the action but warned not to push too hard and risk relations with Siam since the mission was conducted without the knowledge of Bangkok. Strikingly, not only was Chiangmai ready to make a treaty without Bangkok's approval, but for the sake of friendship the king of Chiangmai also happily gave away a portion of territory as a present which the British did not request.[27]

The boundary agreement was simply in writing, however, without on-the-spot marking; Chiangmai, like Bangkok, was not interested in that kind of task. In 1847, the British therefore urged Chiangmai to mark out the boundaries as agreed in 1834. It would be quite simple, Chiangmai replied. Let the British do the job themselves.

Neither the agreement nor the gift was done with Bangkok's knowledge. The British were a little worried about this, but nothing could prevent them from proceeding with their opportunity. Within two years, they had surveyed every fork of the Salween River in order to identify the main stream which would be regarded as the boundary. And with the assistance of the five oldest Karen along the river, they finished the job of marking the modern-style boundaries in 1849.[28]

Another case in which a considerable portion of territory was given away as a present occurred in the southernmost provinces. Captain James Low of Penang suggested in 1829 that a boundary should be marked between Wellesley Province, then leased by the British, and Kedah, a Malay state then under the overlordship of Nakhonsithammarat of Siam (hereafter Nakhon). But the ruler of Nakhon became angry with the request, saying that the Wellesley question was already clear in the treaty between Kedah and Penang. According to the treaty, which was concluded in 1802 without Siam's knowledge, however, it stated only how long and wide the portion called Wellesley was. This might be clear enough for Nakhon's ruler, but not for the empirically minded British.[29]

The question of this boundary became an issue because there was a movement of loyalists to an ousted sultan (raja) of Kedah along the frontier of Wellesley and Kedah who aimed to restore him. Thus the ruling sultan often sent his men across the border, which had not yet been clearly decided, to spy on the movement.[30] Therefore in the following year, 1830, observing that the treaty merely mentioned the width of Wellesley as 60 *orlongs* from the coast, the British suggested that boundaries should be defined.[31] They suggested, however, that they themselves undertake the defining: "His Lordship in Council is of [the] opinion, that instead of alarming the Siamese or exciting their jealousy, it will be better that our own officers should measure out the sixty *orlongs* and establish the line, leaving the Siamese when they choose to take up the question to prove our measurement erroneous."[32]

This action could have been alarming. After the rebellion in Kedah in 1831 was suppressed with British assistance, however, the negotiation for a boundary to be marked by British officers was easier. They erected three brick pillars at three different places east of Wellesley and planned to connect them by a road which would be regarded as the boundary. Because the boundary would help the British to prevent the movement of the ex-raja's loyalists, the ruler of Nakhon, with gratitude for British assistance, did more than the British had expected. He wrote a letter to the British governor-general of India, blessing him and all the British, saying that:

I feel myself deeply indebted to my friend and now return him my sincere thanks. Moreover the Rajah of Singapore (Mr. Ibbetson) asked me to settle the land boundary betwixt the territory appertaining to Penang and that of the Sia-

mese. I was exceedingly pleased at this request, and immediately complied with
it. In an old agreement with the Company the measurement in land from the
sea was considered to be sixty *orlongs.* I have moreover now given much more
than formerly in order to gratify the Rajah of Singapore and Captain Low.[33]

Certainly, this was unexpected. The territory of Wellesley Province was now
twice the size and richer![34] Like the king of Chiangmai's gift in 1834, this
agreement, and the bonus, were made without the knowledge of Bangkok.
Like the king of Siam, perhaps, the ruler of Nakhon was so fond of the British that a year later he too asked for a regular contact with Bengal. Gifts were
given with a request just to see a steam vessel.[35]

When the British wanted Siam to settle the boundaries from Chiangmai to
the Kra isthmus, they sent a letter in April 1845. It was written in an intimidating and didactic tone:

> It is very desirable that there should be one uniform rule as regards the bound-
> ary line from north to south, and that by adhering to that rule all causes of mis-
> understanding should be forever removed.
>
> It is advisable that the Court of Bangkok issue strict orders along their fron-
> tiers so that all subordinate authorities may clearly understand the line of
> boundary. . . . The boundary is clear and mistakes must in future be inexcus-
> able.
>
> Within this boundary no Siamese authorities are to exercise any jurisdiction,
> levy any revenue, and beyond this boundary no British authorities are to
> [do so].[36]

The statements may not seem unusual to us, but for the Siamese this sort
of boundary was unfamiliar and to stipulate such conditions might have
seemed to them an offense. The tone of the court's answer in August of the
same year was no less didactic, therefore, and showed that the court was confident about its full knowledge of the areas. According to the court, however, each area was under the jurisdiction of a local authority. Besides, the
methods of boundary marking were anything but uniform from north to
south. Remarkably, the boundary was identified not only by rivers, mountains, and streams but also by teak forests, mountains upon mountains,
muddy ponds where there were three pagodas, Maprang trees, three piles of
stones, the space between the White Elephant (?) and the Nong River, and
so forth.[37] Definitely none was a line. The letter also complained that the
valuable forests on the borders where people of Burma and Siam were used to
earning their living by collecting honey, sappan wood and teak, and hunting
elephants had been forbidden to them for twenty years since the British had
occupied the area. Did this imply that for Siam a boundary should *not* prevent
people from their customary pursuits?

Another case in 1846 also informs us about the differences in their concepts of a boundary. Following the correspondence cited above, both Siam and Tenasserim Province agreed to depute officials with full authority to decide the boundary on the northeastern edge of Tenasserim. The appointment was made for January 1846. The British officials arrived at the meeting place one month late, however, while their Siamese counterparts, having waited a whole lunar month, had returned just three days before. The British, who had been instructed to negotiate with utmost amity, found that the Siamese officials had advanced as far as a frontier town within claimed British territory and had laid down a pile of stones as the boundary mark to claim the areas as Siam's. The British pulled the mark down.

The British in Tenasserim Province then protested in a letter that was strong and satirical. They asked, for example, why Siam had not marked out the boundary at the center of Moulmein.[38] The internal British communications were more serious. They were alarmed that Siam might have changed its attitude toward the British. The diplomatic-military rationale came into play again when they tried to sort out the cause of Siam's disturbing action. They reasoned that the battle between Burma and Siam for the Red Karen town had just been concluded, so Siam had no urgent reason to reach an agreement with the British as they imagined had been the case earlier.

The Siamese court investigated the case and calmly replied in August 1846. The court's version of the story was totally different. The Siamese officials came back to Bangkok, reporting that they had met no British officials at the rendezvous point. They made no report about any incursion into British territory or about marking a boundary. All of them confirmed that no order had been issued to erect any boundary post or any marking. In fact, they came back with nothing to discuss since they had not met the British team. But, the court added,

> the heap of stones together with a small wooden house for religious purposes on the top of them . . . was erected by the Talien people who stop at the guardhouse of Utaitani merely as a mark to show . . . that they might guard as far as that. The English officer ordering the post to be taken down according to the custom of [Bangkok], no notice can be taken of it.[39]

It is likely that the Siamese team of local guards had in fact gone into British territory. But the mark erected was definitely not a boundary mark, and the officials did not consider their movement as an incursion into the other's territory. Hence no apology and no punishment. Whether or not the story was true, the answer must have been considered a good reply to the British charges. Hence the lack of evasion and embarrassment in telling the British such a story. In fact, the court did ask a guard whether he intended to move into British territory and claim that domain—indicating no complicity of the court but rather that the act was seen as a personal crime. The guard replied that it was a three-day journey from his house, too far for him to go there.

The British were probably stunned by the answer, which must have come as an anticlimax to the purported seriousness of the issue. Though they might not have had a thorough understanding, it was enough for them to realize that their interpretation of the incident was ludicrous—and any more protests about the behavior of the guards would be equally absurd. In any case, there was no further word from the British about this case. Nevertheless, the incident was one among many annoyances which made the court resolve to settle a boundary demarcation.

Siam's willingness to decide the boundary on its side did not guarantee that the demarcation would be decided within a few years, however. For a number of technical, logistical, and other reasons, the task was carried out by the court of Mongkut, which was more cooperative. Equipped with the knowledge to deal with the technicality of a boundary demarcation, and realizing the complication which might cause political problems, Mongkut himself worked out the details on various areas to be marked, including the question of Pakchan, and issued many instructions concerning particular borders to his chief of boundary negotiation—remarkably, his Kalahom. He instructed his officials not to accept British maps uncritically, for there might be incorrect details which could lead to disputes. Yet he disregarded the map done by local officials for its "incorrectness [since] it was done in Thai style, though it was somewhat understandable."[40] It is apparent that the boundary he spoke of was the same kind the British had in mind. But it was not yet the same one as understood by local Siamese authorities.

The boundary on the Siam–British Burma front was on the agenda again in the 1870s and 1880s during Chulalongkorn's reign (Rama V, r. 1868–1910). Two major factors unsettled the matter: the complicated controversy over the timber industry in the areas along the Salween River and in Lanna, as well as the fact that the Anglo-Burmese war broke out again for the third and final time in 1884–1885. A Siamese prince, Phichitpreechakorn, who was sent to supervise the administration of Chiangmai from 1884, found that among many urgent tasks he had to inspect the security of the borders and tighten control over them. He discovered that when the British took over Burma, they regularly watched over the borders whereas the Lanna local chiefs always stayed in their towns, waiting for opportunities to attack the Burmese towns along the borders, plunder them, and force the people back to Lanna. Phichitpreechakorn thus ordered local authorities to set up new villages right along the borders with a number of guardhouses, fortifications, and households in each place. Then he prescribed the need for these guardian villages and local chiefs to inspect the borders regularly—a job unfamiliar to these people—and ordered them to urgently define the boundary of each area by whatever markings. Moreover, he called for a meeting of local chiefs along the frontiers. There they signed a declaration of loyalty to the king of Siam and took an oath of allegiance. In return, they received good-quality cloth plus the Ratchapataen ("raja's pattern")—the semi-Western-style official suit used only at the court in Bangkok—and a sum of money before returning to their duties.[41] Here the confrontation of different conceptions and practices concerning the boundary and border control took place between the Bangkok authority and local ones. The former was conscious of the differences, perhaps, so all the measures were pragmatic and aimed to establish a new kind of boundary via traditional practices.

It was the various disputes involving the timber industry that brought about the first formal Siam–British India treaty signed in January 1874 at Calcutta to mark the boundary between Lanna and Tenasserim Province only.[42] But after the final British victory over Ava in 1885, the boundary of the northern part of Lanna and Upper Burma under British India became a new question. A team of British and Siamese officials was jointly deputed to conduct an inquiry of local authorities about the boundary in that region. To indicate the boundaries, the Bangkok and local delegates tried to use the same geographical discourse as the British. They handled it very well in most cases, though they were not quite familiar with it and sometimes used it awkwardly.

The British persistently ordered local chiefs to provide any treaty or document identifying the boundaries. As these were friendly neighbors who shared understanding and trust, one local chief replied, the boundary did not forbid people to trespass or to earn their living in the area. Hence no document had ever been made. According to them, the borders were "golden, silver paths, free for traders." Moreover, it seems that in some cases local chiefs were ordered to prepare their maps, as one local chief admitted frankly that the map was still being done and would be finished soon.[43] Most confusing for the British was the fact that a subject of a local authority could be at the same time a subject of another authority. This posed a problem in judging what belonged to whom, since there was usually more than one power exercised over a given people who occupied a certain area. On the other hand, the tribal people wandering in the mountain forests were subjects of no power. Furthermore, what caused the most confusion to the British was the fact that for some areas such as Muang Sing or Chiang Khaeng, a small town at the junction of Laos, Burma, and China today, the chief and his people belonged to three overlords at the same time. The first two, Chiangmai and Nan, were Siam's tributaries, but the last one, Chiang Tung or Kengtung, was a tributary of Burma. The head of the British inquiry wisely concluded that "it is a common town . . . since it is not yet decided."[44] We shall consider this situation in the next chapter.

The Nonbounded Kingdom

As we have seen, both Siam and the British talked about boundaries; yet they referred to different things. For modern people, and very probably for the British in the story as well, a boundary of a country is a thing generally understood. Here is a technical definition by a contemporary political geographer:

> Located at the interfaces between adjacent state territories, international boundaries have a special significance in determining the limits of sovereign authority and defining the spatial form of the contained political regions. . . . . Boundaries have been loosely described as being *linear; in fact they occur where the vertical interfaces between state sovereignties intersect the surface of the earth.* Frontiers, in contrast, are zonal and therefore contain various geographical features and, frequently, populations. As vertical interfaces, boundaries have no horizontal extent . . .[45]

Or as an authority on political geography sums it up: "Boundary refers to a line while frontier refers to a zone."[46] For political geographers, the notions of "frontier" and "border" are the same, that is, a zone.[47] It is likely that the British in our story held this concept too, though the one in their head might not have been so technical as the definition cited above.

Siam, however, was not yet in the same world order and was not yet obliged to abide by such European inventions as a fixed national boundary and the laws and customs associated with it. But this did not mean that Siam had no knowledge of the extremity of its sovereign territory. In fact, in the Bangkok Thai language there were many words that had meanings similar to boundary—namely, *khopkhet, khetdaen, anakhet, khopkhanthasima,* and others. The words *khop* and *khet* mean edge, rim, fringe, or limit. The word *daen* means area, territory.

In Khun Prasert-aksonnit's 1891 *Photchananukrom* (Dictionary), there are many words denoting area, country, district, or township, but none for boundary or limit. The word *anakhet* means the areas under control.[48] In Pallegoix's 1854 edition of his English-Thai dictionary the words *anachak, khetanachak,* and *anakhet* mean "limits of the kingdom to which the jurisdiction extends, the power of the king," "limits of the kingdom," and "borders surrounding the whole kingdom, domination over the whole kingdom," respectively.[49] In the 1896 edition, these translations are the same. But there appear the words *khet, khopkhet,* and *khetkhanthasima* meaning "limits," "limits all around," and "boundary of the kingdom," respectively.[50] Bradley's 1873 dictionary, a Thai-Thai dictionary published between the two Pallegoix editions, has no term *anakhet.* The word *khopkhet* means areas in the *huamuang* (provincial areas), the outermost areas of a kingdom.[51]

It is evident that Siam did not lack the terminology and concepts for dealing with the British proposals for boundaries. But considering these definitions closely, we can see that none of them meant exactly the boundary that the British had in mind. To point out only one basic discrepancy, all of the terms tend to signify areas, districts, or frontiers, not boundary lines. They mean a limit—an extremity without a clear-cut edge and without the sense of division between two powers. It is in these terms that Siam understood the British request for a boundary. Hence it is likely that the court was by no means surprised by the British requests but in fact had its own referent.

What were the characteristics of the premodern boundary in Siam's conception? First of all, it was not determined or sanctioned by the central authority. To designate a boundary was probably an unthinkable mission for the Phrakhlang. Nor was it an interesting job for the king of Chiangmai. Rather, it was something the British could do by themselves if they wished or with the help of the local people since it was their responsibility—the guards, hunters, and local inhabitants who earned their living by collecting honey or hunting elephants—to protect the borders.

Second, the *khetdaen* of each town was determined primarily by the extent of surrounding area it could protect. A town may or may not have a common border connecting it with another town, let alone a line dividing the realms of two towns or countries. As a conglomeration of towns, a kingdom was composed of political-territorial patches with a lot of blank space in between.

Third, the *khetdaen* of a kingdom extended to the extremity of these outlying towns and the areas over which their power could be exercised. Beyond these limits there could be vast areas of forests and mountains forming a corridor between the two kingdoms. It was a border without boundary line. Or one could say that it was a "thick line" with a broad horizontal extent.

Fourth, it was not the whole border which was regarded as the area under one's sovereignty and hence the area under control. As the Siamese court wrote in a letter of 28 August 1845, only "whenever there are roads or passes employed by travellers, there are built watch houses for the protection of said roads and places."[52] It was these passages to, and through, the thick forests and mountainous borders that were meant when Siam talked about boundaries. That is to say, these places—not even a whole frontier zone, let alone a "line"—were worth mentioning or guarding and were marked out as the furthest distance under the responsibility of certain local authorities. Only this sort of place could be marked by trees or piles of stones.

This kind of marking is noted in many historical records.[53] Two well-known passages between Siam and Burma, the Three Pagoda Pass and the Singkhon Pass, which were mentioned in most records of wars between the two countries, are also *khetdaen* of this kind. The three pagodas were not in fact pagodas but huge piles of stones intentionally constructed.[54] They were markings of the limit. In many historical records, the word *khetdaen* is mentioned when referring to a path or a passage—such as the words of a Lanna local chief about *khetdaen* being a golden, silver path cited earlier. If the marking was a line, it could be a short line covering only the vicinity of the passage. This was the case when a boundary between Chiangmai and a Kayah state was ritually marked by a bull track at the top of a hill.[55]

As a consequence, only the inhabited areas or the passageways, regarded as limits, were protected by local guards. Thus a guardhouse was also a sign of the extremity of a sovereign power over a particular domain. Remarkably, since no boundary was recognized by Bangkok, the position of a guardhouse and the distance the guard patrolled defined the extent of space under the sovereignty of Bangkok—whereas in modern times the extent of sovereign territory marked by a boundary line delimits the space of a border patrol's authority. Each portion of this boundary was prescribed independently by local authority. It might or might not connect to another portion of boundary. Thus the "boundaries" of a kingdom were discontinuous and, therefore, the kingdom was nonbounded.

Fifth, in some areas, however, a guardhouse meant nothing since the people of both sides were allowed to travel through the areas between the two frontier towns or settle indiscriminately there. In the joint inquiry of boundaries between Lanna and Upper Burma, the British officials were puzzled by the fact that many Shan subjects of Kengtung settled near Chiang Saen, a frontier township of Chiangmai. The Siamese official replied that they were not forbidden to do so, and whether they settled there or not did not matter. In this case, owing to the fact that Chiangmai and Kengtung were not hostile to each other at the time, there was no need to keep watch or to seize the people of the other side. As a result, whether there were many Shan subjects of Kengtung in the forest close to Chiang Saen or not, we don't know, because we regard the town's walls the most important. The nearby areas are branches of the *anakhet*. Whether those Ngieo [Shan] are hiding, living, or earning their living, we do not look around. . . . The watershed on that big mountain is an approximate boundary. But the town is more important than inhabitants.[56]

Sixth, if a corridor border ran between hostile countries, people of one side were allowed to earn their living in the corridor but were not allowed to trespass ontc the areas under the other's authority. In this case, the guards' patrol zones were significant and had to be defined. In our modern definition, a frontier or border is a zone which lies along *each* side of the boundary or interfaces a neighboring country—that is, a boundary is *in between* two sides of borders. But from the account of the Siamese notion of a boundary, it appears that a huge border was between both sides' boundaries of authority. In short, even for Siam alone there was more than one kind of geopolitical extremity. One was the boundary of sovereign authority which was, geographically speaking, well *inside* the border. The other was the border *beyond* the limit of sovereign authority and *without* boundary. Sovereignty and border were not coterminous.

Seventh, it was the boundary of sovereign authority that could be defined without the agreement or ratification of another country. The boundary of a kingdom was of this kind, so it was not necessary to be joined to another—leaving the corridor border outside the boundaries belonging to neither. In fact, when the Siamese court at the end of Rama III's reign talked about the boundary between Tenasserim and Siam, it said that after the Anglo-Burma war was over, "the boundary [of Tenasserim] was *extended to join* the one of Siam."[57] The words precisely reflected this idea. In short, the sovereignty of the two kingdoms was normally set apart without interface.

Eighth, just as open or closed borders signify the health of relations between two countries in modern times, border relations in premodern times did so as well, but in a different manner. On the one hand, there was the "golden, silver path" which never prevented people from traveling across it, earning their living on it, or even settling close to one another's frontier towns without permission. On the other hand, there was the border where the enemy was forbidden to trespass. Generally the rivals preferred to leave space unsettled since it served as a buffer keeping a distance between them.

On an unfriendly border it was the duty of local officials to monitor the enemy's movements by undertaking spying missions into the opponent's territory. At the same time they had to guard the boundary against the enemy's spies. Perhaps the British accusation that the Siamese guards had gone onto their territory was not entirely groundless. Yet the marking of their surveillance point or the religious shrine marking the extent of their responsibility were not boundary marks. On a friendly border, however, as in the early years of the reign, the practice was opposite: "Nowadays, Thai and British are friends. [We] do not have to look after our *khetdaen* as previously when facing the Burmese."[58] For friendly countries, therefore, a prohibition on trespassing as the British prescribed was not welcome. It was probably seen as an unfriendly act since it was traditionally a step short of seizing the enemy. This is why the court was annoyed by the British ban. The prohibition also caused confusion among the local people, who were used to traveling across the boundary without permission in the case of friendly borders. Local people were accustomed to visiting their relatives on both sides of the border; some even migrated from one side to the other from time to time. This has been true for all borders from the Pakchan River to northernmost Lanna.

Furthermore, not only the prohibition on trespassing but also the request to pinpoint a boundary might well have been seen by Siam as a sign of unfriendliness, though the two countries were still on good terms. In 1829, requested by the British governor of Penang to mark out the boundary of Kedah and Wellesley Province at a time when relations between the two countries were very good, especially between himself and many British authorities, the ruler of Nakhon was evidently stunned by such a request:

> Whereas we have always been well inclined to the British, and never charged them with any evil intention in any of our letters, why has our friend sent a letter enquiring about the boundaries of the territories at which we are very much astonished?
>
> Wherefore we have sent Khun Akorn with a letter to our friend in order that he may enquire in a friendly manner, what are our friend's intentions in doing this?[59]

And in another case when the British accused a Siamese local authority of planting a flag over British territory as a mark of boundary, the Siamese court replied with these words: "The Siamese never sent any person or persons to plant a flag. . . . It is against all rules and customs of the Siamese to send and plant flags and point out boundaries."[60]

This may explain why the early British requests were poorly received and sometimes provoked dissatisfaction. When the attitude of Siam toward the British had changed, however, urgent requests from the British received prompt response—positive in British eyes but given by Siam with much irritation. It should be noted here that the replies of cooperation from the court were accompanied by a number of separate letters denying all the charges made by the British about Siam's incursion into their territory. In some of these letters, counteraccusations were put forward. Moreover, it was at this time that the court proposed to have a boundary of the kind which would keep a distance between the two countries. It is likely that the British requests for clear boundary lines with modern rules of border control came close to the behavior of unfriendly neighbors.[61]

From all of these observations, then, we may see numerous boundaries which might not be connected but which were flexible. Some might be thick, some might be blurred. Many had disappeared or never existed. Siam before the last decade of the nineteenth century was not like "an old axe," but a discontinuous, patchy arrangement of power units where people of different overlords mingled together in the same area while only spies were working close to the frontier towns of one another. And those areas far from the center of a kingdom might be generously given away for the sake of friendship. In this case, the border would shrink a bit. It did not matter. In fact, throughout Southeast Asian tradition, as one scholar remarks, "marginal territorial concessions were not viewed as fatal to the kingdom. As long as the essence of sovereignty [the center] was unimpaired, such concessions were a legitimate instrument of policy."[62]

The sphere of a realm or the limits of a kingdom could be defined only by those townships' allegiance to the center of a kingdom. The political sphere could be mapped only by power relationships, not by territorial integrity. Thus to talk about the frontiers of a sovereign unit—*anakhet, khopkhanthasima*—meant those marginal authorities in the remote townships or those chiefdoms at the margin of the sphere of power rather than the frontier space itself.

The British attempt to demarcate the boundary induced confrontations between different concepts of political space. This confrontation, however, went unrecognized by both sides because they used words that seemed to denote the same thing. The words "boundary" and *khetdaen,* or *anakhet* and the like, seemed to be generally translatable. But in fact they confronted each other in every event of communication at the level of the signifying process. The British pushed a concept of "boundary" whose qualification was different from that of *khetdaen.* By doing so, the conception of *khetdaen* held by Siam was disturbed while the concept of "boundary" imposed itself as an alternative of signification. In other words, the "boundary" proposed its concept as a compatible message through the compatible terminology. The signifier became ambiguous, signifying different concepts at the same time. This situation resulted in changing practices—mixing up the practices of the two concepts until an outcome could be determined. Certainly the rules governing such practices were disturbed and changed as well. By agreeing to be involved in practices relating to the concept of "boundary," they already allowed the new rules and practices to be established. The more they agreed with British requests, the more their customary practices related to *khetdaen* were shaken, changed, and moved toward the stipulations of the British.

It was the elite of Mongkut's generation who consciously adopted the alternative concept and its rules and practices, including the methods of marking boundary lines in the modern sense and the use of maps. Although differences in conceptions still prevailed at other levels of the community, particularly among those people along the frontiers, it was not long before the Bangkok regime tightened its control over the borders and by clever tactics—playing on the ignorance of local subjects by employing a traditional ritual of allegiance, for example—stipulated practices which half a century earlier it had not known.

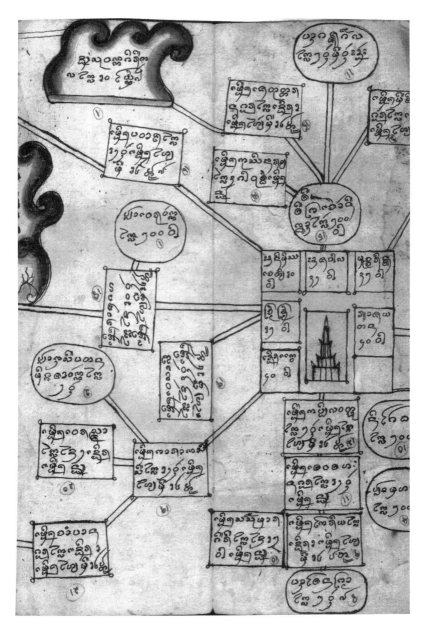

Figure 1. A Map of Pilgrimage from a Lanna Manuscript (From "Northern Thai manuscript: Buddhist Manual," in the John M. Echols collection, by permission of Cornell University)

Figure 2 (panel 1). Tamnan Map from the Traiphum Manuscript
(Courtesy of *Sinlapawatthanatham*)

(Figure 2, panel 2)

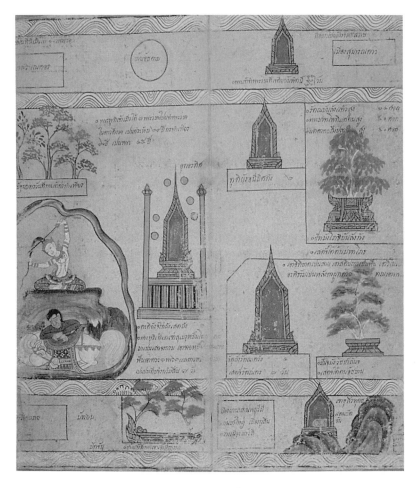

(Figure 2, panel 3)

(Figure 2, panel 4)

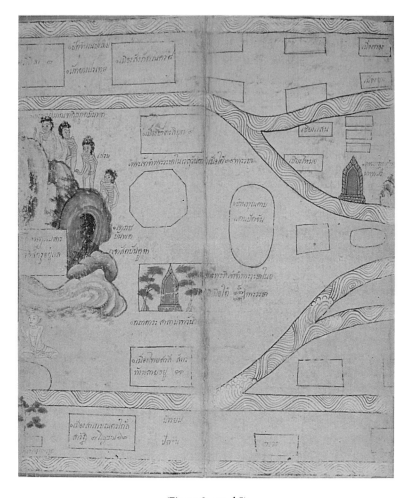

(Figure 2, panel 5)

(Figure 2, panel 6)

(Figure 2, panel 7)

(Figure 2, panel 8)

(Figure 2, panel 9)

(Figure 2, panel 10)

(Figure 2, panel 11)

(Figure 2, panel 12)

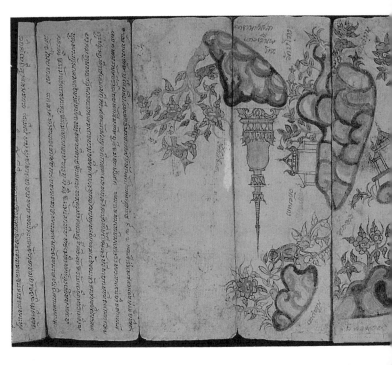

Figure 3. Seventeenth-Century Local Map of the Eastern Bank of Songkhla Lagoon, South of Siam (By permission of the National Library, Bangkok)

Figure 4 (panel 1). Coastal Map from the Traiphum Manuscript
(Courtesy of *Sinlapawatthanatham*)

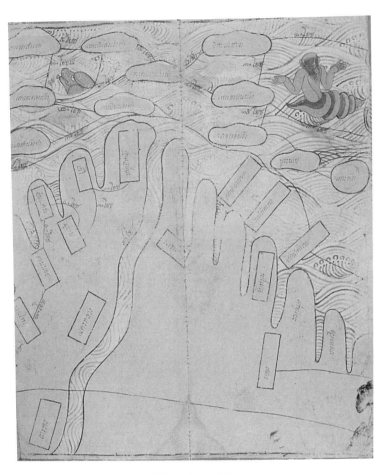

(Figure 4, panel 2)

(Figure 4, panel 3)

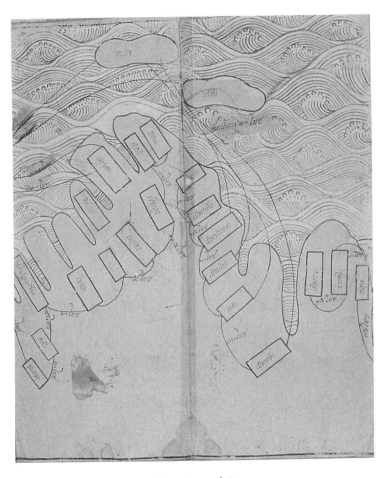

(Figure 4, panel 4)

(Figure 4, panel 5)

(Figure 4, panel 6)

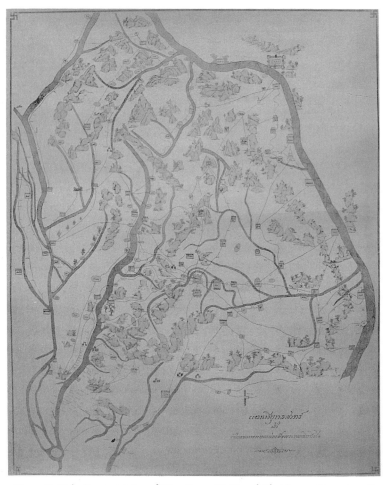

Figure 5. "The Strategic Map of King Rama I" (Royal Thai Survey Department)

Figure 6. "Siamese Map" (F. A. Neale, *Narrative of a Residence at the Capital of the Kingdom of Siam*, 55)

Figure 7. Map of the Kingdom of Siam and Adjacent Countries by a French Cartographer: 1686 (Royal Thai Survey Department)

MAP
of the Kingdoms of
SIAM AND COCHIN CHINA
Compiled by
JOHN WALKER,
to accompany the journal of
Mr CRAWFURD'S
Mission.

Figure 9. George Curzon's "The Siamese Boundary Question": 1893. Borders, left to right, show: 1) hypothetical frontier by F. Schrader (1892); 2) frontier between Annam and Siam by F. Garnier (1866–1868); and 3) frontier by J. McCarthy (1887). (By permission of the British Library)

Figure 8. John Crawfurd's "Map of the Kingdom of Siam and Cochin China": 1828 (From *Journal of an Embassy from the Governor-General of India to the Courts of Siam and Cochin China*)

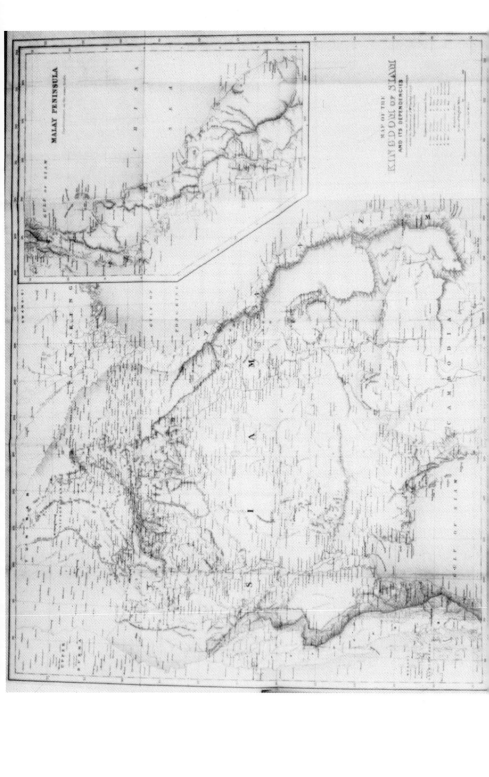

MALAY PENINSULA

MAP OF THE
KINGDOM OF SIAM
AND ITS DEPENDENCIES

Figure 11. Cartoon from Vajiravudh's Time *(Dusit samit)*

Figure 12. Symbol of the Saichaithai Foundation

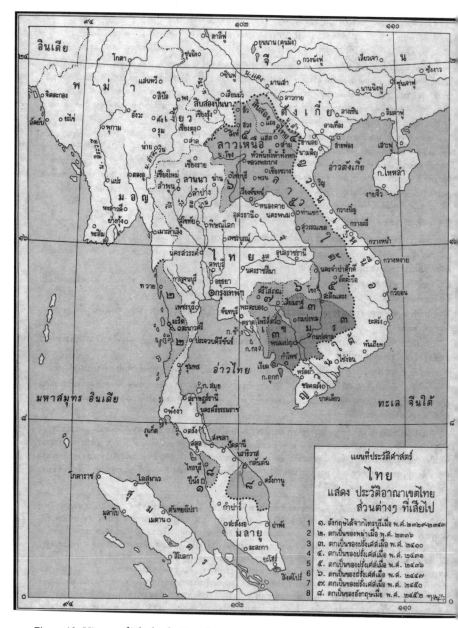

Figure 13. History of Thailand's Boundary (By permission of Thaiwatthanaphanit Co.)

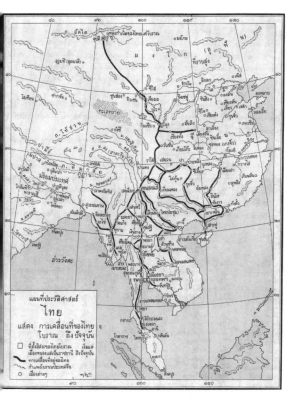

Figure 14. Movements of Thai People from Ancient to Modern Times (By permission of Thaiwatthanaphanit Co.)

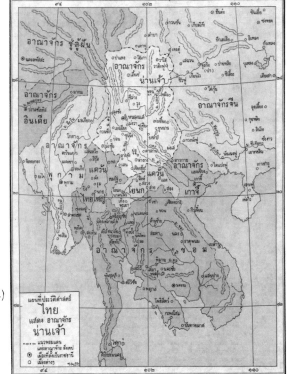

Figure 15. Kingdom of Nanchao (By permission of Thaiwatthanaphanit Co.)

Figure 16. Kingdom of Sukhothai in the Reign of King Ramkhamhaeng the Great (By permission of Thaiwatthanaphanit Co.)

Figure 17. Kingdom of Ayudhya in the Reign of King Naresuan the Great (By permission of Thaiwatthanaphanit Co.)

Figure 18. Kingdom of Thonburi in the Reign of King Taksin (By permission of Thaiwatthanaphanit Co.)

Figure 19. Kingdom of Rattanakosin in the Reign of King Rama I (By permission of Thaiwatthanaphanit Co.)

Figure 20. "Wake Up, Thai People" (By permission of Conrad Taylor)

Chapter Four
Sovereignty

THE TERRITORIAL DELIMITATION of Siam was much more complicated when a border was not a corridor but a frontier town regarded as common to more than one kingdom. A modern boundary was not possible until what belonged to whose realm had been sorted out. But the premodern polity defied such a modern undertaking. Confrontations and controversies over the question of what today we might call "sovereignty" over the Shan states, Lanna, Cambodia, the Malay states, and the left bank of the Mekhong were critical to the formation of the modern Thai state and its misunderstood history.

Hierarchical Interstate Relations

In premodern polities the relationship between political powers was hierarchical. A ruler whose authority prevailed over several local rulers or chiefs of tiny townships, mostly in nearby areas, was submissive to another lord. This pattern of relations prevailed all the way up the pyramid to the most powerful kingship of the realm. Lieberman suggests that even in the supposedly most integrated period of Burmese history, the reign of Bayinnaung (1551–1581), the relationship between the central and local rulers was primarily one of personal subordination under the "High King." The kings of major towns, *bayin*, still held limited power and kingly regalia. The kingdom held together as long as personal subordination to the supreme king remained.[1] In Thai, the unit of status in this hierarchy was indiscriminately called *muang*, which meant the governed area—that is, the area under the righteous protection of the overlord.

This pattern applied also to the relationship among several kingdoms, including the one between a regional major kingdom like Siam or Burma and its tributary kingdoms such as Lanna, Lan Sang, and the Malay states. Fundamentally, these tributaries were regarded as separate kingdoms, that is, separate networks of hierarchical lordship. Not only did each king of these tributaries regard himself as the lord of his realm, but the supreme overlord of the region also tolerated a tributary king with little interference. Each king had his own court, administrative and financial system, tax collection, army, and judicial system. We might say that these lesser kingdoms were generally regarded as having their own sovereignty. Nevertheless, the interstate relations in this region operated by common recognition of the hierarchical world order in which the supreme overlord—because his highest store of merit could be expressed if necessary in terms of force—cast his influence over the inferior kingships. A tributary inevitably had to submit itself to the supreme overlord, recognizing its own inferior status. Based on this world order, consequently, the supreme overlord could enforce his demand or intervene in the affairs of the inferior kingdom whenever he deemed it legitimate. Yet the overlord's store of merit could suddenly expire—hence the decline of his power and legitimacy. In that situation the overlordship might be defied by its tributaries or even challenged by another contending overlord—hence chaos or disorder in the interstate hierarchy. Inevitably the uncertainty of hierarchy relations had to be decided by a concrete measure: a battle. A tributary might dissociate itself from any overlord for a while or might cooperate with another overlord until the order was resumed in one way or another; then it would be forced to enter the tributary relationship again. In Thai a tributary was called *prathetsarat*. This scheme of power relations in Southeast Asian polity has been known to scholars as *mandala*. As O. W. Wolters who proposed this terminology has put it:

> [The] *mandala* represented a particular and often unstable political situation in a vaguely definable geographical area without fixed boundaries and where smaller centers tended to look in all directions for security. Mandalas would expand and contract in concertina-like fashion. Each one contained several tributary rulers, some of whom would repudiate their vassal status when the opportunity arose and try to build up their own networks of vassals.[2]

The tributary relationship had its forms of obligations, sanctions, and allegiance. The most important obligation was the ritual of submission. A tributary had to send a mission of tribute payment to the supreme overlord regularly, mostly annually or triennially, as a sign of commitment to renew the allegiance. Although money and valuable goods were always included in a tribute, the principal tribute was the gold and silver tree—the *Bunga mas* in Malay, small trees fashioned from gold and silver leaves. In return the overlord would honor a tributary ruler with gifts of greater value.

Another important sanction was the appointment of a tributary ruler who had to be approved and conferred by the overlord. This custom always included the ritual of submission from a new tributary ruler, who in return received the regalia, gifts, and the golden parchment of his title conferment. Normally, the supreme king had nothing to do with the succession of a tributary throne, whether it was hereditary or usurped. Only in certain circumstances would the overlord intervene and dictate the outcome. Thus the appointment was on the one hand a sanction by the supreme lord to his inferior kingship, while on the other hand it was a means to guarantee the allegiance of tributaries. In addition, a tributary was obliged to send manpower, troops, goods, money, or other supplies whenever the overlord required. This obligation was significant in terms of material assistance, especially in times of war, as well as a sign of loyalty.

Any attempt to escape these duties, especially the ritual of submission, was a sign of defiance to the overlordship—hence an intent to rebel. In fact, a large number of wars in the history of this region were not contests between rival kingdoms but wars of punishment waged by a supreme lord against the defiance of tributaries. The scale of destruction varied. Some merely forced the replacement of a tributary's ruler; others were no less catastrophic than the battles fought between hostile kingdoms.

The rationale of this relationship has been explained as the necessity of a weaker state to seek protection from a more powerful one as security against the greed of another overlord; in return the weaker state had to repay the benevolence of the protector. Hence it was a reciprocal relation. Yet the fierce punishment meted out to any tributary that wished to quit the relationship indicated that the relationship was far from one of mutual agreement or the relation sought by the weaker. In Thai the manner in which a tributary entered this relationship was described as *khopen kha-khopkhanthasima*, to request to be under the holy sphere of the supreme power, or *thawai sawamiphak*, to give full loyalty to. It meant that, for example, Bangkok had to protect its tributaries from the aggression of any other supreme lord such as Burma or Vietnam and, if requested, from any revolt against a tributary ruler. Thus the submission was voluntary and protection was requested. Although this reasoning is not wrong, it is a half-truth. The notion of protection in this relationship had another meaning.

In the Theravada Buddhist polity of the region, the righteous kingship, the universal monarch or *cakravatin*, was obliged to protect the religion from declining. Protecting the religion and the quest for supremacy were one and the same mission.[3] A powerful Bangkok king had to fight to expand his umbrella of merit and righteousness, *dharma*, as far as possible to bring the lesser kingdoms under the protection of his supreme merit. And it would be wrong to leave those weaker kings unprotected since they might fall into the domain of evil. The acquisition of tributaries in itself became a sign of supremacy. Success in preventing tributaries' disobedience, or quitting their allegiance, or being taken over by another supreme power, therefore, reflected the status of this supremacy. In other words, it was a self-presumed protector who sought the protected to fulfill his own desire to become a *cakravatin.* In this sense the protection was imposed, not requested.

The conventional notion implies that the danger came from a third party, either another kingdom or an internal revolt. But according to the other notion of protection, the threat came from nowhere but the supreme overlord himself, who forced a weaker state to become and remain his protected tributary. A submission, in this circumstance, was unavoidably compulsory rather than voluntary. The two notions coexisted and were manifested by the same practice. In other words, the practice of tributary relations was ambiguous.

The cases of the Malay states and Cambodia will show the different circumstances in which they entered into tributary relationships. In some cases, the oppressive protection was imposed and the tributaries hardly had any choice. In other cases, however, factional disputes within a tributary court led to the request for protection from one or more overlords. In some situations, nevertheless, a tributary sought an overlord to counter pressure from another overlord.

Shared Sovereignty: A Strategy for Survival

Cambodia was a powerful kingdom along the southern part of the Mekhong. It was situated between two more powerful kingdoms, however, Siam and Vietnam. Since its decline in the fourteenth century, Cambodia had been a tributary of the Siamese kingdom of Ayudhya. The situation became worse from the seventeenth century onward as Vietnam grew stronger and demanded submission from Cambodia. Caught in between, Cambodia had no choice but to accept the overlordship of both superior neighbors.[4]

The contest between Siam and Vietnam over Cambodia was further intensified and complicated by factional fighting within the Cambodian court from the late eighteenth century to the first half of the nineteenth. Whenever a faction sought support from one overlord, the loser sought the other's protection. As factional disputes for the throne intensified, both overlords interfered with the Cambodian court through the polarized factions.[5] Not only were there tribute payments and other obligations such as the recognition of the Cambodian king by both Bangkok and Hue, but both superpowers stationed their troops in the Cambodian realm.[6]

In this desperate relationship, the Cambodian kings had always attempted to create a balance of the overlord's power by blurring the line of allegiance in order to make the realm somehow independent.[7] Cambodia in this relationship was perhaps best characterized by a Vietnamese emperor, Gia Long, in a letter to King Rama II of Siam in 1811 begging his pardon on behalf of King Uthairacha who had fled to Saigon, then Gia Dinh, after the dispute with his heir who had fled to Bangkok:

> [The Cambodian king] has depended on both [Siam] and Vietnam for a long time. The Thai king is like his Father and the Vietnamese one like his Mother. Now [King] Uthairacha has committed an offense against his Father, then requested his Mother to beg for the Father's pardon; I could not simply abandon him. So, I write for Your Majesty's pardon.[8]

The feud between Father and Mother themselves increasingly grew out of the disputes among their protected Sons, and finally a war broke out in 1834 which lasted for fourteen years. By the time the parental feud was exhausted, Cambodia lay devastated and neither side could claim victory. The outcome of the reconciliation was the return to the status quo that existed before the war. The Cambodian king had a clear view of this outcome: "Please let me be subjected to the merit and power of both great kingdoms, so that my people can live in peace and happiness."[9]

For Siam, King Rama III regarded the outcome as a success in the sense that "[Vietnam] took *our* Cambodia . . . 36 years ago. Only now have we *got it back.*"[10] Chandler regards this outcome as the restoration of Cambodian "independence."[11] Cambodia's independence in 1847 was not much different from the situation earlier in 1811, however, when the best summary was made by Gia Long: Cambodia was, in Chandler's translation, "an independent country that is slave of two."[12]

For the northern Malay states, the circumstance surrounding their predicament was slightly different. Although they were merely small, disunified principalities, their geographical position was far removed from the supreme powers and thus they were not involved in a confrontation between those overlords. Hence they had more room to maneuver and their strategy to restrain the pressure from Siam was more adventurous. Nevertheless, the outcome was not much different.

Historically, the raja of Kedah was engaged in ongoing struggles against other Malay neighbors and powerful rivals in the region, such as Malacca and Aceh, in order to maintain his own rule. In the 1650s the conflict with the

Dutch, then a maritime power in the region, left Kedah with no choice but to seek assistance from Siam by sending the *Bunga mas,* the gold and silver tree, to Ayudhya. Kedah was regarded by Siam as a tributary ever since. Throughout the rest of the seventeenth century, Kedah survived by alternately seeking help from either the Dutch or Siam to hold one another off. The raja had successfully preserved, to some extent, his independent rulership.[13]

The rise of Ava, a Burmese power, and the fall of Ayudhya in the late eighteenth century meant that Kedah could dissociate from Siam. But Ava asked for Kedah's submission. Kedah sent a *Bunga mas* mission to Ava. Worse, Siam quickly recovered and wanted to resume its overlordship over the former tributaries of Ayudhya. As Bonney tells us, the raja of Kedah wisely "kept peace with both, paying homage sometimes to one and sometimes to the other and often to both."[14]

The Siamese overlordship increased for two reasons. First was the factional fighting for the throne of Kedah, especially in 1803, when a faction requested the presence of Siamese forces.[15] Second, acting as the prime agency of Bangkok to look after Siam's interest over the Malay states, Nakhon actively expanded its power into Kedah for the sake of its own self-interest, beyond Bangkok's supervision or orders.[16] Nakhon's actions, however, led to disobedience and revolts from time to time against Siam.[17] Consequently, a raja of Kedah was ousted by Nakhon's force in 1821.

A similar situation existed in Kelantan, Trengganu, and Perak. The rajas of these petty states ruled their realms autonomously, but had to comply with the burden of demands from Siam. The protection was far from welcome, except when a support for the throne was needed, but a struggle for independence was perhaps unthinkable yet. To avoid punishment from the overlords, the practice of multiple submissions was necessary. Instead of getting rid of all foreign suzerains, a raja needed to cultivate another power's interest in his realm in order to restrain the Siamese overlordship. So when the British company, a new power in the regional maritime trade, was looking for a station in that area, it was invited by Kedah to locate there.

The leases of the port of Kuala in 1772 and Penang in 1785 and the cession of Wellesley in 1800 to the British were more than real estate transactions for money. They were done in the context of the indigenous interstate politics of the late eighteenth century. They were regarded by Kedah as contractual obligations whereby the British would provide protection to Kedah in case of threats from Siam or Burma, particularly Nakhon's ambition. Again, a similar strategy was adopted by Perak, Kelantan, and Trengganu.[18] Perak even offered its realm to the British as a guarantee for help in the event of Siam's intervention.[19] Unfortunately, the British were ignorant of these tributary politics; the politics they knew had different rules; the offers of these rajas were mostly accepted but their wishes were turned down.

The cases of Cambodia and the Malay states show clearly the dilemma these tributaries faced and the delicacy of the strategies they adopted in dealing with pressures from the supreme overlords. The protection was unwelcome oppression and yet it was an alternative to the oppression at the same time. It was a third hand in factional disputes and yet it always turned out to be a mailed fist. Even for the struggle within the Siamese court, for example, in 1874, the British consul was requested to interfere. With patriotism yet unborn, foreign interventions were sometimes welcomed as protection among the ruling people. It was a significant strategy for survival.[20]

Strikingly, most of the interactions in these interkingdom relationships operated via the medium of gifts, especially tribute and the gold and silver trees. In fact, the ambiguity of tributary relationships was also expressed through the ambiguous meanings of tribute. In the light of one of Marcel Mauss's classic works, *The Gift,* the gift exchange in premodern societies was a means of communicating certain messages about the kinds, levels, and circumstances of the relations between the giver and the recipient.[21] In premodern Southeast Asia, various gifts were perhaps codes which could be decoded according to the rules of their interstate relations. This may explain why the documents of relations among these kingdoms and with the West always recorded details of gifts given or received. The point here, however, is that there is a paradox in the archaic practice of gift exchange: "The gift is both apparently disinterested and always interested, apparently voluntary and essentially involuntary."[22]

In the case of Siam, even though the Siamese envoys had always performed the ritual of submission, the tribute mission to the Chinese emperor has been explained by most modern scholars of Thailand as a profit-making enterprise, not a sign of submission, since the Chinese emperor always rewarded the Siamese with commodities of greater value that were salable in the market.[23] Paradoxically the tribute, the gold and silver trees in particular, from an inferior state to Siam was always regarded as evidence of submission. The giver, such as Kedah, however, might similarly deny such a hegemonic interpretation, arguing that it was a token of alliance and friendship, "a mere exchange of civility," and nothing beyond that.[24]

In the tributary relationship, the tribute could be the token for protection of both kinds. It might signify unavoidable submission in order to keep peace with an overlord in one case or merely a ploy in another circumstance. It was simultaneously problem and solution, oppression and alternative, compulsory and voluntary, forced duty and survival tactic, depending on intentions, circumstances, and points of view of both giver and recipient (historians as well take one side or another).

Rulers of tributary states played with the ambiguity of protection and tribute payment as a strategy for survival. Though they could not prevent the imposed mafia-like protection, they could resist by using the same medium—tributes and gifts—to obtain protection from another power. The tributary relationship remained fluid as long as power and resistance occurred within the same relations and practices. Moreover, unlike the modern concept of a sovereign state, a tributary's overt and formal submission did not prevent it from attempting to preserve its own autonomy or "independence," nor did the quest for autonomy prevent a state from submitting itself to more than one supreme power at any one time. Indeed, the practice of multiple submissions was often indispensable if the state was to save its "independence." The tragic side of this strategy was that such a tributary would be regarded by each overlord as its own possession. It appears that both Siam and Vietnam claimed suzerainty over Cambodia while the Cambodian monarch always considered himself independent. The same could be said of Kedah, which was free to give away Penang and Wellesley in exchange for another balancing power, yet which was a customary victim of Siam's imposed protection. The sovereignty over each tributary state was not usurped by the overlords, nor was its realm encroached upon as in modern colonialism. The sovereignty of a state in this premodern polity was neither single nor exclusive. It was multiple and capable of being shared—one for its own ruler, another for its overlord—not in terms of a divided sovereignty but rather a sovereignty of hierarchical layers. And this was what the British inquirer described as the "common" *muang*.

Multiple Sovereignty and the Europeans

Although tacit "influence" over another state is a part of international politics today, the sovereignty of a state must, formally, be exclusive, not hierarchical or multiple, and it must be unambiguous. Even a colony is regarded as an integral part of the sovereignty of an imperial country. Thus in the eyes of the European in the nineteenth century it had to be decided whether a particular tributary was independent or was an integral part or a colony of another kingdom—not somewhere between independent and dependent nor somehow possessed by more than one kingdom at the same time. The ambiguous nature of the tributary relationship misleads even the historians of our time, since the notion of *prathetsarat* had already been displaced by a new Thai word coined during the 1930s and 1940s: *ananikhom,* which denotes a colonyship in modern polity.[25] An authority on Thai history has attempted to classify the status of these tributaries in terms of the degree of independence/dependence as semi-independent, principality, quasi-independent, and peripheral center.[26] Another authority on modern Siam even regards the tributaries as provinces of Siam.[27]

In the case of the Malay states in the nineteenth century, several misunderstandings occurred among British colonial officials themselves, as well as between them and Siam and the Malay rulers. The problem arose as early as 1821 when Nakhon's forces invaded Kedah. The raja of Kedah asked the British for protection. He was rejected. The raja then accused the British of breaking the obligation (implied by the leases of Penang and Wellesley). Finally he was ousted and the British did not intervene.

The British were confused by the ambiguity of the tributary relationship: was Kedah independent or a dependency of Siam? If it was a dependency, the attack on Kedah was an internal affair in which they should not interfere, let alone help Kedah. But in this case the leases of Penang and Wellesley according to the treaties with Kedah in 1786 and 1802 were void without Siam's ratification. If Kedah was independent, on the other hand, the leases were valid but the action of Nakhon must be taken as an invasion and therefore counteracted. The arguments among British officials themselves centered on the question whether the *Bunga mas* was compulsory or voluntary: did it indicate the submission of the giver to the recipient or was it merely a token of respect from a less powerful state who was free to enter or terminate the relations at will, as the raja of Kedah had argued? A historian has noted: "Truth appears to lie somewhere between these two extreme views."[28] Or, more precisely, truth lay in both of them together, interchangeably.

Moreover, the British wondered whether treaties with Kedah implied an obligation to protect Kedah. Again, this question focused on the implications of gift exchange—in this case the leases—in indigenous custom. On all questions, the tributary relationship and the practice of gift exchange divided British colonial officials into two factions; each supported one interpretation and proposed policies accordingly. In the first half of the century, any involvement with native politics was deemed undesirable.[29] Of course the British company preferred the interpretation that the leases were legal but implied no obligation of alliance with Kedah. No such obligation was mentioned in any agreement, they argued, totally overlooking the indigenous view of gift exchange. Not only was the 1821 event which disturbed the region accepted with no interference, but it also alarmed the British that their presence there might be questioned by Siam as well. One of the tasks of John

Crawfurd's mission to Siam that year was to find out Siam's view on the validity of the treaties with Kedah and the British presence.

Eventually Crawfurd was surprised but delighted that the issue was not questioned. He concluded his report, with his undoubtedly European legal rationale, that Siam's thirty-seven-year silence was substantial evidence of the recognition of British rights.[30] Ironically, for some decades after the Crawfurd report, it was the British, not the Siamese, who still had doubts over the validity of the treaties with Kedah, since the status of Kedah with respect to Siam was never clear to them. One finally suggested that even though Kedah was a dependency of Siam, the leases were made with the (mis)understanding that it was independent. The occupation of Penang and Wellesley was, in his word, an "error," but the rights obtained by occupation were later recognized by Siam. Strikingly, in his argument, since the ruler of Nakhon was a high-ranking Siamese noble, the agreement about the boundary demarcation in 1833 was regarded by the legal-minded British as the first substantial legal evidence of British rights over Penang and Wellesley.[31]

Another confusion over the tributary relationship, even more complex, was made evident by the events surrounding the invasion of Perak, another Malay state, by Nakhon's force in 1826. One task of the Burney mission in 1825–1826 was to negotiate a guarantee that Siam would not send troops into the Malay states under any circumstances. He achieved that aim without having to sort out the ambiguity of the dependent/independent status of those states.[32] Siam agreed on condition that the British would not prevent the Malay states from performing the *Bunga mas* ritual as usual. Considering the state of confused knowledge among the British at that time, it is hard to blame Burney for such a contradictory compromise. Nonetheless, it is not surprising that the treaty was the subject of both strong criticism and strong support among the British.[33] They agreed only on the idea that the *Bunga mas* should not be interpreted as a token of submission to Bangkok. Hence in the British view, Siam had no right to interfere in the affairs of the Malay states.[34] For other Malay states, namely Kelantan and Trengganu, the British reached similar agreements with Siam.[35] Both parties were unaware that the agreement was based on misunderstanding.

Shortly after the Burney treaty was concluded, Nakhon sent a small armed force to Perak asking for the *Bunga mas*. Captain James Low was one of the pro-Malay faction among the Penang authorities but considered the *Bunga mas* as a token of submission, so he urged Perak to show its independence by defying Nakhon's demand. Moreover, without authorization, he signed a treaty on behalf of the British company recognizing Perak as an independent state. Assuming that the British had become its protector by Low's treaty,

Perak drove Nakhon's force back. In doing so Perak informed the Siamese that the British would take its side. But after learning of the incident, the British authority at Penang rejected such an understanding, saying that there was no such obligation. Ironically, Nakhon was held off. Perak was told that it would no longer be disturbed by force, but it was still a tributary of Siam. Perak agreed, saying that nothing had changed in the relationship between Perak and Siam. Indeed, Perak applauded the Siamese-British agreements. Perak had already achieved its aim of using the British to hold off Siam, despite British refusal to help. Thanks to the complex and confused misunderstandings, the incident was over.[36]

It seems that Siam regarded the agreement not to send troops to the Malay states as a separate issue from the fact that they were tributaries of Siam. Thus the Siamese court did not quite understand the British position on Perak. As late as 1850, they complained to another British envoy to the court, Sir James Brooke, that Perak used to be a tributary to Siam which paid the *Bunga mas* to Siam but was then taken over by Penang.[37] This claim might have been denied by the British at the time, but the complaint reflected how the court understood British-Perak relations. How can one expect the court to have interpreted the relationship between Perak and the British in any other way but as a "protection" of the former by the latter?

Protection? Many rajas of Kedah had learned, time after time, that the British did not abide by the implied obligation of gifts. The British could sacrifice their ill-fated ally for the peace of the region (read: trade in the region). The British preferred not to be hostile to Siam at the expense of Kedah. They were anxious that if they did not actively cooperate with Siam, Siam's dissatisfaction might affect their presence at Penang and Wellesley. Twice, in 1831 and 1838, when the ex-raja's loyalists attempted to restore him to the throne, the British sent gunboats to blockade the mouth of the Kedah River, directly helping Siam to suppress the revolts.[38] Kedah's cession of Penang and Wellesley did not work, for the legal-minded British, to hold off Siam's interference. The British had acquired good ports and did not want anything that might harm trade. As Bonney puts it, the wishes of the raja turned out to be "the grand illusion."[39]

These cases show the misunderstanding caused by confrontations between the indigenous tributary relationship and the rationalistic European view of modern international relations. Moreover, the requests for protection by these Malay states did give the British an opportunity to claim them as their possessions. Throughout the first half of the nineteenth century, in the best interest of their trade in the region, the British held a noninterference policy. In doing so they left intact the ambiguity of sovereignty over these tributaries. The French were confronted with a similar ambiguity concerning indigenous tributary relationships. Instead of leaving the ambiguity undecided, however, it seems that the French were aware of the situation and exploited it to fulfill their aims in Indochina.

Like their British counterparts, the French first acknowledged the influence of Siam over Cambodia and were reluctant to interfere with its domestic politics.[40] They even refused to lend a hand to a faction of the Cambodian court which, following a palace struggle in 1861, asked for French protection.[41] Later, however, it is clear that they were aware of the other side of the ambiguity—that is, the autonomy of a tributary kingdom. When the first agreement between French Indochina and Cambodia was drawn up in 1863 without Siam's knowledge, Siam lodged a protest. The French navy commander replied legalistically that Cambodia was a sovereign, independent country and could therefore negotiate a treaty with Cochin China without consulting any other country.[42]

The nineteen-article treaty in 1863 making Cambodia a French protectorate was considered by France and later historians as a landmark in this colonial relationship. Yet Siam and Cambodia at that time might not have understood the treaty in the same sense—not because of an anti-imperialist idea but because they perceived such agreements in a different conceptual framework. In fact, despite the treaty, the French did not forbid Cambodia to maintain its tributary relationship with Siam, including the custom of tribute payment.[43] In the following year, 1864, they even invited Siam to participate in the coronation ceremony of Cambodia's King Norodom.[44] Here Mongkut, in a letter to Norodom, describes what the French consul had explained to the Siamese court about the whole situation:

> Monsieur Aubaret, the French consul . . . suggested that both [Siam] and France should together crown the king of Cambodia. This follows the example of [the previous kings of Cambodia], who received the golden parchment [of appointment as king] from Bangkok and then received the Hong (Chinese rank for a tributary king) from Vietnam. . . . In those cases, in correspondence with [Siam], they used the Thai titles; in correspondence with Vietnam, they used the Vietnamese titles. Vietnam and Siam are hostile to each other, hence separate appointments. Each claims Cambodia as their own. On the issue where both Siam and Vietnam claim Cambodia as their own, France remains neutral. After the French took control over the south of Vietnam, however, Cambodia became France's neighbor and a treaty was negotiated for France to foster Cambodia as Vietnam had previously done. Because [France] was on good terms with Siam, all amicable relations between Siam and Cambodia remain. [Both France and Siam] have equal power over Cambodia. . . . What

the French consul said was in accordance with the agreement made with you at Udong (the 1863 treaty). . . . After the consul's briefing, the senior ministers have discussed the matter among themselves and have decided unanimously to depute Phraya Montrisuriyawong to bestow on you the golden parchment and insignia as your coronation.[45]

Whether or not this statement conveyed Aubaret's words correctly is not the issue; the question is how Mongkut and his ministers understood the situation. In another essay on the Cambodian question, Mongkut tells us that at first Siam did not quite understand the French agreement with the Cambodian king. He then details the situation in the indigenous discourse: Cambodia still submitted to both Siam and France. Unlike Vietnam, Siam and France were friends. Thus Siam agreed to let France take care of the Cambodian rulers and two parts of the realm which were too far away for Siam to look after, while Siam still looked after the other two parts which were close to Siam. Hence the Cambodian rulers should still pay respect to both Siam and France.[46] By showing that France took the place of Vietnam in the existing relationship and by allowing the two important rituals of submission—namely the tribute payment and Bangkok's role in the crowning of a tributary king—to be practiced, the French role was not alien to the indigenous polity. France became a new partner of the old mutual patronage over Cambodia. It seems that the French had deliberately exploited the indigenous tributary relationship.

But in this new partnership, the victim was not only Cambodia nor was the victor merely France. Another contest, quietly gathering strength, was the mode of relationship among the countries concerned. On the one hand, the mutual protection over Cambodia provided an excellent guarantee of peace and normal life in Cambodia, as a Cambodian king once said. It had been a condition of stability in the region. This multiple sovereignty was not unusual and needed no adjustment, unless a new struggle for supremacy broke out. On the other hand, however, the recruitment of the French into this partnership provided an opportunity for the European mode of colonial relations to be realized. In this mode, it was unusual for a country to have multiple, overlaying sovereignties. This situation guaranteed neither peace nor stability. Adjustment was inevitable.

Both conceptually and practically, two modes of interstate relations were playing in the same field, making relations among these states ambiguous. To resolve the ambiguity of sovereignty over Cambodia, France appealed in subsequent years to the international community in terms of international law. Mongkut similarly asserted Siam's claim to the world community, but he based his claim on the indigenous polity. In his discourse he presented a Thai version of Cambodian history showing the status of Cambodia (a half-civilized half-barbarian people as he said) as a tributary to the more civilized race of Siam.[47] Within a few years France had repeatedly urged the Siamese court to negotiate the "Cambodian political question." Eventually, on 15 July 1867, the Siamese envoy to Paris signed the treaty recognizing France as having sole authority over Cambodia. The multiple submission for Cambodia's survival had become an opportunity for the French, the agency of the new geography. The premodern polity with its conception and practice of territory and sovereignty became the loser. The modern polity was established as the new legitimate mode of interstate relations, not only for the Westerners but also for the indigenous elite.

On the southern frontier of Siam, both Siam and Britain increased their interference and control over the Malay states in one way or another throughout the last three decades of the nineteenth century by establishing their commissioners in the states in which they had influence. Both guarded their own influence without clashes. By that time the colonialists in British politics had proposed the annexation of the Malay states and the Kra isthmus, though the opposition wishing to avoid any provocation of the French was also strong. The British began establishing full control over the Malay states after a series of conflicts among the Malay rulers broke out in the 1860s and 1870s. Siam, on the other hand, gradually integrated the states it claimed into the new centralized administration. Kedah in particular became a province under direct control of Bangkok in 1871; in 1891 it was upgraded to become a regional center in the new administrative system.[48] Yet Siam faced many difficulties in controlling, let alone integrating, the Malay provinces. They became Siam's burden. Finally, Siam gave four Malay states, Kedah included, to Britain in 1909 in exchange for some benefits, such as the British concession on its extraterritoriality in Siam, and a low interest loan to construct railways between Bangkok and British Malaya.[49] The formal negotiations for boundary demarcation started at this time.

Likewise, the boundary demarcation between Siam and Cambodia under the French Empire started once the political agreement about the sovereignty of Cambodia in the modern sense had been resolved.[50] But when Siam and French Cochin China tried to delimit their territorial boundaries in the areas along the Mekhong, problems emerged because the areas forming the buffer between them were full of multiply sovereigned towns. It had yet to be decided to which country they belonged.

Chapter Five
Margin

THE DISPUTE BETWEEN Siam and France over the Lao region in the decades around the turn of the nineteenth and twentieth centuries has been widely investigated by scholars of Southeast Asia. The issue has been studied basically in only three ways. The first is the perspective of international relations: the diplomatic relations between Siam, France, Britain, and certain other European powers such as Russia and Germany. Studies in this vein have looked at colonialist policies, actions, negotiations, treaties, Siam's foreign policy, and effects of the treaties. The second approach is to look at the domestic politics of the countries involved: the factional disputes within the court or government and the biographies of key figures, Siam's ability to deal with the imperialists in such matters as domestic affairs, the armed forces, administration, and major social changes to counter the imperialist threat. The third approach has been to describe the events: clashes, disputes, heroic episodes, and the French naval blockade of the Chao Phraya River at the Grand Palace in Bangkok in 1893.

Despite the different angles, most studies of the Franco-Siamese dispute have dealt with the same theme: the aggression of French imperialism. The Siamese rulers have been praised for their diplomatic genius, their skill and farsightedness in handling the situation, and their incomparable statesmanship in domestic affairs. It seems beyond doubt, according to these studies, that the incident was a result of the aggression of the French imperialists. Although the dispute itself was about territories, very little attention has been paid to the most critical factor: the nature of space itself.

The reason may have something to do with the nature of the evidence, mostly the correspondence between Bangkok, Paris, and London. Hence the historical concern has been to discover how these territories were divided politically rather than the transforming nature of space. Diplomacy and battles occupy the attention of most descriptions. The more fundamental reason, however, is that scholars have presumed that there was no difference in the knowledge and technology of political space. The preoccupation with modern ideas of sovereignty, the integrity of a state, and international relations is so overwhelming that it leads us to overlook—perhaps even to preclude beforehand—the existence of other conceptions and practices apart from our own. With such a preoccupation, scholars usually try to unravel the sole legitimate sovereignty over the disputed territories by weighing the historical rights of the disputants. The grid of the modern mind renders the unfamiliarity of the indigenous polity and geography more familiar to us by translating them into modern discourse. Such scholars fail to recognize the rapidly increasing role of the new technology of space. Consequently, these studies mislead us into considering only the point of view of those states which became modern nations. Whenever the issue is raised, we hear only the claims of the major nations. The fate of the tiny tributaries under dispute remains virtually unknown. Their voices have not been heard. It is as if they occupied a dead space with no life, no view, no voice, and thus no history of their own.

The situation of multiple sovereignty was common for the smaller kingdoms and tiny chiefdoms on all the frontiers of Siam except that between Siam and Burma, including the whole Lao region along the Mekhong River and beyond. Remarkably, a *muang* in this situation was called in Thai and Lao by the adjective *songfaifa* or *samfaifa*, literally "under two overlords" or "under three overlords" respectively, with the first word *song* (two) and *sam* (three) indicating the number of overlords to which such a *muang* submitted.[1] Sometimes it was called *suaisongfai(fa)* or *suaisamfai(fa)*. The word *suai* means tribute and the final word was sometimes omitted, hence meaning tribute to two and three overlords respectively.[2]

The comparatively smaller kingdoms such as Lanna, Luang Phrabang, and Vientiane were always under many overlords at one time. All of the tiny chiefdoms between Lanna and the Burmese kingdoms, between Luang Phrabang, Yunnan, Tonkin, and between Vientiane and Tonkin or Annam, were also the *muang* of many overlords. They were chiefdoms of the Shan, Lu, Karen, Lao, Phuan, Phuthai, Chinese, and several other ethnic peoples. They were weaker, more fragmented, yet autonomous in their relations to the powerful ones. Consequently, they paid submission to any superior who could provide protection or inflict wounds upon them.

These tiny tributaries were regarded as the frontier of several kingdoms simultaneously. In other words, the realms of the supreme overlords—Siam, Burma, and Vietnam—were overlapping. This situation was indeed the root

of troubles when the notion of a modern boundary with absolute and exclusive territorial sovereignty was applied, since the margins of the major states
in the region were ambiguous.

By the closing decades of the nineteenth century the regime in Bangkok
was well aware of the problem. It voluntarily entered the contest for the
ambiguously sovereign space. The British and French, however, worked
their way through from the west and the east at the same time. Carrying different flags, all of them were agents of modern geography to displace the
indigenous premodern political space. Their only disagreement was over how
to settle the overlapping frontiers. This desire for exclusive territorial sovereignty led to the Franco-Siamese crisis in 1893.

Overlapping Margins

In the north of Siam, Lanna and Sipsong Panna (in southern China today)
were two regional powers. Lanna, with its center at Chiangmai, was one of
the most powerful kingdoms in the region in the fourteenth to early sixteenth centuries. During the late sixteenth to eighteenth centuries, it became
a tributary of the Burmese Toungoo kingdom and occasionally of Siam as
well. In the late eighteenth century, after being devastated by the protracted
war between Siam and Burma during the 1760s to 1780s, it was restored as a
tributary of Siam. In the north of Lanna, Sipsong Panna was a cluster of more
fragmented and smaller states, of which Kengtung (Chiang Tung) was the
most powerful. Lying between Burma, Lanna, and Yunnan, Kengtung was a
tributary of both the Burmese and Chinese overlords, and sometimes of
Siam, while it had its own tributaries in the sphere of Sipsong Panna.

Between Chiangmai and Kengtung, there were numerous weaker chiefdoms such as Jenghung (Chiang Rung), Chiang Khaeng, and Chiang Saen,
which paid tribute to all local overlords as well as directly to the Burmese and
sometimes Siamese supreme overlords. Yet they were autonomous to the
extent that they often defied the overlords and changed allegiance. Nonetheless, any dispute within their courts or between their overlords would always
lead to interference by more overlords.[3]

The status and situation of a chiefdom under many overlords was quite
common and recognized by the overlords. Chiang Saen—an ancient town
under the overlordship of Chiangmai, Kengtung, and Luang Phrabang
throughout its history—was depopulated and abandoned in the late eighteenth century during the wars between Burma and Siam and was not
restored until the 1880s. By that time, however, it was occupied by Shan
people who earned their living around the fortress of the abandoned town.

Remarkably, while reasserting Siam's sovereignty over Chiang Saen, Chula-longkorn (Rama V) did not claim that it belonged to Siam exclusively. He suggested that Chiangmai should allow the Shan to settle there if Burma and Kengtung allowed Chiang Saen to submit to both sides (Burma/Kengtung versus Siam/Chiangmai). Unsurprisingly, the Burmese view on this issue, as reported by Chulalongkorn in the same letter, was not a claim to Chiang Saen but a request for the status quo of Chiang Saen—that is, to leave it as a "common" *muang* where people of both Kengtung and Chiangmai were allowed to live.[4]

Along the Salween River on the western frontier of Lanna was the territory of Kayah people, also known as the Red Karen or Yang. As Ronald Renard has pointed out, the tiny Kayah states formed a dynamic, fluctuating frontier between Burma and Lanna because they gave allegiance to both sides and had defied the authorities of both from time to time since the late seventeenth century. Sometimes the Kayah even demanded tribute from tiny towns under Chiangmai's power.[5]

The Lao region along the Mekhong River was full of chiefdoms in a similar situation. Like Cambodia and Lanna, the Lao state of Lan Sang was among the powerful regional kingdoms, but it became a tributary of Siam and Burma from the late sixteenth century onward. In the 1680s Lan Sang split into two separate kingdoms, Luang Phrabang and Vientiane. And in the eighteenth century another overlord, Vietnam, became involved. From the end of the eighteenth century, both of the Lao centers paid tribute to Siam and Vietnam regularly. In 1826 Prince Anuwong of Vientiane led a revolt of the tributary against its oppressive overlord, Siam. Its failure led to the direct involvement of Vietnam since the prince requested Annam's protection. The entire Mekhong region was contested from then on.

Between Luang Phrabang, Vientiane, and the Vietnamese centers of Tonkin and Annam, there were numerous tiny chiefdoms similar to those in the north of Lanna. The upper part of the area adjacent to southern China was known as Sipsong Chuthai, a cluster of tiny chiefdoms within the sphere of Lai's influence. Lai was an ancient settlement of Phuthai people. It paid tribute to Luang Phrabang, Tonkin, and China (Canton). As its own history tells us, it had been under three overlords for more than three hundred years.[6] It divided its realm into three parts, each of whose manpower and levies were to be paid to each overlord. Its court, administrative pattern, currency, and alphabet followed the Chinese and Vietnamese traditions. Its ruler was known as Kwan Fu to Vietnam, as Hong to China, and as Luang Phromwongsa to Luang Phrabang.[7] Throughout the latter half of the nineteenth century, a large number of Chinese bandits known to local people as the Ho, fleeing from southern China after the failed Taiping rebellion (1850–1864), had troubled the region. The Tonkinese force protected Lai and helped it to drive the Ho away, while Lai's request for protection from Luang Phrabang was put aside. The tribute to Luang Phrabang was thus suspended. In the immediate period before the Franco-Siamese dispute, therefore, Lai was predominantly under the influence of Vietnam both culturally and militarily.[8]

Thaeng, or Dien Bien Phu as we know it today, was a *samfaifa* of Lai, Vietnam, and Luang Phrabang. The ties among them were so strong that not only was Thaeng a long-time tributary of the three overlords, but in the myth of its origin Thaeng was also believed to have a common origin in this world with the Vietnamese and the Lao. Their ancestors were brothers.[9] If the relationship between Thaeng and Vietnam was especially close, Siam's involvement with Thaeng was virtually nonexistent. Yet just before the Franco-Siamese dispute Thaeng was conquered by Siam and became the outermost town where the Siamese established headquarters for their campaigns against the Ho in 1885.[10] It was just at this time that Siam arrested Thaeng's ruler, who was a son of Lai's ruler, because he refused to submit to Siam's force, and replaced him with a new figure loyal to Siam.

South of Sipsong Chuthai was another cluster of tiny towns called Huaphan Thangha Thanghok (hereafter Huaphan). All of them were tributaries of Luang Phrabang, Vientiane, Tonkin, Annam, and sometimes the southern Chinese rulers. After the ill-fated revolt of Anuwong in 1826, Huaphan was handed over by Siam to Luang Phrabang as a reward for Luang Phrabang's loyalty. But at the same time Huaphan was given as a gift from Anuwong to Vietnam for the latter's protection against Siam. Faced with the Ho bandits, Huaphan requested help from both Vietnam and Siam. Consequently, in 1885 the Siamese forces declared the whole cluster to be Siam's.

The case of Phuan was similar. After the Anuwong revolt, it was handed over to Luang Phrabang and Vietnam at the same time. Anuwong himself fled after his defeat and resided in Phuan until the Siamese troops came to uproot him. Siam imposed its loyalist as ruler, though he was executed a few years later by Vietnam. As a consequence, in 1833 Siam launched a campaign of destroying and depopulating Huaphan and Phuan because they were regarded as front-line towns of Vietnam.[11] After the fourteen-year Vietnam-Siamese war, Vietnam restored Phuan's ruler as its tributary and required him to pay tribute to Vietnam annually. Nevertheless, Phuan fell into Siam's hands again in 1885 by the same force which subdued Thaeng, Lai, and Huaphan.[12]

The areas along the Mekhong were full of tiny tributary states. Even though the rulers of these chiefdoms considered themselves as sovereign and autonomous in their own right, they were on the margins of many spheres of overlords' power. In other words, they were frontier towns from the perspective of the overlords—either their own frontier or that of the enemy. As frontier towns, they were left more or less independent and neglected, so long as there was no war between the overlords of the region. But in a war situation, any tributaries en route between the rivals would become the first victims. Under more lenient circumstances, a local ruler might be forced to submit himself to the force of the overlord; otherwise, he would be replaced by a loyalist of that overlord. In the worst case, either they would be forced to supply food and manpower, or they would be plundered, destroyed, and depopulated, in order to deprive the enemy of supplies. As a Siamese commander put it in the case of Phuan in 1833:

> Be careful not to let any Phuan people return to their home town. In the dry season, keep trying to remove those Phuan who are still in the town. If they are cooperative, convince them; if after persuasion alone there are any Phuan left, the king proposes to use force to move them completely. Don't leave any potential food supply for the enemy.[13]

By all these methods, the tiny tributaries regarded as frontier *muang* were forced to change allegiance from time to time for their survival. The sovereignty of these states was therefore ambiguous and complicated by the shifts of allegiance and the reverses following conquests. But an occupation was always temporary, and the aim of a takeover was in fact to compel a tributary ruler to submit his allegiance, which by no means guaranteed the conqueror's exclusive possession. Despite the conqueror's claim, these "frontier" tributaries were still multiply sovereign.

In the indigenous polity in which the power field of a supreme overlord radiated like a candle's light, these tiny chiefdoms were always located in the overlapping arena of the power fields.[14] Unlike the border between Siam and Burma which kept both sides apart, all other borders of Siam were shared by others. Their frontiers were overlapping. In the indigenous interstate relations, the overlapping margin of two power fields was not necessarily considered a problem unless it served as a bridge for the enemy to invade. Multiple sovereignty was well recognized by the parties involved as the status quo. Even Chulalongkorn and his Burmese counterpart preferred leaving Chiang Saen under both overlords.[15] Thus the ambiguous sovereignty of these frontier tributaries was useful and desired by the overlords. Instead of establishing an independent state as a buffer zone, in this indigenous practice the overlords shared sovereignty over the buffer zones as long as the rulers of the frontier tributaries were loyal to all relevant overlords. Not only had Siam never been bounded by the modern kind of boundary but it was also surrounded by "common" frontiers, the shared borders.

For modern polities, however, the overlapping frontier is not permissible. The division of territorial sovereignty between states must be clear-cut at the point where both power fields interface. They must not overlap, and there must be no distance between them. To transform a premodern margin to a modern territorial interface, or to create a modern edge of a state out of a premodern shared space, there could be more than one possible boundary, and all of them would be equally justified because the boundary could be anywhere within the overlapping arena, depending on how the sovereignty of a tributary was decided. Mathematically speaking, the more tributaries and more overlords involved, the greater the number of possible boundaries. Accordingly, the possibility of disputes over territories is infinite.

Nonetheless, to fulfill the desire to have the boundary fixed and sovereignty exclusive, the tributaries in the overlapping frontiers must be determined and allocated. This was done by both Siam and the European powers. Siam operated in its own way to extract its own share of the territories to be allocated. Siam was not a helpless victim of colonialism as is generally thought. The Siamese ruling circle at the close of the nineteenth century was familiar with the tributary relationship, and many of the elite became familiar with the Western political geographical concept as well. It was in the wake of colonialism, armed with the force of the new kind of boundary and polity, that Siam urgently needed to secure its overlordship over its tributaries. On the one hand, the Siamese rulers were aware of the uncertain sovereignty of these tributaries in that they did not yet really belong to Siam. On the other hand, Siam wished to expand and enforce a stronger grip over the tributaries. The difference from previous overlord protection was that this time Siam was equipped with a new mechanism of overlordship in terms of force, administration, and boundary demarcation and mapping. Siam entered the contest with the European powers to conquer and incorporate these marginal states into its exclusive sovereign territory. This expansionist desire was expressed overtly and straightforwardly.

The Making of "Our" Space

In the late nineteenth century, Siam was aware of the presence of the more powerful Europeans. But this did not mean its desire to expand its overlordship over any possible tributary had ended. When Burma was in trouble with the British in 1885, some Shan towns requested Siamese protection. The king responded with an ambitious remark: "The Thai, the Lao, and the Shan all consider themselves peoples of the same race. They all respect me as their supreme sovereign, the protector of their well-being."[16]

The king had a very clear understanding that Luang Phrabang, a major Lao tributary, had been a *songfaifa* to Vietnam and Siam, and its allegiance to Siam was not without doubt. In the period of the Ho disturbance, Bangkok's troops did not provide adequate protection. Luang Phrabang was sacked in 1887, and the king was able to escape only with the help of a French contingent. Although the Bangkok force recovered it in 1888, Chulalongkorn was worried about its loyalty. He feared that the Lao court would be tempted by the French. In his secret letter to the resident commissioner to Luang Phrabang newly appointed by Bangkok, his instructions included details of how to please the Lao rulers, how to make them suspicious of the French, and how to argue against the French. But the most interesting remark was his conscious strategy to turn the ambiguity of a tributary in Siam's favor:

> [We] must try to please [Luang Phrabang] by describing the fact that the Thai and Lao belong to the same soil. . . . France is merely an alien who looks down on the Lao race as savage. Whatever the French do to please the rulers of Luang Phrabang is merely bait on a hook. . . . Although the Lao people habitually regard Lao as We and Thai as They when only the two peoples are considered, comparing the Thai and the French, however, it would be natural that they regard the Thai as We and the French as They.[17]

This was a fundamental aim of the two major efforts which have been known to historians of Siam as measures of self-defense against the European threat—namely the reform of provincial administration and the expeditions to suppress the Ho disturbances in the Lao region. Both were in fact operations to resolve the ambiguity of the overlapping margins.

The reform of provincial administration in Siam in the 1880s and 1890s is a favorite subject for those interested in the modernization of Siam. Reform was first tested in the 1870s in Lanna and then developed and applied to the Lao region along the Mekhong, including Luang Phrabang and many other large and small tributaries. Finally, from 1892 onward it was implemented in other regions including the inner provinces of Siam. It was a gradual process of displacing the traditional local autonomy, especially in these tributaries, by the modern mechanism of centralization. The tempo, tactics, problems, and solutions varied from place to place. But the final outcomes were the same: the control of revenue, taxes, budgets, education, the judicial system, and other administrative functions by Bangkok through the residency. The residents, most of whom were the king's brothers or close associates, were sent to supervise local rulers or even to take charge of the governorship of each locality. It should be remarked that while the relationship between Bangkok and its tributaries was hierarchical and operated through rulers, the new administration was called the *thesaphiban* system, literally meaning protection over territory.

The new administrative methods were very much like the regimes established in a colonial country. Mongkut himself once wished to go to Singapore to learn Western styles of government. Chulalongkorn fulfilled his father's wish from the early years of his reign by going to Singapore, Java, and India where the Thai rulers believed that the government was similar to Europe's and just as civilized.[18] In Chulalongkorn's words to the viceroy of India at that time: "Both I and the council are convinced that there is no country in the East where the science of government is so well understood or the welfare of the people so faithfully attended to [as India]."[19] Thus it is not surprising that the new administration was in many respects similar to what a colonial regime conceived for native people. Prince Damrong, the craftsman of this new system, in his writing about the regime in Java, referred to the Dutch residents as *"Retsiden (Samuhathesaphiban)."*[20] Here he likened the colonial residency to the Thai governorship of the reformed system, putting the latter in parentheses to give his readers the meaning of the former. One should not fail to read the other way round—the term outside the parentheses is in fact the definition of *Samuhathesaphiban*—and to note how similar the two systems were in Damrong's view.

If the reform eradicated the ambiguity of space in a comparatively peaceful manner, the expeditions against the Ho disturbance were more violent. The Ho was the word the Lao used for the Yunnanese in general. In this case it was for the Chinese who had been defeated in the Taiping revolt in southern China in the mid-1860s and then fled southward into the upper Mekhong valley and the Black River valley. They became independent armed bands who plundered, destroyed, or occupied the tiny chiefdoms and even threatened the Lao kingdoms along the Mekhong during the 1870s and 1880s. In 1884–1885 and 1885–1887 Siam sent two expeditions to fight them.[21] But the situation became much more complicated by the infighting among the local tiny chiefdoms themselves.

On many occasions the Ho were merely a mercenary force helping one chief to attack another. In some circumstances they collaborated with a local chief to fight another alliance of Ho and local chief. The forces of the Ho and those of local chiefdoms became mingled. Many Ho Leaders became rulers and officials of local chiefdoms, and in turn many local chieftains were regarded by Siam as leaders of the Ho bandits. The understanding that disturbances arose because of bandits from outside the region was partly true. But to lay the blame for all the disturbances on the Ho was definitely misleading. The sack of Luang Phrabang in 1887, for example, was in fact the retaliation by the chief of Lai for the arrest of his three sons by the Siamese force in 1886.[22] Yet it is true that Lai's force did contain some Ho bandits. The ruler of Lai was therefore regarded by Siam at that time, as well as by historians, as a chief of the Ho gangs.[23]

The Siamese forces against the Ho disturbances in the 1880s did not merely aim at suppressing the Ho; they also intended to reassert Siam's suzerainty over that region by force. Moreover, it was no longer the premodern exercise of overlordship. In the words of Surasakmontri, the field commander, the aim of his troops was to suppress the Ho as well as to "settle the *anakhet*":

> It is an opportunity to settle the *anakhet*. Because France has waged wars with [Vietnam] and is going to demarcate the boundary close to Huaphan and Sipsong Chuthai, it may move forward to set foot on His Majesty's realm claiming that they have been Vietnam's territories. For this reason, and to avoid losing an opportunity, His Majesty gave us the order to mobilize the troops in order to quash the Ho in the dry season this year of the cock.[24]

The phrase "settle the *anakhet*" indicates that there was a problem about the frontier, boundary, or limit of the realm to be solved. The mission was to seize the opportunity to make it clear that these areas belonged to Siam exclusively. Chulalongkorn himself advised at length on the boundary issue and how to deal with the French in anticipation that a confrontation could take place: "Whichever side of the border belongs to whom, let each side make a map in order to negotiate and divide [the territories] by cordial agreement in Bangkok."[25]

After the fourteen-year war between Siam and Vietnam during 1834–1848, the tributaries in the region returned to their status quo as tributaries of Luang Phrabang and Vietnam. The campaign against the Ho from 1884 onward was the first presence of Siam's power over these tributaries. Siam correctly claimed that they belonged to Luang Phrabang. Despite such a claim, Siam recognized the multiple overlordship over these tributaries, even for Luang Phrabang itself. To claim exclusive sovereignty over them meant to expand the realm of Siam under the regime of the new geographical concept over the indigenous ambiguous space. In other words, after conquering these tiny chiefdoms, Siam had to introduce the means to secure its exclusive power, instead of allowing local chiefs to pay tribute to several overlords as they had done before.

Several incidents showed that Siam was quite conscious of its expansionist action. In 1886 when the troops seized a town definitely outside Siam's sphere of power, for example, the king advised the troops to retain the town. If the French raised the issue later, he further advised, an alibi should be given both in the field and in Bangkok that it was a *songfaifa*, or that the ruler of the town had requested Siam's intervention, or that the Siamese force had followed the Ho, the common enemy of Siam and France, and had occupied the town to pacify it, not to invade it.[26] Likewise, when the troops marched into Sipsong Chuthai in 1887, Surasakmontri asked whether he should incorporate them into the Siamese realm. The king, in consultation with his foreign affairs secretary, advised Surasakmontri to annex them: "If the French argued or requested [the return of Sipsong Chuthai], and if it should be relinquished, do so later."[27] The premodern polity did not confuse the Siamese rulers. On the contrary, they exploited it to take over former tributaries. "Peace" and "the Ho" were merely positive and negative tokens to justify their action.

Another important case which must be mentioned is Khamkoet and Khammuan. These were twin towns in the sphere of the Phuan where, in 1893, a collision between the Siamese and the French forces took place. In 1886, Chulalongkorn overtly advised an opportunistic policy on this twin township:

> In the case of Khamkoet and Khammuan, [we] are more disadvantaged . . . because it is evident that [Vietnam] had appointed the rulers. However, there is our claim that it belonged to two overlords. Now France controls [Vietnam] but not yet completely so; thus it may not yet be ready to administer the distant towns. If it is possible to make Khamkoet and Khammuan ours by whatever means, contemplate on this and do it. If it is too ambitious or it will cause a dispute with France, don't try; [we] do not lose anything apart from the fact that our boundary would not be on the mountain ranges.[28]

In 1891, Phra Yod, the first ethnic Thai ruler of Phuan and a historical hero in the Franco-Siamese conflict, recommended that Siam should retain the twin towns not by any historical right but for the security of Siam's occupation of the Mekhong region.[29]

Previously, a conquest would require a submission and, in most cases, temporary exclusive control over the town. The ruler of that town might submit to another overlord to ensure survival after the military presence had departed. But in the conquest in the 1880s the Siamese forces were to be there permanently. The presence of overlord "protection" was no longer remote. The Siamese forces transformed the regime of each small state they conquered. In some cases, previous rulers were replaced by figures loyal to Siam. In many others, Thai officials were appointed to govern these towns. Wherever local rulers were allowed to rule their towns, Thai officials were appointed as supervisors. All new local regimes were directly administered by military commanders from Bangkok. The ambiguous space in the remote Mekhong region was determined by military means. To put it another way, military force concretized these parts of Siam's geo-body.

The new administration was a mechanism to establish a new relationship between Bangkok and its former tributaries, hence a new kind of sovereignty within a new entity. The military operation was nothing but territorial conquest. Both operations established a new kind of political geography in which neither overlapping margin nor multiple sovereignty was permitted. The earth's surface was inscribed in a new way. How important the geographical mission was in the minds of the Siamese elite in the so-called suppression of the Ho is best indicated by the titles conferred on local rulers who submitted themselves to the Siamese forces. Traditionally, titles tended to signify power, merit, blessing, relations to deities or sacred objects, and other magical qualities. This time the titles were weird and had never appeared anywhere before: Phra Sawamiphaksayamkhet ("loyalty to the Siamese *khet*"), Phiaphan Thura-anakhetkosai ("concerning the business of the *anakhet*"), Phra Phithak-anakhet ("protector of the *anakhet*"), Phraya Khumphonphithak-buranakhet ("the commander protecting territorial integrity"), Phra Ratana-anakhet ("the bejewelled *anakhet*"), and Phraya Khanthasema ("the boundaries, domain of kingdom"), for example.[30]

Nonetheless, the local chiefs might not understand the conquest in any terms other than the tributary practice they had known. They might not anticipate that this time the conquest was a new kind of political control, a practice of the new geographical consciousness. The actions taken together constituted a code which signified two kinds of relationship simultaneously. On the one hand, it signified the premodern overlord/tributary relationship. On the other, it represented the new polity and political geography. The shift occurred inevitably once the agent of the new discourse conquered the indigenous one. That is to say, in an action very much like the exercise of an overlord's power, the new conception and practice began to realize the new discourse in concrete terms. As France had stepped into the indigenous tributary relationship by establishing a double-coding protectorate over Cambodia, its action could be understood by the Cambodian and Thai courts as an indigenous overlordship. By a similar strategy, Bangkok imposed a new kind of relationship, sovereignty, and space through colonizing actions, that is, the conquest and reformed administration. The colonial-style relationship bridged the transition in the displacement process. It was a relationship between a superior power and its conquered states, yet it was unlike the tributary/overlord relationship in that the ambiguity of sovereignty and space had been resolved. Certainly, Bangkok never thought of itself as similar to the European imperialists. The most significant distinction in Siam's view was probably that the French and other European powers were alien or foreigners or "They," but Siam was "We" to native peoples in the region. If the word "colonization" is too harsh here, it seems that there were two types of conquest: one by "We," the other by "They." Undoubtedly, this is a powerful distinction which makes the conquests by "We" perhaps more legitimate and worthy of celebration while the other type deserves condemnation. Of course, Lai, Thaeng, or even Luang Phrabang might not consider Siam as much "We" as "They."

New Margins: Siam and the British

Siam did not alone resolve the issue of ambiguous territories. Around the same time as the reform was under way and the Siamese forces were marching through the Mekhong region, the European powers moved to take part in the settlement of the ambiguous territories. In a sense, all of them were working alongside one another to displace the indigenous political space. Confrontations thus occurred not only among these human powers, but also between different realms of geographical knowledge.

After the final Anglo-Burmese war was over in 1885, the frontier between Lanna and Upper Burma became a problem as the region was within the spheres of several powers. Two major areas in question were the Kayah state along the Salween River and the chiefdoms of the Shan and the Lu people between Kengtung and Lanna.[31] As for the frontier along the Salween, small villages with the Siamese white elephant flags and posts with stockades and garrisons were established along the border. Some Kayah were tattooed to substantiate Siam's claim for five Kayah towns.[32] In 1875, however, the Burmese king at Ava had put forward a claim to the British government in India that the Kayah chiefs had sent "virgins to the Burman king as tokens of subjection" and this customary present had been given to Burma "since the beginning of the world." The Kayah people, a Burmese envoy said, "had taken the oath of allegiance to Burma from the earliest times to within the last few months."[33] The British thus supported local rulers who rejected Siam's claim. Then, in late 1888, the British force "resumed possession." Siam protested.[34]

In the territory between Kengtung and Chiangmai, there were several disputable issues. Siam and the British decided to settle the problem by setting up a commission to interrogate local people and survey the areas. The most controversial issue was the case of Muang Sing: did it belong to Kengtung, then under the British, or to Nan of Siam? The chief of Muang Sing was a relative of Kengtung's ruler. But he submitted to Nan and paid the gold and silver trees to Bangkok as well. When the dispute occurred, he even offered the same tribute to the British to express his desire for British suzerainty.[35]

The inquiry and negotiation were carried out throughout 1891–1892. Finally they reached an agreement in 1892 to give Muang Sing to Siam and the five Kayah towns with the rich forest to British Burma.[36] The survey, mapping, and demarcation had been done concurrently with the negotiations during 1890–1891. The final delimitation was done by a joint commission during 1892–1893. The agreement with maps was formally ratified in 1894.

The fact that these disputes did not lead to a violent conflict was owing to many factors. Basically, the British India government wanted to leave Siam as a buffer state on the eastern front of India. Around that time, furthermore, France increased its activity in Indochina, and its conflicts with Siam intensified. Any outbreak of aggression between Siam and the British might provoke the French on the other side.[37] On the other hand, it seems that Siam's attitude toward Britain at that time was a mixture of fear, respect, reverence, and desire for friendship and some kind of alliance. This was quite opposite to Siam's attitude toward the French, which was rather hostile.

The influence of the British in the Siamese ruling circle was considerable. Among the most important signs of this influence was the role of the British in the crisis in 1874 when a civil war nearly broke out because of a factional dispute within the Bangkok court. The dispute was settled by a British arbitrator.[38] Another sign of the special relationship was Siamese-British relations in the conflict with the French. Siam had high hopes that Britain would help. The Siamese rulers informed the British at every stage of the conflict and consulted the British on every move they took.[39] Siam even requested a British "protectorate of a modified kind." But Britain refused to take any action against the French in order to avoid provoking a reaction. On the contrary, Siam was advised to surrender and concede the left bank of the Mekhong as the French demanded.[40]

There were other signs of Siam's special relationship with the British, as well, such as the roles of British advisors in the Siamese regime. A recent study of the formation of the Thai state even suggests that the so-called administrative reform in Lanna was in fact the result of the cooperation between Bangkok and the British for the benefit of the forest industry. The new state mechanism was designed to facilitate British interests, not as a defense strategy against the British threat.[41] All this may remind us of relations between Kedah and British Penang and the indigenous politics of protection through alliance with one superior power against another. Therefore it was not surprising at all that Siam and the British government finally concluded a treaty in 1892 in a peaceful fashion about all matters pertaining to the undecided tributaries. Siam hoped, however, that the agreement would induce the British to intervene in the dispute between Siam and France at that time. Siam also hoped that the agreement would guarantee that Siam would receive assistance and that there would be no arms embargo through their common borders.[42] Like Kedah, such an expectation was a grand illusion.

The Making of Interface by Force

Unlike the British-Siamese differences, the dispute between Siam and France to settle the ambiguous space along the Mekhong River was violent. The French started their campaign to take control over the area about two years later than Siam. As one historian relates, they found that "small Thai guard posts appeared all along the watershed. . . . [The] Thai troops were taking up positions on the crest of the cordillera, virtually overlooking the plains of Annam."[43] Therefore the French put forward their counterclaims against Siam's and against the presence of Siamese forces in the region.

All descriptions and maps done by Europeans in the nineteenth century identified the areas beyond the Chao Phraya valley as countries separated from Siam. As Auguste Pavie, the French consul at Luang Phrabang and Bangkok at the time of conflict and himself a surveyor and explorer, expressed his view, the realm of Siam was confined to the Chao Phraya valley, but it was not clear to what extent the Lao region was under Siam's sovereignty or at what point Siam touched the Vietnamese sphere.[44] The fact that Siam had made the first moves and occupied the most territory under dispute before the French meant that Siam had a slight advantage in terms of actual possession. The French at the time had to protest strongly against Siam's presence and the right of possession. Pavie himself referred to the indigenous practice of multiple submission, arguing that it did not mean autonomy was lost: Siam had no more rights than China, Annam, or Burma. He even consulted a chronicle of Luang Phrabang to argue that Siam was rarely mentioned in Lao history.[45] Ironically, the roles Siam and the French adopted and the tactics of argument they employed in this particular case reversed the ones in 1864 when Mongkut protested the French exclusive possession over Cambodia.

One of the turning points of the contest for the Lao region was when

Luang Phrabang was sacked by Lai's force in June 1887 in revenge for Siam's capture of the sons of Lai's ruler. The king of Luang Phrabang was saved by Pavie himself.[46] Pavie claimed that after this incident the Lao king had told him that Luang Phrabang was not a Siamese conquest. It voluntarily offered tribute to Siam for protection against all attacks. Of course, the king was not satisfied with the result. Here Pavie reports what the Lao king said in the indigenous discourse: "I don't want anymore to do with them [Siamese]. If my son consents, we will offer ourselves as a gift to France, on the condition that she will keep us away from future misfortunes."[47] Neither of the would-be overlords could prevent such a misfortune, however, for they were the sources of it. Moreover, the Lao king did not realize that in the new geographical discourse which both Siam and France then represented, his discourse of gift giving as a submission without conquest would not be allowed to exist.

The method that each side used to substantiate its claim and invalidate the other's—the evidence of submissions—failed to prove anything. All the counterarguments were equally true and false. The ambiguous margin had to be decided arbitrarily, either peacefully or violently, because its nature was logically and historically undecidable. Pavie was right when he remarked that Siam had to resort to military means because the geographic and ethnographic evidence seemed inadequate to justify its claim. He was also right in suggesting that the Ho were merely the excuse for Siam to intervene.[48] But these comments applied equally to the French. As it turned out, the attempt to eradicate the ambiguity of the border in this region was done by sheer force on both sides.

Both the Siamese and French forces marched through the areas, raising their flags over the occupied territories as quickly as possible, until they confronted each other at various points on the left bank of the Mekhong. The confrontation at Thaeng (Dien Bien Phu) in 1888 was an example of how the boundary was determined temporarily. In that incident, both forces "suppressed the Ho" along their way until they faced each other at Thaeng. At first the commanders of both sides claimed their rights and ordered the other to move out. Finally they agreed to settle the dispute by the simple agreement that neither would move forward. They let the territories belong to the conqueror until the negotiation in Bangkok resolved the matter through diplomacy. The agreement at Thaeng in December 1888 applied to all other fronts throughout the Mekhong region.[49]

Not only were tributaries conquered, but the indigenous political geography of multiple sovereign states was also displaced en route. The troops eliminated the ambiguity. Because of the confrontations, the space under the infantries of both sides was joined for the first time. Spatial overlap was thus transformed into the interface of two sovereign territories. The power of the new geographical knowledge exercised by both the Siamese and French forces prevailed and created a new kind of space. The allotment of territory by military occupation was, however, only tentative and temporary. The geo-body of both sides had not yet been fixed, because they could not agree in all cases where the interface should be located.

The Siamese elite by then were concerned for territory—the land about which their ancestors had never worried and even given away as gifts. The object over which sovereignty would prevail had shifted from a governed town and its ruler to an actual territory. For Siam now, every bit of soil was desirable not so much for its economic value but because of its meaning to sovereignty, royal dignity, and nationhood. From the first confrontation in 1888 to the 1893 crisis, Siam had exerted great effort to ensure that most of the borderland would be securely under its sovereignty. Inevitably, the traditional methods of dealing with the borders had to be replaced. Border surveillance became stricter and disciplined. All the localities along the borders were reinforced. Some no-man's-lands were filled by rotating corvée laborers who drew lots to camp there temporarily.[50] Of course, all of these practices and concerns were alien to their predecessors. The battlefield had moved from the defense of a town's fortress to many other points of collision, including those wastelands where there was no living body or possession. Many incidents which led to the Paknam crisis and the blockade of the Chao Phraya River took place in areas which would have been ignored had the premodern geographical ideas prevailed. The major clash occurred in April 1893 on an unpopulated sandbar in the middle of the Mekhong.[51] This led to a regional and then international crisis in which the French sent two gunboats to blockade the Chao Phraya River. It was just another strategic move to resolve the ambiguity of space.

The Franco-Siamese dispute has long been considered a conflict of two nations. But both rivals were actually on the same side as far as the displacement of the indigenous tributary space by a new geo-body is concerned. Both sides utilized the force of modern knowledge which collided with, and subdued, the indigenous one. The overlapping spheres were determined and distributed. The emerging interface imposed limits on the territory of each side —a sharp and clear-cut division between the two realms. Moreover, the domain marked by this new division was transformed into an integral one by the new mechanism of control. All the actions and incidents were moments of shifts where the displacement of geographical discourses took place. The clashes and the blockade can be viewed as moments which led to the emergence of modern territorial sovereignty and international order and a new meaning of native soil.

But military force and the new administration were not the only means to decide the ambiguity of space. The shift in the embodiment of sovereignty to actual territories implied that the form in which sovereignty was represented must shift as well—from traditional rituals and practices of submission to a new representation which dealt directly with horizontal planes. The beginning of full-scale surveys and mapping of boundaries by the Chulalongkorn regime reflected not merely his sympathy for modern geography but also a change in the discourse of sovereignty. To fulfill the desire to have their geo-bodies concretized and their margins defined for exclusive sovereignty, the French and the Siamese alike had fought both with force and with maps.

Chapter Six
Mapping:
A New Technology of Space

GEOGRAPHY HAD BEEN a powerful science inseparable from the knowledge of the East from the early days of the Europeans' journeys until nineteenth-century colonialism. For the Malay peninsula, the Chinese were the customary visitors and had made several coastal maps of the area. Some of them became valuable sources for Europeans such as Marco Polo whose maps were made in 1292–1294.[1] Since then, the map of this region was included in many atlases of classical, medieval, and early modern Europe.[2] Siam in particular, however, appeared rather late in the European maps of this region. It was not included in the Portuguese discoveries until the latter half of the sixteenth century. Thereafter Siam was well recognized by prominent mapmakers.[3]

Siam in Western Maps

The French and Dutch in the seventeenth century were the leaders in cartographic techniques. The French court, in particular, established a scientific society led by many generations of cartographers.[4] Both countries were also among the leading European powers in the Oriental expeditions of the time. France's close connection with Siam in the 1680s resulted in the advance of geographical knowledge and the mapping of Siam. The French envoys and cartographers of the court of Louis XIV published many maps of Siam and passed their knowledge to other European mapmakers. Figure 7 is the map drawn by a cartographer traveling with the French envoy to Siam in 1686. From then on, Siam was prominent on all maps of the region by European mapmakers.[5]

Nonetheless, on all the maps before the second half of the nineteenth century, the detail of Siam was more or less limited to the coastal areas. The interior had been until then *terra incognita* to the European. Only a few Jesuits and travelers had visited the Lao countries in the mid-seventeenth century. In 1636, a Dutchman had tried to make a map of the river route from the Chao Phraya in the central plain of what is today Thailand northward to the Lao countries. It appears that knowledge of the hinterland was quite scant; the Chao Phraya River on the map was believed to be the route to Lan Sang (Luang Phrabang or Vientiane) and northward to Liphi, which is in fact on the Laos-Cambodian border today.

John Crawfurd's mission to Siam in 1821 was partly dedicated to scientific research on the nature of the land. A geographer himself, he made ten maps of the eastern coast of the Gulf of Siam including one of the sandbanks and shoals in the Chao Phraya River's channel from Bangkok to the gulf.[6] Henry Burney also desired to know about Lanna, which was until then, as he said, "unknown to European geographers."[7] But he had no opportunity when he was the British envoy to Bangkok in 1825–1826. Until 1830, Crawfurd continued to remark that the description of the northern border of Siam was little better than conjecture.[8] Figure 8 is the map included in his 1828 account of his missions in 1821–1822 to Siam and Vietnam.

Since Mercator invented the latitude-longitude matrix covering the entire globe, the world has been full of blank squares waiting to be filled in. The New World was "discovered." African Africa was found. The unexplored places were opened up and inscribed on the map. Indeed, modern mapmaking had inspired innumerable missions to fulfill its desire to plot the entire world. Like their predecessors in earlier centuries, Crawfurd and many other explorers and colonial authorities of that generation attempted to produce maps of Siam and the entire region. The desire for geographical knowledge seemed to be an integral part of colonial expansion since it became a master science for colonial acquisition as well as for explorers and administrators.[9] Larry Sternstein relates the case of Captain James Low, who produced a map of the relatively unknown region as a way of advancing his career.[10] Realizing that mainland Southeast Asia was little known but a survey by Crawfurd was about to yield results, Low hastily produced his map of Siam, Laos, and Cambodia, a work which was welcomed enthusiastically by several of his superiors and rewarded with two thousand Spanish dollars. But the map was drawn from information volunteered by native people without the benefit of an actual survey. Although Sternstein spends most of his article denouncing Low's 1824 map, dissecting it in order to show that it was made from outdated data, was ignorant of new findings and indigenous sources, and "almost entirely based on hearsay,"[11] Low's maps and his story conveyed the state of knowledge of the geography of Siam among Europeans at the time, especially its development in the first half of the nineteenth century.

The hinterland in the maps of that time was still *terra incognita*. Sir John Bowring in his famous books in 1857, for example, believed that there was an unknown desert between the central plain and Lanna.[12] The course of the Mekhong River was believed to be straight southeasterly from its headwaters. The great bend, south of Luang Phrabang, which moved eastward before bending southward again, was unknown until the work of Francis Garnier was published in 1864.[13] Until then the whole northeastern region of Thailand today was almost nonexistent, appearing as merely a narrow strip of land between the Mekhong and a mountain range along the eastern part of Siam. Siam in European knowledge until the 1850s looked like anything but an "ancient axe." In fact, an early eighteenth-century description said that its shape was like a crescent.[14] Obviously these maps were based on information obtained from native people who did not have a global reference and who may have had little knowledge of the geography of the hinterland and the Mekhong.

Despite the variety in the maps, all have a striking similarity. Siam was located only in the Chao Phraya valley and the upper part of the Malay peninsula. On the northern frontier, Siam extended only a little above Phichai, Phitsanulok, or Sukhothai, or even south of Kamphaengphet. On the eastern border, the realm of Siam was limited by a huge mountain range beyond which lay the realms of Laos and Cambodia. People like Crawfurd and Bowring acknowledged that the Lao, Cambodian, and Malay regions were under the fluctuating powers of Siam, Burma, China, and Vietnam.[15] But clearly, they were thinking of the alternate occupation of these weaker states by more powerful kingdoms one at a time rather than the simultaneous multiple overlordship without boundaries on the margins. This is not a proof or disproof of any historical claim. Rather, it is an indication of how they conceived Siam geographically and, probably, what the informants, the local people, regarded as Siam and not Siam. The maps and accounts may indicate that in the perception of the Siamese themselves, the Lanna, Lao, and Cambodian regions were not part of Siam.

Western Mapping in Siam

So far there is no evidence on the impact of Dutch and French mapmaking since the seventeenth century on Siamese mapping. Until the reign of Mongkut (1851–1868), surveys neither interested nor bothered the Siamese court except in the case of potential war routes to Bangkok—such as Crawfurd's map of the Chao Phraya channel, which sparked off a protest from the court.[16] Once a British messenger who wanted to travel by land from

Bangkok to Tenasserim Province was led meandering in the jungle on the border by a Siamese official to prevent his knowledge of the land route between Bangkok and the British-occupied territories.[17]

Siam under Mongkut's regime was different. The elite were more familiar with Western ideas and scientific instruments. Globes and maps were among the instruments enjoyed by the Siamese. How important they were for Mongkut may be seen from the fact that among the gifts selected by Western envoys to present to him, maps of many countries and cities were often included.[18] It is hard to say whether the giver wanted the recipient to have these maps, with a certain hidden agenda in mind, or the latter desired to obtain and possess them. It is safe to say that the maps were special enough to be given to Rex Siamensium, the name Mongkut preferred to call himself in the correspondence with foreigners. As for the Siamese elite, having witnessed envoys from so many distant countries and having had knowledge about them for some time, particularly having *seen* those countries on maps, could they resist imagining or desiring to have Siam *be* on a map just as those civilized countries were? Siam was out there, to be included on the globe. Yet it was to a considerable extent *terra incognita* in mapping terms, even to the Siamese elite. It was there; but it had yet to be fully recognized and accounted for.

The Siamese elite of Mongkut's regime were more cooperative and ready to deal with foreigners even with a traditional map. In fact, more than cooperative, the regime was active and creative in expanding the role of mapping in state affairs. In the last five years of the reign Bangkok issued a large number of letters and instructions asking local authorities about the frontiers on the Burmese and Cambodian borders. There were also many communications concerning surveys and mapping of many localities within the realm of Siam proper such as Phitsanulok, Phimai, and Prachin. Some communications concerned the survey with the French at Sisophon (then on the Thai-Cambodian border, not inside Cambodia as it is today).[19] Perhaps this was the first sign of the new concept of territorial administration.

Around the same time, negotiations on many boundaries on both the western and eastern fronts with the British and French were proceeding. But there was no evidence that Siam had launched any attempt to draw a map of its own geo-body. Only in 1866, when he knew that a French exploring team was surveying the areas along the Mekhong, did Mongkut realize that Siam must do likewise. A Dutchman was soon appointed to head a team of surveyors to the Mekhong areas from Nan, Luang Phrabang, then eastward to Mukdahan. He was among the first Europeans to survey the portion of the Mekhong north of Luang Phrabang. To date, however, no details about this mission in any language have been brought to light.[20] Apart from this assignment, there is no record of any Siamese survey of its boundary until the 1880s.

Mapping and topographical surveys seemed to play a much greater role in the modernization projects in Bangkok and certain provincial areas. This role continued and even increased in the following reign as Siam moved rapidly toward modernization. The growth of urbanism and construction projects in Bangkok, particularly roads, railways, and telegraph lines, required the increasing role of mapping technology in terms of knowledge, technicians, and facilities.

Since it was a new technology to the Siamese, however, the task of mapping in those early days was undertaken mostly by foreigners, even by those who were not technicians. Henry Alabaster, an Englishman who had been the vice-consul in Bangkok in Mongkut's reign, became one of Chulalongkorn's most trusted advisors. Though he was not a surveyor or cartographer by training, his ability in engineering was adequate. He was responsible for two major telegraph lines (Bangkok–Paknam and Bangkok–Bangpa-in), as well as many roads in Bangkok and the one from Bangkok to the gulf. His versatility very much impressed the king, and it was likely that he enjoyed his job.[21] Another foreigner employed by the Bangkok regime in 1878–1879 was Auguste Pavie, the versatile French explorer, who was responsible for the telegraph line from Bangkok through Battambang, now part of Cambodia, to join the French line to Saigon.

In 1880 the British India government requested permission from the Siamese court to conduct a survey in Siam in order to complete the triangulations for the boundary map of British India. They had completed their triangulations from India to their eastern frontier, that is, Burma. To accomplish the boundary mapping of this front, however, they needed to make connected triangulations into Siam. Thus the British India government wanted to erect marking points on some of the highest places in Siamese territory. The first proposed site was at the Golden Mountain in Bangkok, an artificial construction only a few kilometers from the palace, symbolically representing the holy mountain for Bangkok, on top of which a stupa of the Buddha relic resides. Another proposed location was at Phra Pathomchedi, the greatest stupa in Siam, which is less than 50 kilometers southwest of Bangkok.[22]

The Siamese court was frightened. An urgent meeting of ministers and senior officers was called to consider the request because many still believed that such a survey was the first step of a foreign invasion. This reaction was understandable, since it was not a survey for a construction project in a particular locality, an undertaking with which the Siamese rulers were familiar. Perhaps not many of them understood what a triangulation was. At that time, there had been no survey of any large area of Bangkok. There were topographical surveys at many points along the borders, but none of them was a survey on such a scale as a triangulation covering a huge area and a great length of the frontier—and including the capital as part of the survey, probably the most threatening matter to the court. The proposed location of marking points, both of them sacred sites, was another cause of apprehension. Indeed the proposal tells us a lot about the imperialistic insensitivity of the British and modern geography. Besides, the initiative came from the British, to be done by the British, for the benefit of the British.

Alabaster had no such apprehension. But presumably to allay Siamese fears, he suggested that Siam should employ a British technician to undertake the task of doing a map of Siam for the Siamese government to connect with the British triangulations. King Chulalongkorn agreed. Thus James Fitzroy McCarthy, known by his Thai title as Phra Wiphakphuwadon, became an official in the service of the Siamese government.[23]

The triangulations from India were completed and became the basis for the surveys for the map of Siam.[24] But after that work was done, McCarthy and his survey team returned to the modernizing projects. Some of their major accomplishments were:

1881: the telegraph line between Tak of Siam and Moulmein of British Burma
1882: a map of Sampheng, the heart of the Chinese community in Bangkok, made to increase the efficiency of the collection of the Chinese head taxes
1882–1883: a map of the boundary between Rahaeng and Chiangmai to settle their dispute over the woodcutting tax
1883: a map of the boundary between Pattani and Perak, two Malay states—one under Siam, the other under the British[25]

Yet this European technology was not so welcome to native people. Phraya Maha-ammat (Seng), a successful surveyor and cartographer trained by McCarthy, remarked that their work was obstructed even by the nobles, who were afraid that their property might be confiscated. The mapping officials were overseen at every step while they were working. McCarthy himself complained many times in his journals that his work was harder than it should have been because of hindrance from local officials. Seng's brother was killed while surveying Sipsong Panna because the local people did not want the work to be done.[26] Nonetheless, the change was coming, as McCarthy noted in 1895 at the end of his successful career in Siam, reminiscing about what he had encountered in his early days in Siam: "Surveying was regarded as of no use in the administration of the country, and as far more likely to serve the purposes of a future invader than of the rightful owners of the country. But it is time for such notions to come to an end, and for the work to be put on a better footing."[27]

For the rulers in Bangkok, the role of mapping had been expanding rapidly. It had become as necessary to Siam as roads, electricity, the telegraph, and railways. The first group of mapping officials was formed as early as 1875 by selecting about fifty men from the Royal Bodyguard, the first Western-style regiment in Siam. It was called the "Military Engineers of the Royal Bodyguard" under the command of Alabaster.[28] But only a few of them finished the training, and the scheme was dropped until McCarthy took the job and began the training again in 1881.

In 1882 Damrong recommended the establishment of the first mapping school to train officials to be assistants to the European technicians. The school limited its students according to demand, and most of them were the descendants of high-ranking government officials. Among the courses offered in this school were Western mathematics and astronomy as well as the use of sophisticated scientific devices. The students also learned to calculate coordinates and many other topographical measurements.[29] In fact, this school was one of the few Western-style schools in Siam at the time. And it was the only school run by the Siamese government which offered intensive studies of English and Western scientific knowledge, since this knowledge was necessary for the job. But perhaps because it was a training school for a particular purpose rather than a school for general education, studies on modern education in Thailand rarely mention anything about this institution.[30]

Three years later, in 1885, the Royal Survey Department was founded. It was responsible for all surveys, planning, and mapping projects of the government.[31] Mapping was no longer a foreign technology in Siam.

The Making of "Our" Space by Maps

Phraya Maha-ammat (Seng) once said that when he joined the Interior Ministry in 1892 he was confident that his superiors knew the frontier towns by name but could not identify their locations on a map. Perhaps, he added, they were not so much concerned with problems on the borders.[32] This reminiscence was exaggerated, since border questions were already high on the agenda of the Bangkok regime in 1892, and the maps of the frontier towns must have been known to a number of rulers by that time. Nonetheless, such a remark suggests that he recognized the transition from a time when the frontier towns were known by name to a time when they were known by a map. This shift took place in rather a short period: the final two decades of the nineteenth century.

A few years after the frightening triangulation request, the needs for mapping increased rapidly. The main impetus from the mid-1880s onward was, however, not the construction of infrastructure. It was the need for the new provincial administration mentioned earlier. As we may recognize from McCarthy's works in 1882–1883, there was a problem of the boundary between a town of Siam and Lanna and another between Pattani, a Siamese tributary in the south, and Perak, then under British power. In fact the whole country began to shift from the traditional hierarchical relationships of rulers to the new administration on a territorial basis.

In the existing system of provincial control, which was based on the hierarchical network of lordship among local rulers under the nobles in Bangkok, a small town could request a change of dependence on one lord to another, mostly after a dispute. The new lord might be the ruler of a town which was not adjacent to it. The domain of a regional lord could even be discontinuous.[33] Thus a town was known by its name, and in most cases Bangkok had no idea about the domain of each regional center. Like the court of Rama III which told the British to ask local inhabitants about the *khetdaen,* the communications from the court of Mongkut to the towns on the frontier inquiring about the boundaries in certain areas indicated that the court did not know its realm territorially.

The reform, which began mostly in the major tributaries in Lanna and along the Mekhong, not only tightened Bangkok's control but also reorganized the administration of the large and small towns. Bangkok officials found that one of the major problems was that the territorial distribution of lordships was chaotic. The solution was territorial redistribution—transferring several towns from one lord to another and abolishing some of them. With the new geographic consciousness, Bangkok introduced two measures necessary for the administration in every redistributed province, namely, mapping and the registration of households.[34]

The reform showed the dramatic transition in the conception of the realm of Siam. For the first time the regime was attempting to know the units which comprised the realm in territorial terms. Undoubtedly, this was a consequence of the new vision created by the modern geographical discourse of mapping. Mapping was both a cognitive paradigm and a practical means of the new administration. It demanded the reorganization and redistribution of space to suit the new exercise of administrative power on a territorial basis. The name of the new system—*thesaphiban* (protection of territory)—reflected these changes honestly. But the redistribution began around the same time as the contest with the French over the Mekhong region. In this case, Chulalongkorn explicitly expressed his desire to have the border areas reorganized and mapped as a measure to counter the French.[35] Formally the reform in that region began rather late, in 1890, but actually it had started earlier.

It is striking that, from its early days in Siam, mapping was involved with the desire to integrate the Lao region into the Siamese realm. In early 1884, a Siamese prince suggested that the court should commission a team of surveyors and mapping officials to make a map of the upper Mekhong basin close to Tonkin and Annam. McCarthy himself warned that trouble over the border of those areas was imminent, so mapping was urgently needed.[36] Of course, mapping had nothing to do with the suppression of the Ho, but the Siamese rulers realized that it was a powerful means of dealing with the boundary question.

For the first time in history, during January–July 1884 Bangkok troops were accompanied by a group of mapping officials headed by McCarthy himself to survey the territories around Luang Phrabang and Vientiane.[37] From then on until mid-1893, the so-called Siamese expedition to suppress the Ho was always accompanied by surveyors and mapping technicians. Indeed mapmaking was a major mission of every expedition. Chulalongkorn's instruction to the Siamese troops in 1885 was straightforward: "The king would like to know all the localities under his sovereignty. . . . For this reason, His Majesty has commissioned a team of mapping officials to explore all localities for accurate information. Hence all commanders and chief officers must support these mapping officials to carry out their mission."[38] Here, to know was to know geographically. Surasakmontri's description of the campaigns against the Ho was full of accounts about the nature of various localities, peoples, and his attempts to identify the exact location of each area with various referential methods. It is obvious that maps were drawn as the troops marched; then they were sent back to Bangkok from time to time.[39]

It seems that Siam expected mapping to be the means which could determine once and for all the boundary of the realm. By mapping, that is to say, the ambiguity of margins was expected to be eradicated and the clear-cut limits of the realm of Siam would appear. Mapping technology was no longer alien or suspicious to them. Apparently they realized that in order to counter the French claim, modern geography was the only geographical language the West would hear and only a modern map could make an argument. Mapping had frightened the court in the early years of the reign. Now it became an indispensable technology to decide and establish the geo-body of Siam.

All the initiatives about mapping, however, also indicate that until that moment Siam had no evidence of this kind in hand to substantiate its claims. To finish such a herculean task within a short time after a few trips was hardly imaginable; but whether or not the Siamese rulers realized this technical imperative is difficult to know. Perhaps a historian's comment that the Siamese elite overestimated their military capability, but were inadequately prepared in real terms, can be applied to their handling of mapping as well.[40] They were ready to use a map to substantiate their claim both on the battlefield and at the negotiation table. But not even one map of the boundary of that frontier was completed before the crisis broke out in 1893.

The 1884 survey was the first such project ever carried out by Siam—apart from Duysart's exploration, whose result was unknown—and was among the first undertaken by any European. Although a number of French explorers had been to the area since the 1860s, a satisfactory result had not been achieved, let alone a scientific map of the area. The 1884 survey failed, however, due to a serious fever which incapacitated almost everyone on the team and took the life of an English technician.[41] The surveys of frontiers were regularly carried out in every dry season—October or November to May—of the following years. By early 1887, the mapping officials had reached Thaeng, Sipsong Chuthai, Huaphan, Phuan, and many other small chiefdoms. But the projects accomplished in those years were merely topographical surveys.

Mapping Cross Fire: A Lethal Weapon Unleashed

Siam did not map alone. French explorers had already been in the region for several decades. They were motivated by a conviction that the Mekhong could be an access to the mysterious but rich southern part of China. Henri Mouhot was the first to reach Luang Phrabang in 1860–1861, but illness took his life before he could travel further.[42] Doudart de Lagrée and Francis Garnier followed this endeavor in 1866–1868, the first Europeans to make a map of the Mekhong countries from actual surveys.[43] The prime agent of the French interest in the contest with Siam in the 1880s and 1890s was Auguste Pavie. After being an employee of the Siamese regime for a telegraph project in 1878–1879, throughout the following decade Pavie and a team of French explorers had been working for the French Indochina government to explore the areas of northern Laos.

In 1886 Pavie, on behalf of the French government, requested Siam's permission to establish a consulate at Luang Phrabang. Chulalongkorn argued that the need for a consul was not to protect French subjects since at that time there was not a significant number of them in Laos. The objective was explicitly for mapping in the region.[44] Although the proposal for a consulate was turned down, Pavie kept working, traveling throughout the region mostly with the protection of the Siamese forces. Pavie and his surveying operations represented French interests before any military presence. His mapping projects spearheaded French colonial power, yet another sign of the new technology's force.

Certainly Siam felt the threat of Pavie's actions. Several times in Pavie's accounts and diary, he tells us he was hindered or obstructed by Siamese officials. Even if the complaints were exaggerated to overvalue his role in the eventual achievement, it seems that they were true to a certain extent. Some of the obstructions are confirmed by Thai sources, which admit them explicitly as measures necessary for Siam's benefit—for example, in 1888 Siam repeatedly demanded recognition of its rights over Luang Phrabang before Pavie could conduct a survey. Siam also sent a number of officials to keep an eye on Pavie throughout his journey. And there are several other initiatives which, from Pavie's view, were assigned by Bangkok to hinder his surveys. Each time the obstruction resulted in a delay of several days.[45] Pavie complained that he was disturbed by these men all the time. They did not understand his work and suspected him for being so interested in collecting insects, flowers, and ancient inscriptions. The Siamese were also suspicious, of course, of Pavie's interest in local traditions and in taking photographs. Once, he tells us, he blurted out: "I am very distressed because you inconvenience me . . . without gain for your side. . . . I only ask you to help me by showing me the boundaries common with ours . . . [names of towns]."[46] In the early years, however, without the presence of French forces, Pavie had to rely on the Siamese for protection, supplies, and preparation for every step of his journey. So he could not avoid Siam's interference. But nobody could show him what he wanted: boundary.

It is not surprising that Siam's mapping officials urgently advanced their survey, trying to cover the areas claimed by Siam as extensively and quickly as possible. At one point McCarthy requested authority from the king to move forward to areas where troops had yet to go but had been delayed by administrative work in the conquered towns. Enthusiastically, McCarthy suggested that he could ask local people about the histories of these towns to decide where he should locate the boundary and map it. "We, then, can know the land where we live," he wrote to the king. The king, perhaps not less enthusiastic, praised him but warned: "It seems that [McCarthy] will decide the boundaries by himself."[47] Consciously or not, that is precisely what McCarthy was doing. He realized the power of mapping. On one occasion he told local rulers and warlords that the king had sent him to survey the region, "so that the peoples in the outer towns will know for certain up to which points the Thai territory extended."[48]

Eventually, the French force arrived. At the Thaeng confrontation in 1888, not only did each side demand that the other retreat, but they also put forward the intention to send surveyors into the territory occupied by one another. Surasakmontri reported Pavie's saying that his map of Sipsong Chu-thai was good enough for determining the boundary and there was no need for Siam's surveyors to advance into that area.[49] Pavie reported that Surasak-montri tried to persuade him twice in 1887 and 1888 to use the map Siam had made, which, of course, showed the realm of Siam extending beyond the upper Mekhong basin.[50] While both claimed the territory and proposed their maps as the basis of negotiation, they implied that their maps were not yet complete, so more surveys were needed. Finally, despite the military status quo, they accepted the fact that their maps were only preliminary ones. They therefore allowed each other's surveyors to continue their work in the oppo-nent's occupied territories for the benefit of the supposed negotiation in Bangkok.

The competition in surveying and mapping by both Siam and France accompanied the political turmoil in the Mekhong region. For Siam, the sur-veys for boundary mapping from 1884 can be summed up as follows:

1884: topographical survey of the northeast frontier around Luang Phrabang, Sipsong Chuthai, Huaphan, and Phuan

1884–1885: travel to Luang Phrabang by a different route through Nan and topo-graphical survey of the country around Luang Phrabang

1885–1886: travel to Luang Phrabang but failure to do any work owing to late arrival of the troops

1886–1887: travel to Chiangmai, Luang Phrabang, and Thaeng and survey for military and administrative purposes

1887–1889: survey for the Bangkok–Chiangmai railway

1890–1891: mapping of the boundary on the frontier between Siam and Burma

1891: triangulation of the northern frontier to connect with the system of triangulation from British India's eastern frontier; survey of the northwest-ern frontier and completion of the boundary map of this part

1892–1893: continuing triangulation from the northwest and north of Lanna east-ward across Luang Phrabang and the areas northeast to south of Luang Phrabang[51]

A map which has provided crucial evidence in supporting Siam's claim—both in those days as well as retrospectively in the argument by historians today—is the so-called 1887 McCarthy map.[52] Drawn up six years before the 1893 crisis, it is regarded now in Thailand as the first modern map of Siam. Thai historians of the Franco-Siamese conflict always refer to the map as it was illustrated in an article by George Curzon, however, without having seen the original. Lord Curzon, a prominent colonialist in British politics, a geographer, and later a viceroy of British India, wrote that article published in July 1893 mainly to discuss British policy in the wake of the French advance in Indochina. His map shows three proposed maps of the boundary between Siam and Vietnam: one by McCarthy in 1887, the other two by French explorers in 1866–1868 and 1892 (see Figure 9). He challenged both French maps, exposing their unreliability and confusing data. Strikingly, he did not say a word about McCarthy's map.[53]

In 1985 the Royal Thai Survey Department reproduced a map entitled "The 1887 Map of Siam and Its Dependencies" by James McCarthy. It is definitely not McCarthy's 1887 map, however, since it shows Siam's boundary after the 1893 treaty with France and in fact gives several names of provinces which had not been so named until 1899 (and one not until 1906).[54] From 1884 to 1887 McCarthy had two failed and two successful seasons of surveys, all carried out in the upper Mekhong basin between Luang Phrabang and Sipsong Chuthai. All were topographical surveys. The actual measurement, which had to start with a triangulation connecting from the western border, had not begun until the 1890–1891 season. McCarthy returned to England briefly in 1887, giving an address on his surveys in Siam to the prestigious Royal Geographic Society in November of that year. Actually, the map was printed in 1888, not 1887.[55]

The original map was similar to the one appearing in Curzon's article. It covered the entire Siamese realm, with focus on the Mekhong region. A colored line supposed to be the boundary was drawn from Chiang Khaeng (on the Burma-Laos border today) to the Black River, covering parts of Sipsong Chuthai, the whole of Huaphan and Phuan, then southward along the mountain ranges parallel with the coast to latitude 13 degrees north, then westward to join the boundary already agreed on at Battambang (Figure 10). As it appears, it was a rendering into map form of the conviction and desire held by the Siamese elite to see Siam on a map. Like all other proposed boundaries which were interpretations of the ambiguous territorial margins by the new code of space, McCarthy's map was just another spatial speculation and the encoding of desire.

Pavie, on the other hand, mentioned several times in his books that the boundaries had yet to be decided. He claimed the territory on behalf of the French, but he was also aware that there was no boundary yet. In most of the maps published in his books no boundary was identified, except the short one on the Battambang-Siamreap front between Siam and Cambodia which was the result of the 1867 treaty between Mongkut's envoy and Paris. No one knows for sure whether the absence of boundary lines between Siam and French Indochina in Pavie's books was cunningly deliberate—to leave the question open for additional claims—or was due to his scientific rigidity which did not allow him to specify a boundary line while the demarcation was not yet finished.

Although the Siamese rulers were confident in their cause, either by conviction of their historical rights or by unrealistic overconfidence in their military capability and map or both, they wanted to avoid a collision. Chulalongkorn strongly warned that any dispute which might lead to a military clash should be deferred to the negotiation table in Bangkok. One of the solutions to avoid such an undesirable clash was to establish a joint commission to survey and mark the boundaries since 1887.[56] But the commission yielded no result. As is usual in this sort of conflict, both sides accused one another of undermining the commission and thereby the negotiation in several ways, while professing firm determination for a peaceful solution.[57]

The relation between map and military force was remarkable. The desire of the force was to make the territory exclusive and map it. In actual practice, the operation of the force was planned and guided by the preliminary maps of the areas.[58] As the case of McCarthy's request may suggest, sometimes mapping advanced one step ahead of the troops; then the military operation followed, making the mapping proposal of the areas come true. Mapping spearheaded the conquest. Nevertheless, since the spheres of influence of both sides had never been defined and in fact were overlapping, a modern boundary could be anywhere in those marginal—in every sense of the word—areas. A proposed boundary therefore was a speculation which, depending on one's point of view, was equally truer and falser than another proposal. In actual practice, the survey of an area by one side was done alongside the military advance. The military decided the extent of territorial sovereignty and provided the authority under which mapping could be executed, not vice versa. Force defined the space. Mapping vindicated it. Without military force, mapping alone was inadequate to claim a legitimate space. But the legitimation of the military presence was always substantiated by a map. Mapping and military became a single set of mutually reinforcing technology to exercise power over space in order to define and create the geo-body of Siam.

The relationship between a mapmaker and the military operation in this process was even more striking. James F. McCarthy was not merely a surveyor and technician. From the 1884 start of the operation in the Mekhong region, he was involved in a great deal of strategic and operational planning as one who knew the area best. His findings led him to point out that the Siamese force could effectively take control of the entire Phuan and Huaphan plateau by concentrating on the Phuan area and restoring Chiang Khwang, the Phuan center, as its headquarters. The successful military campaign of 1885–1888 that resulted was generally attributed to his recommendation. Throughout the operation, McCarthy's reports of his surveys played a great role both in the field and in Bangkok. Geography lent him the authority to recommend the occupation of specific towns. Through McCarthy, geography gave the Siamese force the knowledge of where to establish a border control and boundary markings. It was McCarthy who drafted the operation map and the map of the boundary of Siam in 1887 to support Siam's claim and support the military operation.[59]

By 1893 tension was high. Sporadic minor clashes erupted along the borders while mapping officials of both sides carried out their work. McCarthy led the survey teams for the triangulations from the west and north of Lanna, urgently moving eastward through the Lao regions from 1890 to 1893 without returning to Bangkok as usual until the Paknam crisis broke out in July 1893. This continuous project was supposed to map the boundaries between Siam and British Burma and then make triangulations from that point eastward through Nan, Luang Phrabang, Phuan, Champasak, and Ubon to join the existing boundary at Battambang. The work was brought to an abrupt halt by the crisis, however, when only a little over half of the projected areas had been covered.[60] McCarthy was on a mountain when the news about the French blockade of the Chao Phraya River arrived, along with a dispatch from Bangkok ordering him to return to Bangkok immediately. Mapping was under way on the mountain while the issue was about to be decided in the river. The geo-body was being created literally on paper. A new life for Siam was about to begin.

Chapter Seven
Geo-Body

THE MAP OF BOUNDED SIAM appeared for the first time after the Paknam crisis of 1893. Ironically, it was eventually an outcome of cooperation between Britain, France, and Siam. By 1893, only the boundary and map of the western front between Siam and Burma were finished. On all other fronts, except for a short boundary at Battambang and the one between Kedah and Perak, there were only topographical surveys and sketches. So all the data and work done by the Siamese and French mapping officials were gathered together with British cooperation. In 1897 two maps were produced by Siam. The first one was published in England.[1] The other map, published in Calcutta under the title *Phaenthi phraratcha-anakhet sayam r.s. 116* (Map of the Boundary of Siam 1897), was drawn by two Thai officials named Son and Baeb.[2] Both maps stated clearly that whenever there was a gap in the survey by Siam, the maps drawn by the British and French had been copied to fill in the missing sections. Practically and symbolically, Siam had its first geo-body and its representation made, filled, and shaped, at least in part, by Western powers.

Auguste Pavie published a detailed map of the area in 1902. His map, regarded as the most reliable and informative of its time, was basically a topographical map showing details of natural features. No boundary line was shown on any frontier except that separating Siam and British Burma, probably copied from the work done by McCarthy and the British between 1890 and 1891. There was no boundary in the Mekhong region.

The geo-body of Siam was reshaped by many treaties with Britain and France in 1893, 1899, 1902, 1904, and 1907 and by means of cartographic techniques. Siam and both superpowers set up many committees to decide the boundaries and many detailed ad hoc agreements for each section of the boundary with specific maps for each.[3] It is an irony that Pavie's map was the

128

authority for all later maps of Siam for a long time. Even in the time of Vajiravudh (King Rama VI; r. 1910–1925), the so-called nationalist period, Pavie's map, an updated 1909 version, was reproduced as the official map of Siam.[4]

Emergence of the Geo-Body: A Victory of Mapping

It depends on one's point of view whether the contest between Siam and France for the upper Mekhong and the entire Lao region was a loss or a gain of Siam's territory. But it certainly signaled the emergence of the geo-body of Siam. And the ultimate loser was not in fact Siam. The losers were those tiny chiefdoms along the routes of both the Siamese and the French forces. Not only were they conquered—a fate by no means peculiar to them—but they were also transformed into integral parts of the new political space defined by the new notions of sovereignty and boundary. Another ultimate loser was the indigenous knowledge of political space. Modern geography displaced it, and the regime of mapping became hegemonic.

It was this triumph of modern geography that eliminated the possibility, let alone opportunity, of those tiny chiefdoms being allowed to exist as they had done for centuries. In other words, the modern discourse of mapping was the ultimate conqueror. Its power was exercised through the actions of major agents representing the contending countries. The new geographical knowledge was the force behind every stage of conceiving, projecting, and creating the new entity.

From the beginning, it was a new knowledge—a new geographical "language" by which information originated and the new notion of the realm of Siam was conceived. It became a framework for thinking, imagining, and projecting the desired realm; it became in effect the language in which Siam was to be discussed. But since the reality did not yet exist, the new geography served as the vision for the geo-body of Siam still to be created. Its requisites—the new kind of boundary, sovereignty, and margin—were formed at various moments in time and place and in different fashions. When all parties involved became preoccupied by the new conception of a state, drafts and sketches of the limits of Siam were drawn even before an actual survey was carried out. Siam's geo-body was anticipated, and desired, by all parties. But the anticipated extent of the entity to be created was varied. The imperialist concept of the two European powers and the royal hegemonic ambition of Siam were in conflict.

At that point, mapping was no longer merely a conceptual tool for spatial representation. It became a lethal instrument to concretize the projected desire on the earth's surface. Not only was mapping a necessary device for new administrative mechanisms and for military purposes—functions that seemed modest and merely instrumental—but indeed the discourse of mapping was the paradigm within which both administrative and military operations worked and served. In other words, mapping turned both operations into its mechanism to realize its projection, to concretize its "enunciation." It transformed human beings of all nations, people whose actions were heroic or savage, honorable or demeaning, into its agents to make the mapped space come true. Siam was bounded. Its geo-body emerged. Mapping created a new Siam—a new entity whose geo-body had never existed before.

Communication theory and common sense alike persuade us that a map is a scientific abstraction of reality. A map merely represents something which already exists objectively. In the history of the geo-body, this relationship was reversed. A map anticipated a spatial reality, not vice versa. In other words, a map was a model for, rather than a model of, what it purported to represent. A map was not a transparent medium between human beings and space. It was an active mediator. In this case, all the requisites of the map of a nation had not been given in premodern Siam and thus had to be created to meet the demands of a map. The outcome was the result of the contending anticipation expressed on each claimant's map. Perhaps more than has been realized, the regime of mapping did not passively reflect Siam. Rather, it has actively structured "Siam" in our minds as well as on earth.

In fact, the ambiguous relationship between a map and its anticipated object—and the potential of the reverse relationship—can be found in the ambiguity of the notion of geography itself. In English, "geography," as well as *phumisat* in Thai, refers to the knowledge or study of a spatial object as well as to such an object itself. The ambiguous and intricate relationship between the two notions indicates that an object can be what a knowledge of it allows it to be. Of course, we may question the relationships of other branches of knowledge and their object (subject of study), especially those whose double notions are signified by the same term, such as history.

In a conventional history, the making of modern Siam was often seen as the outcome of the reform and modernization undertaken by the Siamese elite. Siam's territory was the outcome of the "national integration" which consolidated its formerly disintegrated units by means of "internal" mechanisms. The West was an "external" power which jeopardized the survival of Siam and dismembered "parts of its body." Siam appeared as much victimized as the West appeared cruel. In the history of the geo-body, however, the annexation of the otherwise autonomous units was executed ambitiously and aggressively by the new administrative mechanism as well as by military force. But together they were only one side of the attempt to inscribe the geo-body of Siam on the earth's surface. They were the positive identification of the realm of Our space.

The other side of the emergence of Siam's geo-body was the making of the Others' space by the imperialists. Through diplomacy and military conquest, they delimited the extremities of the domain of Siam's space by identifying the limits of domains of their colonies. The Others surrounding Siam were also concretized and delimited in the same process. What distinguished Siam from the Others was not language, culture, or religion, since Siam took over many formerly "foreign" tributaries as parts of its realm. It was simply the space that was left over from direct colonialism. Siam was the space in-between. This was a negative identification of the geo-body of Siam. Whether Siam lost its territories to the imperialists or simply was the loser in the expansionist contest depends on one's perspective. But the indisputable fact remains: the colonial powers helped constitute the present geo-body of Siam.

The emergence of the geo-body of Siam was not a gradual evolution from the indigenous political space to a modern one. It was a displacement of the former by the latter at various moments both by foreign powers and by the Siamese themselves. Strategically, the new discourse threatened, destabilized, or simply made the existing discourse ambiguous and then displaced it. The presence of the geo-body of Siam is an effect of the hegemony of modern geography and mapping. It is a phenomenon in which a domain of human space has been inscribed in one way rather than another. This phenomenon will last as long as the knowledge that inscribes it remains hegemonic. Not only is the geo-body of a nation a modern creation; if we perceive history in a *longue durée* of the earth's surface and humankind, it is also ephemeral. There are other knowledges of space, either residual or emerging, operating to contend with the geo-body. The presence of the geo-body is always subject to challenge.

The Geo-Body Empowered

The fetishism of nationhood in modern times is mysterious and begs explanation. Robert Sack suggests that people tend to think about territoriality as a natural entity, as the place to which they belong emotionally and spiritually.[5] In one of the latest attempts, Ben Anderson resorts to the relation between a nation and nature. He argues that by making a nation natural, the sense of belonging naturally to a common identity is created—hence the sacredness and the grip of nationhood.[6]

The birth of many early European nations was based on long-standing common features like language, ethnicity, or even political adherence. These features were regarded as almost intrinsic parts of the identity. The boundary of a community was thus easily seen as natural as well. But an undeniable fact remains: every boundary is artificial. All are prescribed, not naturally given, although some may seem more natural than others.[7]

Prescriptive methods range from the adoption of natural features like a mountain, a river, or a watershed to the calculation of coordinates (as in the case of many African countries), or an extremely arbitrary line on a map (as in the case of India-Pakistan which cost thousands of lives), or the construction of a road, fences, posts, or The Wall. The question, however, remains: how has an artifact like a geo-body been made natural?

A simple lesson in one of the earliest geographical textbooks in Siam illuminates a strategy of intellectual indoctrination which helps naturalize, in every sense of the word, the geo-body. Here Uncle teaches two boys:

> Uncle: You already know that the earth is spherical, but do you know how the earth divides?
> Chun: The earth divides into three parts of water and one of land.
> Uncle: Right. But how does the land divide?
> Chom: Into continents, sir.
> Uncle: Can a continent be divided?
> Chun and Chom: No.
> Uncle: Our earth can be divided into large portions called continents, and a continent can be divided into nations *(prathet)*. Many nations are all different. China is one of the big countries; Siam is a small one."[8]

This lesson about the earth's surface is simple but remarkable. What is striking is the mixture of geographical categories: nations and natural features. A nation becomes a natural component of the earth's surface like the *terra firma* and the oceans. The only distinction between them is simply one of size. A similar pattern of description can be found in most of the early geography books in Siam mentioned earlier and perhaps in most of the ones today. Van Dyke's book, an elementary atlas of nations, started from the earth's surface and then divided it into nations on each continent without describing the natural features. Perhaps everyone in our generation has experienced this phase of geographical learning which posits the concept of a nation in the same category as natural features. It should be noted, however, that in the case of Siam the only exception among the books of that earliest generation is *Tamra phichika-phumisat* (A Text on Physical Geography), written in 1901 but first published in 1918. This book's description of the physical features of the earth's surface, from the atmosphere down to the core of the earth, did not include a nation.[9]

The naturalization, literally, of the geo-body can be done at one stroke since its material basis is the earth's surface. Its representations, including terms like *phumisat* and *prathet*, maintain their referent and root in the earth or soil. For most Southeast Asian cultures, the soil is a crucial part of human genesis and civilization. Either the *naga*, the underworld serpent, or the goddess of the earth (soil) is the mother of humankind. The notion of motherland is indeed deeply rooted in every culture in one form or another. In premodern times, that soil or motherland could be the land marked by temples, natural limits, the soil of the tribes or clans who shared the same myth of genesis, the sphere of the same supreme overlord. In our time, that motherland is represented by the geo-body. The geo-body supplies the new objectification for the beloved motherland or common soil and, reciprocally, acquires the human loyalty originally given to the soil. As the soil had been an identification of commonality, the geo-body has been given the concrete magnitude of the soil while it makes itself an identification of commonality. Not only was the geo-body naturalized but it was also given what Clifford Geertz might call the primordial sentiment by the soil.[10]

Being natural, however, is not the only strategic discourse by which the geo-body can create the sense of belonging to the same community. The significance of soil or the earth may vary from one culture to another, while there may be other mediation for communal identification. The geo-body can become a powerful totem of a national tribe by its association to these other kinds of communal identification. Its fetishistic power does not depend on its "naturalness" alone. It also comes from the conjunction with other totems, especially indigenous or traditional ones. A splendid example in the case of Siam is the relationship between the geo-body and kingship.

In many premodern societies in Southeast Asia, a realm, a kingdom, or a country was believed to be an extended body of the divine kingship, which is in turn a personification of sacred power. But a realm was not a bounded, territorial state. As Shelley Errington suggests in the case of the Buginese society, the body of kingship is not merely the biological body. It is the entire entourage, including his followers and the subordinate rulers within the realm.[11] A comparable case can be found in the Mon notion of a realm as a federation of princes and *nat* (local spirits). In the case of Siam, the body of kingship was not only the biological body either. A passage in *Ramakian*, the Thai version of the *Ramayana* believed to have been composed by King Rama I of Bangkok (r. 1782–1809), says:

> All the cities are the body,
> The king is the mind,
> Which is the lord of the body.[12]

The country, the kingdom, or the realm is always expressed as the royal property, such as *phraratcha-anakhet* (the royal sphere) or *phraratcha-anachak* (the royal kingdom). This means that territory was not profane; it was a component of the royal body. When the geo-body displaced the premodern nonbounded, hierarchical realm, the manifestation of the royal body emerged in a new form. But it was still very much the royal body. After the 1893 crisis had passed, the king was deeply saddened. Yet he ultimately recovered, and, according to one of the courtiers, he had a good reason to console himself: "The loss of those margins along the border of the *phraratcha-anachak* [the royal kingdom], which we could not look after anyway, was like the loss of our fingertips. They are distant from our heart and torso, and it is these we must protect to our utmost ability."[13] The semiological transaction is always a two-way exchange. The royal realm, then, had taken a new embodiment. The king's extended body was now a little patchwork on a blue planet, no more the center of the universe or the southern continent of the Hindu-Buddhist cosmology. But in that semiological shift, the sanctity of royalness was transferred and transposed to the geo-body as well.

Perhaps the most significant semiological conjunction and shift involve the notion of *chat* or "a nation" itself. Etymologically, *chat, cha-ti, cha-ta* mean a birth or a collective noun for being born of a common origin, ethnically, temporally, or socially. In Bradley's 1873 Thai dictionary, *chat* still meant such. Thus his examples of the word included *chatna* (next birth), *chatthai* (born as a Thai), *chatphrai* (born as a serf), *chatkasat* (born as a king), and *chatma* (born, and behave, like a dog), which is still a famous swearword even today. The word for "ethnic" in Thai now is *chatphan*. And *cha-ta* still preserves its original meaning as a birth. Around the end of the nineteenth century, the meaning of *chat* shifted significantly.

Two scholars have studied this shift by using Anderson's idea of the official nationalism.[14] Basically they explain how the Siamese state at the time had nurtured the notion of a "nation" out of traditional concepts embedded in the term *chat*. What they also show, though unintentionally, is the trace of semiological shifts and conjunction caused by the force of the newly emerging geo-body.

Formerly, to talk about a country, a governed spatial unit, the term was either *muang* or *banmuang*, literally town and village-town respectively. Despite its connotation of space, however, *banmuang* was not spatially defined. It was a generic term meaning a country, the realm of a monarch. *Chat* had no semantic relation to a space at all; it referred to the commonality of origin. After only a slight shift in the late nineteenth century, *chat* came to mean a community of people who shared a cultural commonality particularly defined by being the subjects of the same monarch. Both *chat* and *banmuang* therefore came to signify a common cultural and geographical community defined by the royal power. The geo-body then provided the new spatial definition for the royal sphere of such a community. As mentioned earlier, it came via modern geography—via the word formerly signifying an unspecified spatial unit: *prathet.* A semiological conjunction took place in which the power and values imbued in the terms *banmuang* and *chat*—common origin, cultural commonality, soil, and royal sanctity—met those of the geo-body and were transferred to each other. The rendezvous of this conjunction is at the terms *chat* and *prathet. Chat,* whose root is in the sense of a common identity, and *prathet,* whose root is in space, became synonymous; each conferred meanings and values upon the other. In fact, since then they are usually expressed as one word: *prathetchat* or *chatprathet.*[15] The words are a meticulous invention combining traditional values with a modern concrete embodiment.

The conjunctions of the concept of geo-body with other communal identifications have generated broader and more complex significations for the geobody. Powerful values are added to it once its signification extends beyond territoriality—encroaching upon the notion of soil, *chat,* and the royal sphere of power, for example. It now represents not only the territory but also the organic community to which people belong as well. It is obvious that the fetishistic power of the geo-body not only lies in its fabricated naturalness, but significantly increases by means of its intercourse with other powerful discourses, especially by transferring traditional values to enrich its presence. Its life is diabolically generative.

Beyond Territory and Geography

As a two-way traffic of signification and values, however, while the geobody gains additional meanings and values, it becomes a force pushing for the shifts of meanings of other discourses too. Again, a good example is the relationship between the geo-body and kingship. A specific case is the concept of *ekkarat* and *itsaraphap.* Nowadays, both terms are equivalent to "independence." An *ekkarat* country means an independent one. The loss of *ekkarat* means becoming a colony. In all Thai dictionaries compiled in the nineteenth century, however, *ekkarat* and *itsaraphap* never meant independence. Take, for example, Pallegoix 1854 (Thai-English-Latin):[16]

> *ekkara:* superior; one who does not fear others; bold, haughty
> *ekkaraat:* king, superior to others
> *itsaraat:* king, superior to others
> *itsaraaphaap:* supreme power

itsaaraphaap: having supreme authority
itsara, itsaro: first, excellent, domineering over others

Or Bradley 1873 (Thai-Thai):[17]

ekkara: one who is bold, haughty
ekkarat: one king
itsaro, itsara: superior to others such as a king
(There is no *itsaraphap* in this dictionary.)

Or Khun Prasert-aksonnit 1891 (Thai-Thai):[18]

ekkarat, ekkarajaya: the king in a *prathet*
itson, itsara, isuan: the king, the god

In Smith's English-Thai dictionary of 1899, the words "dependence" and "dependency" find their nearest counterpart in the term *muangkhun.*[19] Of course, the term denotes the hierarchical relationship of overlordship rather than a colony. For "independence," Smith found no specific Thai word and thus explained it as "not dependent on anyone, not under the subjection of anyone, to be master of oneself, to be free and not in bondage to anyone."[20]

As these dictionaries inform us, *ekkarat* and *itsaraphap* at that time denoted the supreme monarch—a double notion of being the supreme one and therefore being second to none. Both terms signified the status at the apex of the hierarchy. In *Sangkhitiyawong,* for example, a Buddhist text in Pali written by a monk in the late eighteenth century, an *ekkarat* king, not country, was jealous of the *itsaraphap* of other kings.[21] Another example: in every version of the royal chronicles, all written before the mid-nineteenth century, there is a story of when Siam was defeated and became a tributary of Burma in the late sixteenth century. Later the Burmese king was suspicious that a Thai prince was about to revolt. Here every chronicle says that the Burmese king plotted an assassination of his adversary in order to achieve "a greater *itsaraphap* than other cities." *Itsaraphap* meant supremacy, not independence. It was Burma that sought *itsaraphap over* Siam, rather than Siam attempting to do so *from* Burma.[22] In the hierarchical relation of kings, to say that a tributary king suddenly fought for *itsaraphap* would seem senseless since it would take him some time to achieve that supremacy.

When the context shifted from the hierarchical relation to the international and the units of relation were territorial states, the notion of *ekkarat* thus shifted from the supremacy of a monarchy to the status of a modern state in relation to others. Without hierarchical overlordship, the old meaning no longer made any sense. The shift eradicated the notion of supremacy in a hierarchy while preserving the other notion of the term which meant depending on no one. From the early decades of the twentieth century onward, the notions of *ekkarat* and *itsaraphap* have nothing to do with the status of kingship. A new denotation given to them is equal to "independence." Etymologically, both terms might have lost their condition of existence when the indigenous concept of hierarchical relation was displaced. The conjunction with the new geographical concept, however, shifted their meanings and let them survive. The geo-body actively takes part in generating new ideas, new values, and new culture even beyond its primary task of spatial definition.

The role of the map of Siam has been similarly active not only in representing the territory of Siam but in conveying other meanings and values as well. A map is frequently used to represent nationhood—to arouse nationalism, patriotism, or other messages about the nation. Figure 11 shows the leadership of the Siamese monarchs lifting Siam above the level of Burma, Cambodia, and Vietnam who are left pleading for help. This cartoon, however, is slightly different from the original which won the contest of King Vajiravudh. In the original, on the swing was not a man but the map of Siam.[23]

As a symbol of nationhood, the map of Siam has become one of the most popular logos for organizations, political parties, business firms, and trademarks. The use of a map may become more serious if it is indispensable for conveying the proper message of a particular symbol or is designed to arouse sentimental effects. Figure 12 is the symbol of the Saichaithai Foundation under the patronage of the Thai royal family. The foundation works for soldiers, the police, or members of other paramilitary forces injured or disabled in the course of fighting all sorts of "enemies" to protect the nation. The symbol of the foundation is composed of the map of Thailand, a pagoda, the royal emblem, and a heart with blood. The symbol is powerful indeed; it is dense with obvious meanings. It is a deliberate combination. The map is here to control its proper meaning. A similar densely meaningful symbol is that of the Village Scout. This popular royalist organization was active in Thai politics in the late 1970s, especially in the massacre of the student movement in October 1976.[24] The key symbol of the Village Scouts is the crimson scarf carried by each member. The emblem on the scarf is the map of Thailand in yellow with the word "Thai" in blue across the map.

Sometimes the appearance of a map is not serious since it is not designed for any sentimental effect. In commercial usage, for example, a map may be decorated, distorted, or transformed for visual appeal. It may not look like a map at all. It may be a caricature of the map of a nation used in a very casual manner. Imagine what would happen if a casual or distorted map replaced the serious map in the emblem of the Saichaithai Foundation and on the scarf of a Village Scout. Can a proper meaning be transmitted? Can a caricature of a map arouse nationalism, royalism, or other serious sentimental responses?

A map is usually taken out of its contextual origin, that is, the earth's surface. In many cases, there is no symbol to indicate the coordinates or the surrounding countries as in a geographical textbook. A map may float. Moreover, there may be no mapping symbol or any convention. Yet floating maps even without mapping conventions can communicate to anyone familiar with the map. This is because all the maps in the emblems and advertisements cited above are no longer maps. They no longer represent the nation's territoriality. Rather, they are signifiers which signify the map of a nation. They are signs of the map of a nation. They have meanings and values and can send messages because they refer to the map of such a nation, which has been loaded with the meanings and values of nationhood. In other words, the map of a nation becomes a signified. In the words of Roland Barthes, it becomes a metasign: it has become an adequately meaningful sign in itself, not necessarily with a further reference to the territoriality of that nation. By signifying the map of that nation, these maplike signs can signify other meanings and values carried by the map. And in the reverse direction, becoming a metasign, the map of a nation can generate values and meanings which have nothing to do with territory at all.

At this point, we may realize that the relationship between a map and space becomes even more complex. It is hard to confine a map to its assumed nature as a spatial representation. It has moved too far away from its technical origin to return to its creator, the cartographer. It no longer belongs to the cartographer, who has lost control over it completely. Independent of the object as well as its human creator, it becomes a common property in the discourse of a nation.

In many ways, a map contributes its share to the human knowledge of a nation. As a sign, it is an effective and active mediation which can even create a geo-body; as a metasign, it is an object of reference in itself and can create more meanings and values beyond its origin. In addition to the fact that it monopolizes the means of human conceptualization of the artificial macrospace called a nation, both roles allow it to reign comfortably over the domain of knowledge of nationhood and also bring it close to being a natural entity.

By way of example, we can perhaps point to a never-ending number of cases in which the geo-body and a map as a discourse, knowledge, a sign, a metasign, operate to generate meanings and conceptual shifts. But one of the most significant effects the geo-body and a map have on our knowledge is their power to shape our conception of the past. Here the issue is the conjuncture between the new geographical knowledge and that of the past. How did the geo-body and map generate history? In what ways must history be changed in order to come to terms with the emergence of the geo-body and its disruptive origin?

Chapter Eight
Geo-Body and History

Historical sites are our nation's prestige. Even a single
block of old bricks is valuable to preserve. With no
Sukhothai, Ayudhya, and Bangkok, *prathetthai* [Thai-
land] is meaningless.
—KING BHUMIPHOL (the present king of Thailand)

HISTORY IS INDEED SIGNIFICANT to the life of nationhood. The king's words
quoted above reflect that fact, reproduce it, and transmit it persuasively. But
why is *prathetthai* meaningless without the former centers of the Siamese
kingdom? Why would Thai people today find the word unambiguously
intelligible? How has the intelligibility of the king's statement been established? How did the discourse of the nation's history come into existence?

To talk about the past, one may think about what happened. But the fact is
that only what we can recall can constitute the body of the past which is
meaningful to us. In English, the past is what can be re-collected. The past
exists in relation to our constitution of the knowledge of it. The past we can
know, therefore, is always a representation of it which is created from our
own conceptions but believed to be the true past. History, a field of study, is
always a discourse of the past. It is a language that can make the elements rec-
ollected meaningful and intelligible. It is not so much a matter of discovering
fragmented facts as a matter of how to re-member them.

Like geography, the premodern indigenous conception of the past was
utterly different from—and displaced by—the Western notion of history.
This question, however, deserves a separate project. Our question remains
how the emergence of the geo-body was involved in the creation of Siam's
past. How has it generated or affected other knowledge or discourses in order
to make them conform to the force and demand of the geo-body? This examination will give us a complex but illuminating example of how the conjuncture of two powerful discourses could happen and its results. In fact, a
demand for a completely new history emerged with the geo-body since the
latter was such a disruptive moment for the life of Siam. The formation of a
new kind of past was needed to mend the rupture in its continuity.

140

The Scar of 1893 and the Discontinuous Past

The French blockade of the Chao Phraya River by gunboats, even holding the Siamese palace at gunpoint for days, was a shock to the Siamese elite. It was hard for them to believe they could be defeated so easily. Besides, the elite had an illusory trust in British support in the dispute with the French. In the course of events, that confidence was broken and the British turned out to be an unreliable ally. Britain never wanted to enter into serious conflict with France on behalf of Siam and had informed Siam more than once that it would not be "mixed up" with the incident. In reply to Siam's request on the day of the blockade, therefore, London told Bangkok to "dispel any idea that we are contemplating joint action to defend Bangkok." Worse than expected, the British urged Siam to meet the French demand for the left bank of the Mekhong, and when Siam hesitated they accused Siam of not being cooperative.[1]

Siam finally retreated. Confidence in its skillful diplomacy, its military forces, and its natural right to the disputed territory diminished dramatically. A historian puts it well when he says the 1893 incident became "a crisis of morale" for the Siamese rulers:

> [Siam's] sense of insecurity mounted, her self-respect cracked. . . . The king, who had been ill throughout the crisis, suffered a physical and moral collapse. He lost some forty-two pounds in weight between August and November and openly declared his loss of interest in life.[2]

Not many people thought that the king could survive. Jockeying for the regency position to manage the throne for the young heir got under way.[3] But ultimately the king did survive, due in large part to a critical but inspiring poem by one of his brother-associates, Prince Damrong.[4] Not only did he survive, but he also made a remarkable recovery as captain of the Ship of Siam, as Damrong put it. He fortified the spirit of the ruling circle for the tasks ahead.

But who could deny the observation that the king, and certainly others too, "was permanently scarred by the 1893 crisis"?[5] To them it seemed that Siam's independence was imminently threatened, more so indeed with every passing year. The perceived "loss" of territories, the shock of mid-July 1893, the sudden exposure and proof of the empire's failure, the disillusionment of any unrealistic confidence in oneself and trust in civilized diplomacy, the crisis of morale in the immediate months following the event—all amounted to what has been recognized as a moment of deep agony in the history of Siam. Certainly it was an agony for the Siamese rulers.

In this sense the 1893 crisis was a moment of great contradiction. It was the time Siam lost many of its former tributaries to the French. Yet it was the culminating moment of the emergence of the geo-body of Siam. It represented a sharp break in geographical concepts and practices and the displacement of the old notion of nationhood. Ostensibly, Siam was then in the process of modernization and the crisis appeared as an interruption of this process. Yet no one could deny that the post-1893 Siam was not the same as before, even in the minds of the rulers. They continued their tasks, but in a different situation, and in a different Siam, both on the earth's surface and in their own minds. The 1893 crisis marked a sharp discontinuity in the life of Siam. This rupture in the life of the nation needed to be sewn together and required appropriate accounts of the turbulence to mend it in order to reassure everyone that the life of the country was a continuous stream of time.

The demand for a new account at a time when there was tension in the moments of continuity/discontinuity is not a new phenomenon. Nor was it for Siam. Many studies have emphasized the role of historical writing as a political instrument to legitimate new regimes against their rivals in a propagandistic or even an Orwellian sense.[6] Few studies, however, have analyzed the relationship between a rupture and a reassuring account of the past that emphasizes the continuity of the familiar or even the revival of golden days. At the start of the Bangkok period in the late eighteenth century, for example, a new dynasty in a new palace at the new city—that is, a new microcosm —tried to restore order following the collapse of the previous center. The tension of the continuity/break was calmed by a religious account of the reordered world and by the creation of the court's history which gave assurance of the continuity of the previous world order.[7] Given its distortions and misplaced accounts, perhaps such writing was not so much a political device to legitimize the new regime as an ideological one to help them come to terms with their immediate past. Another rupture was the 1932 revolution which ended the absolute monarchy and began the new Siam under military regimes. This time the rupture was sutured, simply by suppressing the divisive nature of the event or leaving it out. Instead, the Thai past is framed as a series of struggles to liberate the country from foreign rule or to defend its independence, a familiar anticolonial theme. Moreover, post-1932 Siam is cast as the revival of the golden age of Sukhothai, supposedly the first kingdom of Siam.[8] In this scheme, despite vicissitudes in the life of the nation, the present would witness a continuation of the good old days. Nothing was lost and nothing would be unfamiliar in the nation's future life without the absolute monarchy.

The turbulent times were never suppressed or erased from memory.

Rather, they were fully recognized but only to be shaped and explained in such a way that the ruptures were accommodated to an enduring past. To what extent, then, was the modern account of Siam's past affected by the rupture of 1893? Could it have happened that, in order to dissolve the discontinuity, the emergence of the geo-body and the role of maps must be concealed? Was there any relationship between the post-1893 Siam, particularly with the emergence of the geo-body, and the emergence of modern historical writing in Siam? Let us look at how the story of the 1893 disruptive moment has been depicted. The strategies that such a historiography employs may indicate how the entire body of Siam's past has been constructed.

The Assumed Geo-Body in the Thai Past

The first product of the conjuncture between the geo-body and history we will consider is the historiography of that critical period. For Thai historians, the last two decades of the nineteenth century have never been known for the emergence of the geo-body. Rather, the period and the incident are known as the loss of territories and the integration of provincial administration. Both were related but, in this view, were separate processes. And this Thai view has been taken for granted by Western scholars. What are the measures this conventional historiography has employed to produce such a history, which certainly has effects on the remembrance of that disruptive moment?

A typical account begins with the desire of French colonialism to occupy Southeast Asia in order to counter the expanding influence of Britain in the region and find a route to southern China, which was believed to be an economically profitable project. The problems started after France occupied Vietnam and further claimed the left (east) bank of the Mekhong. Rong Sayamanonda, in one of his textbooks about Thailand in English, says that the French had taken over Sipsong Chuthai and Huaphan from Siam in 1887, but they were not yet satisfied. Rong depicts the unreasonable French aspiring to the whole of Laos even though their own maps showed Laos as part of Siam. The French had acted aggressively in various disputes along the borders. They were consumed by greed.[9]

A similar account of the unreasonable, greedy, untrustworthy French is given by another prominent Thai historian, Khachorn Sukhabhanij. He says that despite Siam's reasonable and sincere offers to settle the disputes peacefully, the French were evasive, procrastinating, and constantly lying. As the next innocent victim, Siam was in jeopardy and had done its best merely to protect itself from the predator. But when violence occurred, the French complained that Siam had molested them along the borders for years and thus deserved a proper retaliation. This was the way the French justified their expansion, he explained.[10]

Neither Rong nor Khachorn wrote a detailed history, but their supervision of history graduate students bore many offspring: first they carefully work out the details of the incident; once the view becomes conventional, it is capable of reproducing without the presence of the progenitors. Many studies share the same idea. We are told about France's wicked tactics, lies, and dishonesty to achieve its greedy and aggressive ends. Siam had done everything possible to protect itself, including the reform of the administration to control its tributaries directly from Bangkok and the suppression of the Ho bandits in the disputed territories. Finally, without any reasonable motive but to ensure its success, France resorted to gunboat diplomacy with which Siam could not contend. In brief, it is a sad story of the devil defeating the virgin.[11]

It goes without saying that every account argues that the whole left bank of the Mekhong undoubtedly belonged to Siam. Wyatt, in the book now becoming a standard text on Thai history in English, adopts the same view. In sympathy with Siam, he argues, retrospectively, that the French had not a single piece of evidence to support their claim, apart from the alleged protector status inherited from Vietnam. Regrettably, Siam should not have trusted the British so much and was wrong in believing that "the French would never sustain their ridiculous claims in a supposedly civilized world."[12] Here is an apt summary with which all the conventional accounts would no doubt unanimously agree:

> In a real sense, Siam was being *forced* to agree to *outrageous* demands simply because the kingdom had *defended its own* territories against *foreign invasion*. It was as if a new government coming to power in Britain had revived the eighteenth-century claims to the United States, and then punished the American government for resisting a British invasion sent to enforce those claims.[13]

While Wyatt has opted for a fiction in Anglo-American history to capture the theme of the whole incident, Khachorn has chosen one of Aesop's most popular tales as his analogy: "We have seen clearly that France adopted the ploys of the Wolf who, first, picks a quarrel with the Lamb, then jumps over and executes it."[14] Does this analogy come out of the story? Or is it the other way round? Has this famous tale in fact become a grid to make the confusing story elements orderly, organized, intelligible, and familiar to the reader? To what extent is the metaphor in fact the frame for conceptualizing this episode of the past?

In Siam's view, the history of that moment was tragic. This is not because the desire of the prime actor has not been fulfilled as in a Western tragedy, but because in this episode of history the *adharma* (evil) was victorious over the *dharma* (good). If this is so, which runs somewhat counter to Buddhist rationality, the historiography of the reform will relieve the sense of loss and irrationality.

The memory of such relief first appeared in the form of a personal recollection of Prince Damrong, who himself administered the reform between 1892 and 1915. Written in the early 1940s but unfinished at his death, *Thesaphiban* reports that Chulalongkorn reminded Damrong of foreign threats to Siam at the time and thus encouraged him to undertake the reform. If Siam did not quickly tidy up its provincial administration but carelessly left it in such a mess, the country would be in danger. Siam might lose its independence.[15]

This theme was taken up a few decades later by Tej Bunnag, whose book became the authority for many later studies in Thailand about the reform. Tej reminds us of the legacy of Damrong by choosing to study only the period in which Damrong was the interior minister. He subscribes to Damrong's perspective faithfully, saying that he wrote the book "in the belief that [the reform of provincial administration] was one of the factors which helped Siam survive as an independent nation in an age of the European imperialism."[16]

Tej begins with a description of the administration before 1892. The pre-1892 Siam was, in his words, "in theory" unified. Siam's sovereignty over the outlying provinces and tributaries, thus its integrity, was never in doubt. The potential problem lay, he argues, in the fact that until 1892 such a theory had not yet been properly implemented "in practice."[17] This theory/practice discrepancy became a dangerous condition only in the face of colonialism. In January 1896, the king warned his commissioners over the former tributaries that foreign powers were ready to use any "internal" conflict as a justification to intervene in Siam's affairs. They must protect Siam "against internal and external dangers."[18] The tributaries were the weakest points and needed reform if the country was to "defend" itself. Therefore the government centralization was the key to the problem, Tej explains, despite much opposition and resistance. The rest of the book proceeds to describe in detail how the integrated administration was implemented in practice step-by-step throughout the country.

Tej's book provides the foundation for a number of later works by Thai historians who simply apply the same idea to a particular area or specific aspect of the reform, to an expanded period before and after Damrong's incumbency, or to the works of other princes.[19] The theme of foreign threats —hence the necessity for a reform to "defend" the country—becomes a presumption, not a thesis. In many cases, it is even advanced at the beginning as an undisputed fact if not a truth. In the conclusion, unsurprisingly, most express relief and confidence. Thanks to the reform, Siam survived. For Tej, Siam had passed one of the most difficult periods in its life with great success. Siam reemerged more glorious than ever. It was not just a reform; it was a glorious revolution:[20]

> [Prince Damrong] and the Thesaphiban system of provincial administration had indeed helped to preserve the Thai kingdom as the only independent nation of Southeast Asia in the age of European imperialism. . . . During that period [1892–1915 under Damrong's incumbency], Siam was transformed from a conglomeration of states and provinces without clearly defined boundaries to a compact state with a definite frontier. The foundations were laid for a modern central administration and a centralized provincial administration. A start was made in the development of economy. *The people were emancipated from a semivassalage and slavery and initiated in self-government.* . . . [The reform] generated dynamic forces which are still shaping modern Thailand.[21]

In both the stories of the loss of territories and the reform, European imperialism, particularly French imperialism, takes on the role of the Wolf. Siam is the Lamb whose survival was at risk amidst a situation in which its neighbors had already fallen. Standing alone, Siam protected itself gracefully, reasonably, and wisely. In one story, the end is rather tragic, but only because the Wolf was beyond Siam's capability to deal with reasonably. In the other story, the end is a happy one. Not only did Siam defend itself, but it survived with a great leap forward.

Both the loss of territories and the reform appear to be the consequence of the same cause—the external threat—which became the only thread uniting the two stories. They transmit the same message: the external danger and the need for defense or sacrifice. They appear as a two-sided outcome of the same moment in the past. Subconsciously kept together in our memory, they form a binary discourse of the same episode which generates a number of nationalist historical discourses. Of course, they never appear as the two operations in the contest for the exclusive margins which led to the emergence of the geobody. In fact, some studies say a lot about mapping and something about multiple submission. Tej also mentions the absence of modern boundaries as one of the problems of the pre-1892 administration. But mapping and the boundary problem were merely technical issues that played no significant role in either the cause or its resolution.

Considered closely, these two stories rely on a number of common assumptions without which the stories would be read and remembered differently. I call these assumptions "strategies," since they were not simply ineffectual ideas. Rather, they have command functions by which the stories must be organized or rearranged accordingly in order to produce the proper plot and to sustain certain desired meanings and values, both intellectually and emotionally.

The first strategy is to assume the prior existence of the geo-body of Siam. All the accounts about the loss of territories must establish that the geo-body of Siam was always there and extended well beyond the left bank of the Mekong. There was no fundamental difference between the indigenous and the modern kinds of political space and interstate relations. Hence there was no ambiguity of space. Without this assumption, there would be no ground for agony because there could not have been any "loss." In the history of the reform, this strategy is even more necessary for the justification of direct control by Bangkok. Without it, Siam's attempts to control the disputed territories would be seen as anything but self-defense, and its actions to quell the former tributaries anything but internal affairs. The command function of this strategy is to prevent any "improper" interpretation which may point at Siam's expansion, conquest, or even contest. The assumed geo-body helps control the ideas of internal/external and defense. This strategy, furthermore, leads to the view, now taken for granted, which considers the whole question from Bangkok's perspective, another strategy we shall consider shortly. This means the suppression of the perspectives of tiny states in the region. Above all, the prior existence of the geo-body, at least "in theory," directly prevents any recollection that it was in the process of being created. The role of mapping as its precedent is thereby concealed. In doing so, the nature of the rupture is fundamentally changed. The moments no longer involve a struggle to eradicate the ambiguity of space. The moments become a critical time merely to preserve the existing integrity and implement the unified geo-body and exclusive sovereignty.

The second strategy is to establish the stories within the context of modern international politics, particularly colonialism. First of all, this context commands the story to be perceived in terms of the relations between Siam—an integrated nation-state—and the Western powers. The international context imposes a grid to reduce, classify, or exclude the voice of those tiny states which were never born later as nations, despite their active role at that time, and allows only the story of the emerging nation to be heard. It is the context of the event as seen from the metropoles only. From a local perspective, it is a misplaced and anachronistic context.

Seen against a different context, the role of Siam in relation to foreign nations would differ. Within the local context of hierarchical powers without the geo-body, they were rival expansionists contesting for the same prey, albeit with unequal capabilities. Within the global context of international politics of the colonial era, however, the conflicts became unfair disputes between the world superpowers and a remote nation in self-defense. The anti-imperialist outlook, proudly adopted by many historians of the postcolonial era, alters the terms of these relations. Siam in this global reference was no longer a contestant, a hegemonic force, or an indigenous expansionist. It became a Lamb instead of a Lesser Wolf. What should be a history of regional hegemonism turns out to be a glorious anticolonial history performed by the Siamese elite. The threat from the immoral power has become a famous cause of whatever Siam did in that period, making Siam's actions a just struggle for its "survival."

The third and final strategy is to take Bangkok's point of view. In the context set by the previous strategy, it seems proper, politically correct, hence justified, for a good historian to take Bangkok's side. The agonies of the tiny states, their voices, and their interests are overlooked or suppressed, as if they were the inevitable cost of security. The conquests by the Siamese force and the implementation of the centralized regime have been celebrated as proud accomplishments. As Tej puts it in the quotation cited above, people were emancipated and self-government was initiated. Whose self-government? Who was emancipated from whom?

Indeed, if we merely change our point of view, the entire story about the administrative reform and the battle against the Ho reads very much like a colonial history in which Siam always claimed its natural superiority over the regional horizon. Because of this, the function of the external threat as the causality of the stories is vital for the history of Siam. Not only can this element alter the contextual reference as suggested. It can also shift Bangkok's perspective from a view toward its victims to another view toward the external powers. The shifting perspective conceals the expansionist desire but magnifies the anticolonial pretension.

This has been the perspective of most historians on the modernization of Siam. They admire, glorify, celebrate the ability to retain Lanna and some of the Malay states, including the suppression of the resistance against Bangkok's centralization, such as the rebellions in 1902.[22] The local resistance was, seen from Bangkok, trouble for "national" survival; hence the occasional subjugation of tributaries was necessary for "internal" stability. Furthermore, the agony of the Siamese rulers in Bangkok—a result of the defeat in the contest and the shock of mid-July 1893—became a national agony which has created a common sentiment among Thai against foreign threats.

In many cases, moreover, the elitist nationalist blindness takes another toll:

the evaluation of the sources. For generations, from Khachorn to his students, the studies of this issue have relied on the map and the article by George Curzon, as mentioned earlier, as their authoritative evidence retrospectively against the French claim. Khachorn even praises Lord Curzon as one who was familiar with Siam and thus his article must be a reliable source. As we may guess, McCarthy is among those who are classified as eminently reliable.[23] In fact, in his article Curzon stated clearly that he did not want to see the French move further westward since it would jeopardize British Burma and Malaya. But he strongly opposed any British involvement in the Franco-Siamese dispute. Nowhere in the article did he support Siam's claim. George Nathaniel Curzon was a renowned colonialist who later became viceroy of British India, but he might not have known much about Siam. As Edward Said describes him,

> Lord Curzon . . . always spoke the imperial lingua franca, and more obtrusively even than Cromer he delineated the relationship between Britain and the Orient in terms of possession, in terms of a large geographical space wholly owned by an efficient colonial master. For him, . . . the empire was not an "object of ambition" but "first and foremost, a great historical and political and sociological fact."[24]

It appears that the national agony has been perpetuated by historians themselves to the extent that it works blindly in repudiating the French in the past.[25] Their basic criterion of reliability is simply who took which side in the conflict. In this regard, even though it is now a century after Siam's trust in the British alliance turned sour, it seems that these historians still play the same game with a similar tactic of relying on the authority of British colonialism to rally against the French.

In brief, the conventional history of the loss of territories and provincial reform can exist only if the ideas of premodern hierarchical polity and the nonbounded realm are suspended or suppressed. Then the whole scenario is read in the light of the modern concept of international relations and the vision of modern territorial states with boundaries and exclusive and absolute sovereignty. The agony is also concrete, identified by signs of the new conceptions such as territories that were "lost." All of these strategies have arranged the recollection of that critical moment of Siam's biography for a certain desired effect. Perhaps the most significant result is that the moment becomes almost identical to the anticolonial or nationalist past of neighboring countries. And the glorious survival and successful reform are attributed to the intelligence of monarchs and prince-rulers. All of them become national saviors.[26] This kind of history is capable of turning the rupture into continuity and the proud accomplishment of the monarchs, the familiar theme in Thai historical consciousness.

Historical Atlas

If the agony of defeat by a European power has scarred Thai memory up to the present day, there is no doubt that half a century after the disruptive moment such a memory was firmly marked in the minds of the Siamese elite of that generation. After the 1932 revolution which overthrew the absolute monarchy, however, the wound was not that of the royal dignity but was transferred to the nationhood. The monument to that agony was the "lost" territories themselves. The issue of the lost territories was raised from time to time in many writings until it became high on the national agenda again in the late 1930s.[27] In the absence of the monarchy, which abdicated in 1935, the regimes after 1932 had to build up legitimacy and credibility. Following the global current of fascism, the Phibun government (1939–1944) espoused the chauvinistic notion of the Thai civilized nation. They changed the name of the country to "Thailand" in May 1939.[28] Many nationalist ideas and practices proliferated under the guidance of the government which stipulated cultural and economic norms of behavior from the public level to the family and the individual.[29]

In politics the government propagated the notion of the great Thai race and the brotherhood of Tai peoples in mainland Southeast Asia. Moreover, to rally popular support they promoted the movement calling for the return of the lost territories. Their commitment to "recover" the lost territories, especially the right bank of the Mekhong handed over to the French by the treaties in 1904 and 1907, was so significant to the Phibun government that its reputation was at risk after the Vichy government had rejected the request in 1940. To avoid a political catastrophe, the government decided to cooperate with the Japanese in 1940 in return for the latter's powerful support in the international community. This led to military cooperation in December 1941, and in return Thailand was given the western part of Cambodia, a temporary possession which lasted only until the end of the war.[30]

It was during this situation that a map titled *Phaenthi prawat-anakhet-thai* (Map of the History of Thailand's Boundary) was produced and became influential (see Figure 13).[31] The map assumes that the extent of Siam's bounded territory before any loss is the total legitimate realm of Siam. It is not clear, however, where this legitimate extent came from. The history of the boundaries accounts for those losses of territories which reduced the legitimate realm until the present boundary of Siam came about. But there are many versions of the losses. In the popular version shown here, each loss was marked by different colors with the numbers 1 to 8 assigned to each of the eight losses:

1. Penang and Wellesley were ceded to Britain during 1786–1800.
2. Tavoy, Mergui, and Tenasserim were taken by Burma in 1793.
3. Most of Cambodia was ceded to France in 1867, except the western part which became the Eastern Province of Siam until loss no. 7.
4. Sipsong Chuthai were occupied by France in 1888.
5. Laos of the left bank of the Mekhong was ceded to France in 1893.
6. The Lao regions on the right bank of the Mekhong, opposite Luang Phrabang and Champasak, were ceded to France in 1904.
7. The western part of Cambodia (Siamreap, Sisophon, and Battambang) were ceded to France in 1907.
8. Kedah, Perlis, Kelantan, and Trengganu were ceded to Britain in 1909.

Most of the losses accounted for in this map were surrendered to European powers from the late nineteenth century, except for the first and second, which happened a century earlier (and the second was taken by Siam's traditional arch-rival). But the 1935 version of this map accounted for only seven losses. In many writings about the issue, the number and areas of losses are varied. Some omit the fourth loss on this map, suggesting that it never belonged to Siam. Many omit the first two or three since they took place in different contexts from the rest. One includes Singapore, Malacca, and Jahore among the losses. Some add the Shan states and Sipsong Panna to the list of losses while failing to mention Sipsong Chuthai.[32] Besides, none of them mentions Chiangmai's cession in 1834 and Bangkok's cession in 1892, both to the British.

Likewise, Western scholars on the issue present a similar situation. The losses they account for are varied, and their maps are anything but uniform. Minton Goldman does not consider Sipsong Chuthai as a loss, for example, and includes Huaphan as part of French Indochina even before 1893.[33] Most Thai scholars would not agree with him. Wyatt, on the other hand, follows the 1940 Thai map closely. But the territory lost in 1888 to the French appears larger than in any other version, even the Thai maps, while he does not include the loss to Burma in his map. The total legitimate realm before any loss in his map therefore differs from the Thai prototype. In the Thai map, the total realm before a loss includes the Mon region of Lower Burma but excludes Sipsong Panna. In Wyatt's map, it includes the huge Sipsong Panna but excludes the Mon.[34]

This kind of map is generally supposed to be a representation of the territory of Siam before and after the losses. But, as we have seen, it is impossible to figure out exactly what was Siam before the loss or even whether there was really a loss of territory. By what means can a historian establish a legitimate realm, with all modern geographical conventions, before the end of the nineteenth century in order to identify or talk about the loss? How can any of these studies say with authority which parts counted or did not count as Siam's realm and hence which constituted a loss or not?

As it happens, there are several versions of the presupposed legitimate realm. None of them ever explains why they propose it as such; all of them dodge that question to identify the deductions from that total realm. But if the total territory before any loss is logically speculative, the loss of territory is, at best, also a logical speculation imposed by the agonized elite onto the populace in order to communicate the same emotion. The map is merely a creation out of the two fundamental elements: an elitist memory of the crisis and the modern geo-body of Siam. Based on the perception provided by the former, the map is in fact a retrospective projection of the present geo-body of Siam. The result is twofold: first, a geo-body which had never existed in the past was realized by historical projection; second, the agony is visually codified by a map. Now the anguish is concrete, measurable, and easily transmittable.

This map is in no way a scientific record of any geographic reality outside itself. It is a visual text of a historical proposition, a codification of the crisis, indeed a purely semiotic manufacture. The theme of this map is not how Siam was created but how Siam's present axe shape came about. It does not hesitate to tell its own history—which not only cleverly rejects the existence of anything like Bangkok expansionism but also refutes any view that Siam was delimited for the first time by the European powers. If the greater, homogeneously bounded Siam had existed long before, the numerous incidents vividly show Siam's cruel and irrational enemies forced it to sacrifice its body time after time. Sometimes the losses are calculated in square kilometers —as if to quantify the amount of suffering—which is nearly half the legitimate body. The map seems to say, nonetheless, that despite that amount of agony, the most important task is to preserve independence. And Siam survived.

In 1940 this map was distributed to schools and government offices throughout the country. The British consul regarded this as a gesture of, as he put it, Siamese "imperialism" that wished to encroach upon the left bank of the Mekhong, Lower Burma, and the four Malay states. He and the French chargé d'affaires protested.[35] The Ministry of Defense, which was responsible for the publication, explained it away, saying that it was used exclusively for historical study. But later it was used in the movement calling for the return of territory from the French. The British were alarmed that the movement might demand the territory taken by them too.[36] Phibun gave his word to the consul that such would not be the case, and he would stop the distribution of the map. But one of Phibun's close advisors who was said to be the most pro-Japanese figure in the government had it published again and sold at the price of one-tenth of a baht per copy.[37] Again, the government denied any involvement in its publication and ordered its sale to be stopped. Even now, the map is still easily found in school textbooks and most Thai atlases. Owing to a new situation after World War II and the postcolonial era, the map has lost its immediate political thrust. But its function as a sentimental visual code of history persists. Its power over the discourse of the nation's biography has not been diminished.

Another set of powerful historical maps covers not a single episode of crisis but the entire scheme of Thai history. Produced in 1935–1936 by the Royal Survey Department under the Ministry of Defense, the maps show Thai historical kingdoms from the eighth century up to the early Bangkok period, as well as the movement of the Thai peoples since the first millennium (see Figures 14 to 19).[38] Sternstein calls this set of maps *"The* Historical Atlas of Thailand."[39] Like the Map of the History of Thailand's Boundary, this historical atlas is very well known in Thai textbooks and atlases.

The title of the set in different editions varies slightly. Thongbai's atlas, the most popular one in Thai since 1963, emphasizes the word "Thai" in the title of every map, while the 1935–1936 originals did not. Each map is designed to show specifically only the Thai "Kingdom of . . . in the Reign of . . ."[40] The following list gives the translated title of each map appearing in Thongbai's atlas:

Figure 14: Thai Historical Map Showing the Movements of Thai People from Ancient to Modern Times
Figure 15: Thai Historical Map Showing the Kingdom of Nanchao[41]
Figure 16: Thai Historical Map Showing the Kingdom of Sukhothai in the Reign of King Ramkhamhaeng the Great, 1277–1317[42]
Figure 17: Thai Historical Map Showing the Kingdom of Ayudhya in the Reign of King Naresuan the Great, 1590–1605
Figure 18: Thai Historical Map Showing the Kingdom of Thonburi in the Reign of King Taksin, 1767–1782
Figure 19: Thai Historical Map Showing the Kingdom of Rattanakosin (Bangkok) in the Reign of King Rama I, 1782–1809

Considering this atlas as "the most comprehensive and accurate account of the number, location, and status of centers known to have been in existence during several important periods prior to the nineteenth century," Sternstein nonetheless points out a number of errors and shortcomings.[43] He also correctly comments that the maps do not show the complication of hierarchical status of centers within the realm. But how can a modern map do that? The function of a modern map to suppress the indigenous space has never been an issue. On the contrary, the ability of modern geographic technology to invent the space of the past, to control it, and then to put it on paper has been praised. Sternstein even joins the attempt to pinpoint the precise delimitation of these kingdoms.

The question is this: how does this atlas create emotional effects and shape our memory? First of all, it goes without saying that there are at least two basic requisites that make these maps intelligible: the historical knowledge needed to understand what these maps are about and the knowledge of how to read a map. But, like the Map of the History of Thailand's Boundary, these maps have no direct relation to Siam on the earth's surface. As a visual coding of historical knowledge, they are retrospective speculations based on the present geo-body of Siam. If one had never seen the present map of Siam, these historical maps would not make any sense. But if one has in fact seen Siam's map, even without any travel beyond a few miles from home, or even as a foreign student who never visits Thailand but has read Wyatt's book, one easily receives the message of these maps. The origin of these historical maps is not the remote past as it is purported to be. The origin is the geo-body of Siam in the present.

According to these historical maps, the geo-body is not a modern creation. The maps reject any idea that the Thai nationhood was conceived only in the recent past as a result of the intercourse between the old Siam and Western powers. Likewise, the notion that modern Siam is the result of ruptures, not continuity, is precluded. The disruptive moments are tamed and endurable. It is ironic that the recent birth of the geo-body and nationhood was suppressed by a map, the same technology which gave them birth. As the humble origin of the geo-body in the operation of mapping is concealed, the geo-body of nationhood becomes naturalized as having existed with the Thai since time immemorial.

It appears that the operational domain of the mapping discourse extends far beyond the knowledge of space and enters our memory as well. In fact, it is through this mediation of historical maps that the domains of space and memory, with knowledge and sentiments, are transgressed. Commenting on how a Thai historical play can produce such an emotional effect, a historian has suggested one method: "The term *prathetthai* [Thailand], for example, was used for Sukhothai and Ayudhya regardless of its anachronism. [This] was done purposefully in order to blur the time span, so that the past could be lifted out of its context, reshaped to suit the author's needs, and presented to the audience to cause particular sentimental effects."[44]

The function of the geo-body of Siam's past in historical maps is the same as the term *prathetthai* here. Anachronistic devices make the past familiar to the present—hence the possibility of transfering values, emotions, and other meanings, particularly patriotism and chauvinism, from the present back to the past and thus into our memory. Without anachronism, plays and historical maps are doomed to fail. The geo-body in the historical maps has a similar function. It provides a channel, an access, and an opportunity to expropriate the past in the light of present needs. As an anachronistic device, in short, the geo-body helps to represent the continuity of Thai history despite its historic effect as, ironically, a disruption of that continuity. It mediates a continuum of the life of the nation.

What else, apart from the mediating function of the geo-body, makes this historical atlas effective in shaping the perception of the Thai past? It is quite true that the maps represent only the period of the Thai ascendancy in the region. The atlas neither indicates the fluctuations of the domains and power in the intervals, nor does it constitute a true historical sequence of the regional politics.[45] But such is its strength, not its shortcoming. The atlas is so selective that it is able to highlight Siam's biography by demonstrating the movements and growth of its body—thus the nationhood—from the beginning to the present within seven frames (six historical maps plus the History of Thailand's Boundary map). The maps tell us the story, beginning in the childhood of the nation, of how the Thai were forced by a foreign threat, the Chinese, to emigrate southward where they believed the golden destination was teleologically placed. The migrations signify hardship as well as love for independence since time immemorial. Eventually the Thai arrived at the Golden Peninsula where the Khmer had occupied most of the land. Again, despite hardship under foreign domination, independence was in the Thai heart—hence the struggle to establish a great kingdom of their own until their coming-of-age was achieved at Sukhothai. Throughout hundreds of years in this setting, however, Thai kingdoms faced foreign threats from time to time, especially from the Burmese. The highlighted periods show that at these turbulent times the heroic kings always led the Thai people to fight back to restore the country. Indeed, each time Siam was consolidated, its power was greater than ever. Despite hardship and foreign enemies, Siam was great and prosperous. The atlas makes the nation's past alive. All the maps operate as a single set of visual codes, not individually. Operating together, they represent the entire plot of Thai history.

Another emotional effect which can be visualized in these maps is the grandeur of Siam. One cannot help noticing how great Siam's body was in the past in comparison with its neighbors. The maps help one imagine the good old days when Laos, the Malay states, parts of southern China, the Shan states, and the whole of Cambodia as well as Lanna were integral parts of Siam. So great was it that the historical arch-rivals, Burma and Vietnam, look humbler on every map. This signifies the efforts of the ancestors to establish and preserve the nation and to ensure its progress up to the present time.

The maps are not for a study of historical geography, but for historical consciousness about the life of the nation. Data and facts are necessary to make them look realistic and objective. What is the value of producing a map of, say, 1569–1584 when Ayudhya was defeated and Siam was said to have lost its independence? If such a period were visualized in the same fashion as this atlas, Siam would appear in the same color as Burma on the same map, with Ayudhya integrated into the Burmese kingdom. What is the value of publishing a map of, say, the fifteenth century when Lanna was independent and fought against Ayudhya to control Sukhothai? These two "if" maps would confuse or destroy the ideology for which the whole set is designed.

The Past Plotted

It appears that the conceptual strategies and literary techniques constructed around the deployment of the geo-body are crucial in both the historiography of the 1893 crisis and the historical atlas. They command the presumptions and perspective as well as create the desired sentimental effects to tame the disruptive moment in the life of the nationhood and, in turn, produce an anticolonial biography of which the nation can be proud.

As many thinkers now argue, the past, historical narrative, and literary construct are not quite separate realms. Not only are anachronism and selective emphasis responsible for the desired effects, but the arrangement of the story elements in the historiography and atlas has also produced a particular way of recollecting the past. Astonishingly, a closer look at the arrangement —the plot—of the history of the 1893 crisis and the atlas will find that they resemble a typical plot of popular Thai historical fictions and plays.

Luang Wichitwathakan (Luang Wichit) (1898–1962) was the most influential and the most prolific creator of nationalist cultural works in Thailand —an exponent of the powerful nationalist historiography, a novelist of many historical fictions, a renowned playwright of historical plays, and writer of many well-known militaristic songs.[46] A brief examination of his plays is perhaps the best way to understand the relationship between literary techniques and Thai history. The themes of Luang Wichit's plays are quite limited: the origin of Thai people, the establishment of the Thai kingdoms, the struggle for independence, the battle against foreign enemies, and the unification of the Thai nation. Only a few are about the impermanence of life, all of which were written in the sudden decline of his official career after World War II. Within these themes, despite the various complexities of the story, the plot is generally the same: the peaceful nation beset by foreign enemies, actions attempted to solve the problem, then the celebrated resolution. In Hayden White's scheme, it is a comedy plot. In my perspective, it is a familiar Thai melodrama.

An example of this typical plot will be helpful. Luang Wichit's first historical play, "King Naresuan Declares Independence," performed for the first time in 1934, is the story of a heroic Thai king in the late sixteenth century. The story starts with a narration and an opening dialogue between Naresuan and a noble about the suffering the Thai people have faced since the country was defeated by Burma fifteen years earlier. Seeking revenge, they are now looking for an opportunity to restore the country's independence and, in one particular phrase, to recover the realm *(dindaen):* "We must recover our independence. Independence is the heart of our life. For any *prathet* without independence, people of that *prathet* are not human."[47]

The opportunity came when Nandabayin, the Burmese king, ordered Ayudhya to send a troop to help him fight a rebel at Ava in 1584. But when the troop reached Khraeng, a Mon town near the border, the two Mon commanders who received the order from Nandabayin to ambush Naresuan changed their minds and defected to the Thai side. Charging the Burmese king with dishonesty and conspiring to assassinate him, Naresuan then performed a ritual declaring the independence of Ayudhya. After that, the Mon people there voluntarily joined him to attack the Burmese capital at Pegu.[48] The play resumes at the final episode, one of the most fabulous stories in Thai history. According to the play all Thai and Mon people under Naresuan's leadership crossed a river on their way back from Pegu without a single casualty, but a Burmese troop followed closely. Naresuan then fired a single shot across the river and miraculously struck the Burmese commander dead.[49] Naresuan finally made a prophecy that his soul would look after the country forever; but the Thai people must follow his example in bravery, sacrifice, and never-ending effort against the enemy.

The play's story follows the Thai chronicles closely. For a more complex story, there may be more actions and, of course, more problems or conflicts added to the major plot. But the additions are always problems at another level, mostly individual issues such as gratitude, personal animosity, and, the most popular choice, love. The different levels of problems generate more complex actions and plot. In most cases the individual interest will eventually conflict with the national interest. For a nationalist, of course, the former is always secondary to, and must be sacrificed for, the latter. Furthermore, in the introduction to each story the problem always anticipates a desirable end, such as the liberation of the country, which is always accomplished. Besides, many plays end with the sacrifice or death of the hero, which makes the story more sentimental. Even so, such an end is far from tragic because it is a sacrifice for a noble cause. Sacrifice and preparation for hardship, not complacency, are the message to the audience. The conflict between individual and national interests has a similar function. The sacrifice of individual interest is very sentimental, either sad or exciting, and is the climax of many plays.[50] The strategic plot is not an explanatory or logical expression, but a very emotional one which already subsumes all necessary explanations and reasons. In many cases, especially between lovers, Luang Wichit cleverly uses dialogue to resolve the conflicts with reason and not without sentiment—for example, he plays with the word *rak* (love), which is part of the word for patriotism in Thai, *rakchat* ("love the nation").[51] His audience will be stimulated to think and feel the *rakchat* through the sacrifice of the personal *rak* of the lovers.

Luang Wichit once admitted that historical plays are not history. Although they must be based on history, they are colored, embellished, or even invented stories to create particular effects.[52] Some of them should not even be called "historical" plays *(lakonprawattisat),* since their only link to history is a name or an event as background for the story. Characters are usually flat, one-sided, portrayed in black and white, and predictable. Dialogue is not natural, and is sometimes like a written statement. Yet what is upheld as historical in these plays is not the invented story or character, but the messages transmitted by the themes and plots.

Modern historical writing in Siam has never been considered akin to literary and fictive works. How does the historiography of the loss of territories and the reform of provincial administration make use of the strategies and techniques of fiction? For one thing, it uses perspective to approach the story from a particular viewpoint. Just as in fiction, this creates effects such as the exaggeration and detraction of certain characters. With the contextual discourse of international politics, actors are classified and the two major characters, Siam and Imperialism, are distinguished. Accordingly, conflicts and problems are classified into various levels of unequal value, importance, implications, and priority of concerns, such as external and internal, international and domestic, national and individual. Sentimental attachment is induced according to the classification of the conflicting interests. Therefore, a sacrifice of lovers or individual interest for the national interest is celebrated—like the celebrated suppression of former tributary status for "emancipation" and "self-government" when the nation's independence was endangered from the "outside."

The historiography and maps discussed in this chapter use anachronistic assumptions and devices such as the geo-body, boundary lines, the modern concept of independence, and so on, similar to the anachronistic words and dialogue in Luang Wichit's dramas. By this method they make the stories intelligible and familiar to the present audience. By doing so, the transmission of values, ideas, and sentiment is possible. Furthermore, to generate values out of the past, the two major characters in the primary conflict are relatively flat, and presented in black and white, to the extent that one of Aesop's fables about good versus evil is applicable. In the historical maps, the technique of highlighting is necessary. If all the maps are put in the proper order, with the map of the ancestral movement serving as the introduction to Thai history, followed by the maps of the heroic periods, and the Map of the History of Thailand's Boundary serving as the immediate episode before the present, the course of Thai history becomes the development of the Thai territorial states.

Now apart from these strategies and techniques, the plots of the historiography, the maps, and Luang Wichit's plays are strikingly similar. The stories always arise from the major conflict between Siam and foreign enemies. From that point on, actions ensue. There can be additional conflicts, all of which are subordinate to the major one, and more actions complexly interwoven around the core of the major conflict. The story of administrative reform has at its climax the successful implementation of the new system in former tributaries. It has a happy ending in which we see the expansion of the new system throughout the country and praise for the accomplishments of the prince-administrators. In the story of the loss of territories, of course, the climax is the 1893 crisis. The story is rather tragic. Yet as Luang Wichit realized, sacrifice is a blessing in disguise. As long as the country's eventual survival and independence are known, it is not tragedy or complacency that comes to mind. The story reminds us of hardship, sacrifice, and the necessity of patriotism and unity. And these values will come across to us in a very stimulating and moving fashion. For the historical atlas, although it contains multiple episodes of Thai history, the plot is similar and the values are the same. It is not a collection of unrelated maps. The whole set is a synopsis of the entire history of Siam, comprehensively saying that throughout the life of the nation the major problem has always been the danger from outside: foreign enemies, external threats, the Chinese, the Khmer, the Burmese, the

French, the Wolf, or whatever. External enemies are recurrent and imminent. This is a repetitive motif from the early episode up to the present. The orderly sequence of these repetitive motifs becomes the "master plot" for the entire biography of the nation up to the present time.

This master plot contains two somewhat paradoxical subplots. On the one hand, it demonstrates development, change, or progress during the course of the nation's life. On the other hand, the motif of external threat and the struggle for independence is repetitive. The seemingly dynamic history is just a recurring phenomenon. The repetitive theme seems redundant. Yet redundancy has an important function in our memory. As Edmund Leach notes in his study of the Genesis myth,

> in the mind of the believer, . . . the redundancy of myth is a very reassuring fact. Any particular myth in isolation is like a coded message body snarled up with noisy interference. Even the most confident devotee might feel a little uncertain as to what precisely is being said. But as a result of redundancy, the believer can feel that, even when the details vary, each alternative version of a myth confirms his understanding and reinforces the essential meaning of all the others.[53]

Nonetheless, both subplots complement each other, and together they formulate the master plot which accounts for the entire past of Siam's life. Siam grows up, moving ahead, while the essential meaning of the life of the country—independence—is reinforced. According to this master plot, Siam has lived through many turbulent periods, facing enemies, threats, the hardship of migration, defeat, disunity, and so on. But Siam survives. The agony at the end of the nineteenth century was nothing but another turbulent episode in which Siam's freedom was at risk. Thanks to the monarchs and Siam's love of independence, the country survived yet again. Biographically, the body of the country has survived different phases and sometimes endured tragic wounds. The sacrifice of the body around the turn of the century was crucial for survival, however. And the fact is that Siam did prosper again. This time the nation was even more progressive and more civilized. If the emergence of the geo-body and the 1893 crisis constituted an acutely disruptive moment for the life of Siam, a historiography of the kind we have discussed so far has performed a special function in reestablishing continuity of the nation's life. There is no rupture, no break, no displacement. It has been concealed or erased from our memory. Rather than being a critical disruption, the turbulent times even serve to stimulate unity behind the nation's leadership, especially the monarchs of the present dynasty.

It is this master plot, not the actual past, that is so generic and provides an inexhaustible reservoir for Luang Wichit's fictional histories. For the history of the loss of territories and the reform, the master plot provides the preconception, the given plot, necessary to understand the late-nineteenth-century crisis as a recurring phenomenon similar to previous crises, only with different story elements, actions, characters, and dialogue.

Does the premodern literature about the past, on which modern history relies, really contain such a master plot? Or is it the reading of the premodern narrative by a modern mind?

The Past Remade

The preceding question leads us to another set of questions of even greater importance. In the late nineteenth and early twentieth centuries, the modern historical study emerged in Siam. The pioneering scholars in the field introduced new methods and new concepts for reconstructing the past. Like geography and other disciplines, the new kind of past, though ostensibly based on traditional texts, represented a sharp break from the indigenous notion. Did the rupture at the end of the nineteenth century have any effect on this formulation of the new kind of past? If the experience of a few decades around the turn of the century was so traumatic in the minds of the Siamese rulers, did that terrible moment shape their preconception about the country's fate both in their present and the past? Was the new past inscribed, directed, and plotted by new ways of thinking and a new sentiment after that moment? Is it possible that the master plot of the history of Siam as we know it today was a result of the post-1893 trauma?

So far I have argued that the emergence of the geo-body demanded a new history to seal the rupture in the life of the nation. The historiography of that crisis has performed that function well. Although the writing on the loss of territories and the provincial reforms was reconstructed much later, it is likely that the crisis itself and the memory of it helped generate a new past of Siam. In other words, the impact of the geo-body's emergence was so great that Siam's past had to be completely remade in a new light. To a large degree, the new history was remade by the discourse of the geo-body and its associated conceptions and practices—for instance, the anachronistic assumption about the prior body and homogeneity, the necessarily misplaced context of international politics, the concept of exclusive sovereignty of a state, and above all the use of maps. The "misrepresented" history of the loss of territories and the reform, as well as the anachronistic maps, have done much to create and perpetuate the new discourse of the Thai past with its new plot, preconceptions, values, and techniques. This new discourse has been reproduced by media, schools, and many other institutions of ideology. It is predominant.

Given its important role in the creation of a new kind of past for Siam, the discourse of the geo-body should have generated or shaped many other aspects of the new history. The instance I wish to discuss here is the scope of the new past: its subject. The question is: which past was worth accounting for? On 2 December 1907, King Chulalongkorn gave a speech for the inauguration of the Antiquarian Society—known in Thai as Borankhadi Samoson —which was a landmark of historical scholarship in Siam. The content of the speech clearly represented the new discourse of Siam's past. The king urged members of the society to study the past of the *prathetchat* (nation) as distinguished from the traditional chronicles of kingship, known as *phongsawadan*. The *prathetchat* in his view, moreover, was not merely the realms of Ayudhya and Bangkok but also included other major cities in *prathetsayam* (Siam):

> The history should begin with Muang Luang, or some call it Hang or Chang, which was the site of Thai people originally, followed by Chiang Saen, Chiangrai, Chiangmai, Sawankhalok, Sokkhothai [Sukhothai], the old Ayudhya, the new Ayudhya, Lawo, Lopburi, Nakhonchaisi, Nakhonsithammarat, or those *muang* [cities] which ruled over other *muang* like Kamphaengphet, Chainat, Phitsanulok, San, Suphan, Kanchanaburi, Phetchaburi, for instance. All of them had been powerful at times and made up the unified *prathetsayam* [Siam] of today.[54]

The space of the new history was obviously set by the recently emerging geo-body. Indeed the geo-body was the only logical reason why those towns or cities should be included in his scheme. Nor should the new history be confined to the time set by the royal chronicles. The temporal span of the new history should be a thousand years, he suggested.

With this polycentric perception of the past, many histories of regional centers were collected and written. But the following generation of historians—especially his son, Vajiravudh, and Prince Damrong—altered Chulalongkorn's spatiotemporal parameter. The new scheme, which went unchallenged until the 1980s, focused more on the histories of the great centers, namely Sukhothai, Ayudhya, and Bangkok. The influence of the discourse of the geo-body was still obvious, however. The focus on capitals and the absence of other major cities did not mean that the space of the new history was fragmented as in traditional time. Rather, by the early twentieth century the unified country was represented by its center (hence the representation of a country by referring to its capital or even the residence of its leader). Indeed the idea of a capital in this new historiography implies awareness of the integrated geo-body. In fact, Sukhothai has been regarded as the first capital of Siam because it is believed to have ruled over most of the present territory of Siam and beyond whereas other major centers had not. As Damrong put it in 1929:

> Those Thai who had established kingdoms in Lanna had only occupied the territory of the present Northwestern [Region] and then declined. But the Thai who established the independent kingdom at Sukhothai were able to expand the realm so vastly that it reached other countries. Since then they have ruled and occupied *prathetsayam* [Siam] up to now. Thus Sukhothai should be regarded as the first capital of *prathetsayam* under the Thai people from B.E. [Buddhist Era] 1800 [1257] onward.[55]

Perhaps the famous Ramkhamhaeng inscription has been excessively celebrated partly because it is believed to be one of the oldest pieces of evidence that the realm of Sukhothai was almost as great as the present geo-body.[56]

It is very likely that the changing perception of the geo-body was responsible for this changing spatial parameter of the past. Chulalongkorn's polycentric Siam seemed to imply the contiguous relation of the spatial units, while the history of centers makes capitals the representatives of the whole. In this light, the growing interest in so-called local history in Thailand in the 1980s and the changing political and economic conditions of Thailand in that decade, especially the state-promoted growth of capitalism and urbanism in regional centers, may have some correlation.

Of course, the knowledge of Siam's past has been greatly affected by the discourse of the geo-body in different fashions and in various degrees. Even the essence of the indigenous past as the story of *dharma* (virtue) versus *adharma* (evil) was displaced by the story of the national struggle for independence.[57] The past is perceived as the life of the Thai versus other nations. From the early twentieth century onward, the most powerful and effective theme of Thai history has emerged. It is the history of *"Thai rop phama"* ("the Thai fought Burma").[58] Nationhood, patriotism, and the like become burdens compelling us to read the past in one way rather than another. History has therefore become one of the most significant instruments in the identification of Thai nationhood.

Perhaps, as in the displacement of geography, there is an arena of confrontation between different discourses of the past—an arena in which the new past has been unable to expropriate the old one completely. Hence there may be discrepancies, ambiguities, and traces indicating how the new past has been created.[59] This territory, however, is beyond the scope of this book.

Conclusion
Geo-Body, History, and Nationhood

THE GEO-BODY AND HISTORY have become powerful technologies of nationhood. The most powerful effect is their operation in the identification of Thainess, or We-self, as opposed to otherness. The political turmoil in many places around the world now shows us, as Edmund Leach suggested long ago, how a boundary violently, arbitrarily, divides ethnic peoples into different nationals.[1] Along the frontiers of Siam, there are many ethnic peoples who are considered as Thai nationals as opposed to Burmese, Laotian, Cambodian, or Malaysian—or in fact as opposed to being Mon, Karen, Kayah, Shan, Lao, Hmong, Lu, Lua, Phuan, Khmer, or Malay. Yet by the same power of geo-body, today it is equally evident that ethnic peoples find it eminently desirable to have a political entity whose boundary defines their identity.

The Creation of We-Self vs. Others

In the indigenous Southeast Asian tradition, a subject was bound first and foremost to his lord rather than to a state. People who lived in one area might not necessarily belong to the ruler of that area, although they might still have to pay tax or rent to the lord of that land. As the surveyor James McCarthy noted with puzzlement, it was a peculiar custom in which the power over individuals and land was separated.[2] As a modern Western man, he did not realize that this custom was quite common in the region and throughout Asia.

It was a puzzle as well for those modern administrators who wanted to determine nationality—hence national allegiance and loyalty—by geography. On the Lao-Thai border, once the 1893 treaty was concluded, the Siamese authorities wanted the boundary just settled to mark the distribution of population as well. Those people who belonged to the lords on the left bank of the Mekhong (French Indochina) but inhabited the other side (Siam) were permitted to return to their homeland. If they did not, they would become Siamese by virtue of their residency. The French rejected such an idea, proposing birthplace as the first and foremost determination of naturalization— that is, the Lao of the left bank were always French subjects no matter where they lived.[3]

The politics of this controversy, which lasted for a decade, was the contest for the control over population, hence humanpower, since the region is well known for its underpopulation. The Siamese and French authorities tried to make these people become their subjects by several measures, including the abolition of taxes, handouts of money and clothes, and intimidation.[4] Both proposals, however, similarly pushed for the shift in the identification and assignment of bondage or allegiance from the traditional personal ties to the new geo-body, based either on birthplace or on residence. Siam's proposal seems to be the more conscious departure from the old practice.

The consequence was twofold. On the one hand, the traditional system of bondage for control of humanpower became ineffective. This was one of the crucial changes which eventually led to abolition of the system. On the other hand, a new system of identification to make people "Siamese" was urgently needed. The result was the registration of households throughout the country and the change from traditional lordship to local administration on a territorial basis.[5] In addition, a Thai prince-governor of the Lao region on the right bank issued an order to his local authorities to abandon the practice of identifying people by their ethnicity in the census and household registration. Instead, all people must be identified in the same way as "Siamese subjects."[6] Although the new identification could not be fully implemented in a short time, the geo-body had set the direction and established the foundation for the new classification of people. In 1941, one of the Phibun regime's chauvinistic *ratthaniyom* (state prescriptions) was to call all Thai people from whatever regional and ethnic backgrounds "Thai" without identifying the diversity of their ethnic origin.[7] As late as 1967, Charles Keyes reported that the people on the right bank of the Mekhong still identified themselves as Lao, although they were more and more becoming "Isan" (northeasterners). He also observed that by the time of his study the Isan regionalism which had posed a potential problem of separation during the Phibun regime was no longer a threat. The regional community had become an identity *within* the Thai national domain, and no insurgency demanded a separate state of Isan.[8] The "Lao" became "northeasterners," a very spatial ethnic/cultural identification within the frame of the newly created body of nationhood.[9]

Today the territorial identification of people is newly introduced on some of the margins of Thailand. In 1986, the Thai government conducted an aerial survey to map the Thai border confronting Burma and Laos. They found minority people in the area who had been living without interference and moving back and forth in the territories of the three countries for a long time. In addition to the map, therefore, a census and household registration were conducted, as they explained, for security reasons.

As for the task of history in constituting Thainess, the past has also been created on the basis of binary opposition between what is Thai and what is otherness. Here the geo-body offers the entities of otherness to history. The nations nominated as Others are mostly modern states rather than a fragmented kingdom or a major city as had been the case in the premodern polity. Moreover, the contrast between what is Thai and what is otherness is not confined to political entities alone. The Burmese, according to Thai historical perspective, were aggressive, expansionist, and bellicose, while the Khmer were rather cowardly but opportunistic, attacking only when Siam was in trouble. It is not hard to see that the Thai characteristics were the mirror image of these traits. The Thai were a peaceful and nonaggressive, though brave and freedom-loving, people. This is exactly what the Thai national anthem tells us.

Here, as pointed out at the beginning of the book, the otherness serves as a token of negative identification regardless of what that nation is or does. Other nations have always been blamed for damage and evil. It is convenient for Thai historians to blame the Burmese even for the loss of historical documents, for example, which was quite possibly a result of the lack of modern historical consciousness more than anything else.[10] But this historian's myth is in no way exclusive to the Thai.[11]

The Enemy Function

The theme of struggle for independence—or, to put it more precisely, the imminence of a foreign enemy—has become the magic box to generate the discourse of national security in history as well as in the present. For a striking example in history, consider how a prominent Thai historian has justified the Thai system of serfdom. Khachorn Sukhabhanij, once again, wrote one of his classic essays about the *phrai*, a type of serfdom in Thai society, in response to a Marxist view of the system as evidence of class oppression and exploitation in the Thai past.[12] He argued that suffering and hardship (and oppression?) were necessary and a complaint did not deserve sympathy, because the enemy's threats and war were imminent: "Individual freedom when the country was in trouble was thus properly secondary to the independence of the country and the freedom of the whole nation."[13] Besides, this Thai situation might not be as bad as the plight of Others: "If the reader feels that our ancestors were oppressed by their society, I would like to inform [him or her] that the ancestors of other societies such as Laos, Cambodia, Vietnam, Burma, and Malaysia were equally or even more severely oppressed than ours."[14] To put it another way: suffering is tolerable as long as it is for national security. This strategy of classifying the problem is the same one that Luang Wichit employed in his plays. The reference to otherness is ideologically meaningful and effective even though it might be academically meaningless.

The discourse of national security is undoubtedly a very effective paranoia put into Thai people's heads by the Thai state. The creation of otherness, the enemy in particular, is necessary to justify the existing political and social control against rivals from without as well as from within. Without this discursive enemy, all the varieties of coercive force, from a paramilitary organization on every border of Thailand to the professional army, would be redundant. In contrast to the general belief, the state and its security apparatus survive because of the enemy. Discursively, if not actually, what actively creates the enemy and produces most threats to a country if not the state's security mechanism? The enemy must be presented, produced, or implicated and then discursively sustained. It is always projected—if not overtly *desired.*

When Vajiravudh established a paramilitary force for himself in 1911 in competition with the institutionalized army, he named it Suapa—presumably after the guards who patrolled the frontiers of Siam in history. The name referred to the past, to the border between Thai(ness) and Others, and to the threat from the enemy. Suapa therefore symbolized the active force which safeguards Thainess against the enemy.[15] The same reasoning is put forward, less symbolically, to justify the role of the military. Take one of the present king's speeches, two months after the October 1976 student massacre in Bangkok, as an example:

At a time when our country is being continually threatened with aggression by the enemy, our very freedom and existence as Thais may be destroyed if Thai people fail to realize their patriotism and their solidarity in resisting the enemy. . . . Accordingly, the Thai military has the most important role in defense of our country at all times, ready always to carry out its duty to protect the country.[16]

Who or what is the enemy? Where does the projected threat come from? Although the wars in Indochina have been a persistent discursive reference for many decades, the fact is that since the establishment of the professional military in the late nineteenth century, the Thai military force has been very active in the domestic theater for the sake of its own political domination. Fighting against other nations has been rare, and even then one can question whether it was for the defense of the country or otherwise: namely the disputes with the French over the Mekhong territory, the regiment sent to France in World War I, the troops sent to the Korean and Vietnam wars, the semiofficial mercenary force secretly operated in Laos, and the sporadic battles along the Thai-Cambodian and Thai-Lao borders. To confirm Thainess, it does not matter if the enemy is relatively abstract or ill defined. The enemy must always be present.

The creation of enemies has profound effects on the people's perceptions of those presumed enemies. In 1985, a little-known survey was conducted on the nationalist attitudes of local leaders, mainly the headpersons, medical practitioners, and teachers at the district or village levels. The results showed, unsurprisingly, the strong view that Thailand is a wonderful nation in which the respondents would love to be reborn. As for the nations they hate most, Vietnam, Cambodia, and Laos scored the highest. Peoples of these nations—with whom they said, Thai should not have a close friendship or marriage—were the most untrustworthy. The Burmese came fourth on the scale of disliked nationals.[17] If one asks why these peoples are classified as enemies, there will be no clear rationale. The function of otherness does not need an objective explanation. The enemy function needs only to be concrete, real, and identifiable as the opposite of We-self, regardless of who or what that otherness actually is.

The fact that the geo-body and history have played a great part in the production of Thainess and the creation of its enemies is perhaps best illustrated in a poster which may not be widespread but is strikingly typical of its kind. Figure 20 shows a map floating without any global reference in the background. But it is easily recognizable as the map of Thailand. On the eastern frontier is a picture of a soldier armed with full cartridge belts. His eye is glaring at the Thai map and his mouth is wide open as if he is intimidating—or going to devour—the map. Obviously he is a communist, easily identifiable by his uniform, the star on his hat, and the hammer and sickle tucked into his belt. The most striking feature of this soldier is his shape, which is drawn upon the figure of a combined map of Vietnam, Cambodia, and Laos. At the top of the frame is a strip of the Thai tricolor flag above the symbol of the organization producing this poster. The symbol itself also contains the tricolor flag and the map of Thailand. The caption below reads: "Wake up, Thai people." In the map of Thailand, the statement says: "We have already lost 352,877 square kilometers of our territory. Only 514,000 square kilometers are left." Below the map is another slogan: "Unity is strength; protect the nation; stop corruption; the nation prospers." At the bottom, the name of the poster's sponsor is "Luangpho Samniang Yusathaphon." He is a senior Buddhist monk.[18]

The Border of Thainess

The internal/external dichotomy is one of the most effective strategies to differentiate We-self and otherness. Yet the demarcation between internal and external, We-self and otherness (or enemy), is sometimes obscure. Even the geo-body, which should be the most obvious and solid identification of the Thai nationhood, has limits at those locations where its boundary is not coterminous with the boundary of Thainess. The domain of Thainess is rather ambiguous; it can be quite extensive or quite restricted. In 1988 the country as a whole, with the Thai in the United States at the forefront, rallied against the Art Institute in Chicago for the return of an eleventh-century Khmer lintel to its sanctuary now inside Thai territory. In fact, the lintel is a piece, perhaps not even the most important one, of Khmer art in the period before the Thai ascendancy in mainland Southeast Asia. But as the awareness of national identity is peculiarly high these days, it is regarded as an invaluable treasure of Thai national identity. The entire nation was angry that the Americans had stolen this national treasure from Thai soil. Finally the entire nation was moved by the return of that piece of national identity to its motherland—Thailand, not Cambodia.[19] Thainess here is culturally extended beyond Thailand to include the threshold of the Angkorian empire. Its operative arena is even in Chicago. Remarkably, a Khmer specimen can generate a world-wide Thai response simply because of the present location of its sanctuary within the Thai geo-body.

Another striking example at the opposite extreme is the perception of communism and Thai communists. Communism in Thai discourse has not much to do with Marxism as a corpus of theories, political and economic programs, or a sophisticated ideology. Communism is simply the enemy of the Nation, Religion (Buddhism), and Monarchy. It is simply Enemy Number One of Thainess and thus external to Thainess. In Cold War propaganda, communism was normally equated with other countries like Russia, China, and North Vietnam. But the presence of Thai communists contradicted this definition, particularly in the late 1970s when socialist ideas were widespread and thousands of middle-class Thai students joined the Communist Party. Yet one of the most persistent strategies of counterinsurgency is to link socialists, communists, and the Left with the external threat. As a result, these students were called "the Deceived," or "our children who are deceived" (by communists? by Others?), a created category between Thainess and Others. Later the "Deceived" category extended to all Thai communists, including those in the Politburo. After laying down arms and ideology, most of them were granted amnesty and became known as "participants in the development of the Thai nation." They become "one of us" in the Thai state.

One of the counterinsurgency forces is the Border Patrol Police, whose main task is to fight Thai communists in the rural areas. Here the term "border," as it turns out, signifies the demarcation of otherness from Thainess, rather than signifying a geographical definition. The discourse on the geo-body provides an effective figuration to equate the subversive elements within Thai society with the external threat. Thus the Border Patrol is the force to safeguard the border of Thainess against the enemy—who are definitely outside such a border, no matter where they really locate. As it happens, this police force can be found operating anywhere from the border areas, among the minorities (to teach them the central Thai language and introduce to them the Thai flag, a Buddha image, and pictures of the king and queen), in a village of Thai peasants well inside Thai territory (to organize a counterinsurgency unit), to an urban center like Chiangmai. It was also the main force which stormed into a university near the Grand Palace in Bangkok in the October 1976 massacre.

The "external" may not really be external; the "internal" can be made alien or external. In every situation, the discursive domain of Thainess remains homogeneous and unified. In turn, moreover, the terminology of the geographical discourse, terms such as border, becomes ambiguous. It may signify something other than space or geography. In the example cited above, the Border Patrol operates everywhere on the border of Thainess, even well inside the geo-body. The border of Thainess is much more limited than its geo-body. The Thai geo-body is not necessarily equal to Thai nationhood. We may think about all sorts of minorities who are well inside the geo-body but are on the edge of Thainess, ethnically, religiously, or ideologically, and are not well accepted into the domain of Thainess. These are the sensitive areas where a confrontation is imminent.

The Power of Symbols

A code or a symbol, like the word "border" or the map of a nation, does not necessarily signify the original signified. It can be generative, producing many more related meanings. In other words, each symbol has the inherent potential for multiple signification. The struggle to take control over the signification of symbol is therefore a serious battle—a contest to destabilize and eliminate certain meanings while asserting another. Hence loyalty or resistance to the dominant meaning of a symbol signifies either submission to or sedition from the hegemony of a discourse . . . and power.

The symbolism of nationhood is normally the conjugation of several discourses, each of which is effective in itself. That makes the symbol of nationhood a rich and potent icon. It has power. One of the best examples is the national flag. A history of the national flag of Thailand is so far merely a superficial record of the changes of color, shape, and emblem.[20] But such a history could instead trace the discursive formation of identification of nationhood. What did it mean when Mongkut invented the flag of "Siam" as a distinct symbol separate from the emblem of monarchy? What did it indicate when he chose a white elephant as the symbol on the flag, while the flag of the monarchy showed Mongkut's personal emblem? What did the major step of introducing the tricolor as the national flag mean? It has been said that King Vajiravudh's decision to take the white elephant out of the flag's design was the result of an accident in which the white elephant flag was raised upside down.[21] Even if this is true, how did the tricolor become the symbol? In what ways was power invested in this formulation?

The tricolor flag has gone through several upheavals without change, while several other symbols of the nation from the absolute monarchy period were challenged. The 1932 revolution which abolished the absolute monarchy tried to introduce the constitution as the nation's supreme symbol of reverence.[22] The next regime commissioned the composition of a new national anthem to replace the songs that had represented the royalty in public events.[23] Moreover, the anthem for Their Majesties was shortened and many competing symbols were invented.[24] Despite these struggles, the tricolor flag survived virtually untouched. Why was it so powerful? Or was it simply weak, ambiguous, and therefore malleable? If this is the case, was there any shift of emphasis, interpretation, or function in the regulations and rituals surrounding it?[25]

As the flag was produced and sanctioned by the power of the Thai state and its discourse, however, its meaning and identification are circumscribed by the discourse of Thainess, which does not include, and may not be accepted by, the dissidents. Since 1982, when communist armed forces defected to the government, they handed over their rifles and red flags to the government officials. In return, they would receive the tricolor flag and a picture of Their Majesties, and finally they would join in singing the national anthem together. This political rite of passage with the tricolor flag and other symbols transformed these Thai communists under the red flag into members of the hegemonic society under the tricolor flag. Did it mean that they were not fully Thai until the ritual was performed?

The power of the flag, and the seriousness of the issue, are acknowledged by most political forces. On the eve of the popular uprising in October 1973, the military regime at that time accused the student movement of being communists and said that all the chaos was planned by the Communist Party. To counter this accusation, when several hundred thousand people began their march against the junta, they were led by a troop of students who, instead of arms, held huge national flags and pictures of Their Majesties.

How powerful the symbolism is can be recognized when it is used improperly or challenged. Once a man was arrested because he wore a pair of socks with the national flag printed near the heels, which is regarded in Thai culture as an offense to the symbol.[26] In another case, in October 1975, on the second anniversary of the successful uprising just mentioned, a ceremonial march along the route of the event was planned as the climax of the commemoration. The organizers prepared thousands of small paper flags for the march, but not the tricolor flag. Instead, they invented a new flag especially for this occasion. It was in sky-blue with a well-known image of a heroic moment printed on it in white. At first the artist was criticized on the grounds that the sky-blue and white failed to convey the uprising's radical spirit. Finally, alerted by army propaganda, the leadership of the student movement said that the hero flag should be abandoned altogether because it could be interpreted as an intentional challenge to the national flag, which might then lead to an unthinkable political disaster. The heated argument among the organizers went on virtually throughout the night before every hero flag was securely put away and thousands of the small tricolor paper flags were purchased throughout Bangkok in the early hours of the morning. Were they too timid? Properly cautious? Or should they not even have tried the new flag instead of having to abort it at the last minute?

A Final Word

The identification of nationhood is a kind of totemism. It has as its basis the binary opposition of We-self and Others. Certainly there are several kinds and levels of identification—class, school, region, occupation, nationhood— and one may be in conflict with others. But their power varies according to the hierarchies of identities. Communists argue that workers should have no country, for example, and it might be logical to wish that the world of nations would give way to a new world of internationalism. But Marx and Engels were too optimistic and deluded by the supranational character of capitalism to recognize that being a worker is secondary to being a national—or even an ethnic, a Croat, Serb, Slav, Czech, Ukrainian, Karen, Mon, Tamil, Sinhalese, or southern Thai. Workers hardly united; they usually untied. Even unity on the basis of one kind of identity may one day be dissolved in favor of a new differentiation on the basis of another kind of identity. Even a nation—still a strong and desired primordial identity—can dissolve. And one day nations will dissolve, perhaps for another communal identity, presumably a superior one.

The identification ascribed to nationhood does not represent any intrinsic quality of it. It represents what it creates. The definition and domain of nationhood are not given. They are constructed, carved, inscribed, fabricated. Nor is its unity given. The identification is formed by the composition of effects of discourses which define its domain, confer meanings, or confront each other from time to time. It is always unfixed, ambiguous, self-contradictory, too restricted, yet too extensive. The presence of identity is merely a temporary discursive conjuncture in which certain discourses have stabilized their hegemonic forces upon the domain. But other discourses always exist marginally in certain areas, and new ones can emerge to challenge, destabilize, and displace the dominant discourses—thus reinscribing the domain and hence the identity. Identity is always in a crisis of contention and displacement; thus it is always changeable. The life of such an identity is neither stable nor continuous. It is full of moments of shift, disruption, and displacement. The study of nationhood should therefore dispense with the illusory notion of identity. Moreover, since the creation of nationhood is full of contention, struggle, and displacement, a study of discursive identification becomes a study of ambiguities, misunderstandings, unstable moments of signification, and the extrinsic forces which nurture such identification.

The map has long played a subordinate role in most historical studies. Now we should recognize its power. Has it been exaggerated here? Perhaps. But elsewhere it has been definitely undervalued. It is not merely a means, a verb, of the human subject. It may be the other way round. Perhaps the same can be said of other technologies. They can be nonhuman subjects which are able to turn humans into the agency or even the object of their mediators. The supposed creator, like a cartographer, is always anonymous and cannot be held responsible for the fact that the product has gone far beyond control. Human beings are too often given the central role in a historical narrative. They deserve a much humbler place in history—as servants of a technology, perhaps, which is what is really happening now.

A conventional history of a nation is always full of stories of heroism, ingenious leaders, struggles for independence, suffering caused by the enemy, and so on. They are worth remembering as how we used to remember our past. But in fact a history of the birth of a nation is full of embarrassing, irrational, accidental, unintentionally charming, and amusing happenings, including ideological and psychological cover-ups. No matter if it is worthy and useful, it is undeniably another history within the same past.

A map created a nation, though not single-handedly. But to give credit to a map, which is comparatively young and humble in its technical origin, is inconceivable because it would withdraw the glory the nation has deposited in the historical account. Yet why is a search for the origin of a nation in the immemorial past so worthy? Why not look at its obvious components in order to analyze them discretely to see its ephemeral conjuncture? It is as simple as saying that the birth of "Siam" locates in the composition of the characters S, I, A, and M. Likewise, its geo-body is born in a map, and nowhere else.

Note on Sources

THE BURNEY PAPERS. Reference to *The Burney Papers* will be in the form *BP* (volume)/ (part). For instance, *BP* 4/1 means vol. 4, pt. 1. The volume number here means the manuscript volume no matter in which bound volume it appears, since it does not necessarily correspond to the number of the bound volumes. For example, vol. 2 of the manuscript extends to two bound volumes. Moreover, the method of page numbering is not consistent throughout the entire manuscript. In vols. 1 and 3 the page numbering runs consecutively through their four and two parts respectively. In vols. 2 and 4 the numbering runs afresh in each of their six and two parts respectively. Volume 5 has only one part. Therefore, the reference to part number is necessary for vols. 2 and 4 but is omitted for other volumes to prevent confusion.

PRACHUM PHONGSAWADAN. The series of *Prachum phongsawadan* (Collected Chronicles), a collection of historical documents and essays of various types, comprises eighty parts. In the Khurusapha edition consulted here, however, the series is divided into fifty volumes of more or less similar size, regardless of the beginning and end of each part. So the reference will always be *PP* (volume)/(part). For example, *PP* 34/62 and 35/62 mean vols. 34 and 35 in which pt. 62 appears; *PP* 11/13 and 11/14 mean pts. 13 and 14 which are in the same vol. 11. In most cases, the title of each document will be given, as in a reference to an article in a book.

PHRARATCHAPHONGSAWADAN KRUNG RATTANAKOSIN. The reference to Thiphakorawong, *Phraratchaphongsawadan krung rattanakosin* (Royal Chronicles of the Bangkok Period) for the third and fourth reigns, which comprises two volumes each, will be shortened to Thiphakorawong, *Third Reign* and *Fourth Reign* respectively, followed by the volume number.

Notes

THE REFERENCES in this section are in a concise form. For works frequently cited and with lengthy titles, the full titles and translations, if in Thai, are given in the first reference and are abbreviated thereafter. The complete details of each reference are in the bibliography.

Introduction: The Presence of Nationhood

1. *Sydney Morning Herald,* 9 June 1986.
2. La-o-thong Ammarinrat, "Kansongnakrian paisuksato tangprathet tangtae ph.s. 2411–2475" [Sponsorship of students studying abroad], pp. 99–100.
3. Ibid., pp. 212–213.
4. Sirilak Sakkriangkrai, ed., *Phraya suriyanuwat (koet bunnak) naksetthasat khonraek khong muangthai* [Phraya Suriyanuwat (Koed Bunnag): the first economist of Thailand], pp. 27–30.
5. Prince Damrong Rajanubhap, "Laksana kanpokkhrong prathetsayam taeboran" [The Siamese government in ancient times], pp. 6–7.
6. Thamsook Numnonda, *Thailand and the Japanese Presence 1941–1945,* pp. 21–41.
7. Ibid.; see also a collection of the government's prescriptions in that period in Kromkhotsanakan, *Pramuan watthanatham haengchat* [A collection on national culture].
8. *Rai-ngan kansammana ruang ekkalak khong chat kap kanphatthana* [Report of the seminar on national identity and development], p. 1.
9. Commission for National Identity, *Ekkalak khong chat* [National identity].
10. From the speech of M. R. Kukrit Pramoj; ibid., p. 19.
11. Edmund Leach, *Political Systems of Highland Burma,* pp. 285–286, 290–292.
12. *Far Eastern Economic Review,* 18 June 1987, p. 53.
13. Prudhisan Jumbala, "Interest and Pressure Groups," p. 130.
14. Interview of Dr. Khian Theerawit in *Matichon* (a Thai daily newspaper), 8 April 1985, p. 2.
15. Edward Said, *Orientalism.*
16. Mark Hobart and Robert Taylor, eds., *Context, Meaning and Power in Southeast Asia,* p. 7.
17. Benedict Anderson, "Studies of the Thai State," p. 196.

18. Thongchai Winichakul, "Siam Mapped: A History of the Geo-body of Siam," (article) pp. 155–156. This point is also expressed by the convener in postconference comments; see "Postscript" by Gehan Wijeyewardene in vol. 3, pt. 2, pp. 650–652.

19. From the introduction by Amara Pongsapich in *Traditional and Changing Thai World View*, p. 8.

20. Sit But-in, *Lokkathat chaothai lanna* [The worldview of Lanna Thai people]; *Sangkhomsat chabap lokkathat chaolanna* [Journal of social science]; Chamroen Saengduang-khae, *Lokkathat chaothai phaktai thi prakot nai phlengklomdek* [The worldview of the Southern Thai as it appears in nursery rhymes]; Sutthiwong Phongphaibun, ed., *Lokkathat thai phaktai* [The worldview of the Southern Thai]; Charuwan Thammawat, *Lokkathat thangkanmuang chak wannakam isan* [Political perceptions from the literature of the northeast]; Panya Borisut, *Lokkathat khong khonthai wikhro chak wannakhadikhamson samai sukhothai* [The worldview of Thai people: an analysis of teaching literature from the Sukhothai period]; and Saowapha Phaithayawat, "Lokkathat khong khonthai samai ton rattanakosin 2325–2416" [The worldview of Thai people in the early Bangkok period].

21. Especially in Panya's book cited above: what he calls an analysis is almost verbatim from his sources.

22. See the transcription of the program in *Phua phaendin thai* [For the Thai land].

23. There are similar broadcasts on radio and television. Although not all of them are popular—indeed, some gain only a limited share of the audience due to their poor style of presentation—they too are part of the effort to standardize Thainess. See *Yuyangthai* [Living as Thai], an annual publication of the radio and television scripts of the programs of the same title.

24. Seksan Prasertkul, Review of *Thailand: Society and Politics*, p. 406.

25. The view is perhaps best represented by the works of a well-known social critic and prolific writer named Sulak Sivaraksa and his followers. In English see, for example, *Siam in Crisis; Seeds of Peace: A Buddhist Vision for Renewing Society;* and *Religion and Development*. See also Donald Swearer, "Sulak Sivaraksa's Buddhist Vision for Renewing Society," pp. 17–57. This current of thought is popular and well recognized by scholars as well as among social activists. Another ideological leader is a medical doctor-turned-social-critic, Professor Prawes Wasi.

26. Sulak was charged with lèse-majesté twice in 1984 and 1991. The second offense included the charge of defaming the army's commander-in-chief. But in fact Sulak is well known for his royalism: many of his writings are biographies and interviews of members of the royal elite, and his ardent support of the monarchical institution is explicit in many writings. Nonetheless, these people do not propose to put back the clock but urge the observation of traditional values and institutions, which they regard as the Thai way of looking to the future.

27. See Aphichat Thongyoo, *Watthanatham kap chumchon: thangluakmai khong nganphatthana* [Culture and local community: an alternative for development works]. Among people well known in Thailand for this kind of thinking are Bamrung Bunpanya, Dr. Seri Phongphit, and Dr. Kanchana Kaewthep.

28. The quote here is from an advertisement for the book *Charukwai thamklang yuksamai an sapson* [Recording amidst the complex age] by Aphichat Thongyoo, as it appears in the journal *Sangkhomphatthana* [Social Development], 5–6 (1983), p. 104.

29. Sa-nga Luchaphatthanaphorn, ed., *Wikrittakan ekkalakthai* [The crisis of Thai identity].

30. Phra Pracha pasannathammo, "Than phutthathat kap kanpatiwat watthanatham" [Buddhadasa Bhikku and cultural revolution], p. 76.

31. For the Thammakai see Peter Jackson, *Buddhism, Legitimation and Conflict: The Political Functions of Urban Thai Buddhism;* for Sulak's attack (in Thai) see *Matichon rai sapda* [Matichon Weekly], 13 July 1986.

32. *Far Eastern Economic Review,* 18 June 1987, pp. 53–54. For this monk see Charles F. Keyes, "Political Crisis and Militant Buddhism in Contemporary Thailand," and David Morell and Chai-anan Samudavanija, *Political Conflict in Thailand,* pp. 246–248.

33. See Pornpirom Iamtham, "Social Origin and the Development of the Communist Party of Thailand," pp. 205–209 and 212–215; and Gawin Chutima, *The Rise and Fall of the Communist Party of Thailand (1973–1987),* chap. 1 and pp. 44–60. It is hard to measure to what extent this "China factor" was the actual cause of the rift between the CPT and young intellectuals. Apparently, however, it is one of the most common reasons given by those who turned away from the CPT. (See Yuangrat Wedel, *The Thai Radicals and the Communist Party*).

34. See, for example, the article "Ratthai kap chakkrawatniyom" [The Thai state and imperialism], pp. 15–35, by Santisuk Sophonsiri.

35. See Craig J. Reynolds and Lysa Hong, "Marxism in Thai Historical Studies," pp. 77–104, for the historical context of Thai Marxists in the 1950s and its application and effects in the 1970s.

36. Somkiat Wanthana, "Rat somburanayasit nai sayam 2435–2475" [The absolutist state in Siam 1892–1932]. See also a panel discussion among young scholars on this topic in *Pacharayasan* 8, no. 3 (June–July 1981): 14–57.

37. Andrew Turton et al., *Thailand: Roots of Conflict.*

38. Anderson, "Studies of the Thai State," pp. 211–215, discusses ethnic minorities. The article as a whole criticizes the myth of the homogeneity of the Thai state in other aspects as well.

39. Charles F. Keyes, *Thailand: Buddhist Kingdom as Modern Nation-State.* See also Andrew Turton, "Limits of Ideological Domination and the Formation of Social Consciousness," on the heterogeneity of a society and domains of consciousness.

40. Kenneth R. Hall and John K. Whitmore, eds., *Explorations in Early Southeast Asian History: The Origins of Southeast Asian Statecraft,* introduction; and David Marr and A. C. Milner, eds., *Southeast Asia in the 9th to 14th Century,* introduction.

41. Donald K. Emmerson, " 'Southeast Asia': What's in a Name," pp. 5–14.

42. Benedict Anderson, *Imagined Communities: Reflections on the Origin and Spread of Nationalism.*

43. See, for example, a classic work about the identification of Kachin and Shan people in Leach, *Highland Burma.* For more on ethnic identification see Fredrik Barth, ed., *Ethnic Groups and Boundaries: The Social Organization of Cultural Difference,* introduction; and Charles F. Keyes, ed., *Ethnic Adaptation and Identity: The Karen on the Thai Frontier with Burma,* especially the chapters by Keyes, Kunstadter, Lehman, and introduction.

44. The reimagining of time has yet to be explored in depth and indeed deserves a separate project. Apart from Anderson's work, the study which tells us how much the mechanical clock is involved in our modern life is David Landes, *Revolution in Time: Clocks and the Making of the Modern World.*

45. Robert D. Sack, *Human Territoriality: Its Theory and History.* The definition here is a combined quote from pp. 19–20, and 216.

46. Ibid., p. 30. For the three effects see pp. 21–22 and 31–34.

47. Edmund Leach, "The Frontiers of Burma," pp. 49–68.

48. Tej Bunnag, *Provincial Administration of Siam 1892–1915*, pp. 2–3, 17–19.

Chapter One: Indigenous Space and Ancient Maps

1. For a translation of *Traiphum Phra Ruang* and discussion of this cosmography see Frank E. Reynolds and Mani B. Reynolds, *Three Worlds According to King Ruang: A Thai Buddhist Cosmology.*

2. Michael Vickery, "A Note on the Date of the Traibhumikatha," pp. 275–284.

3. B. J. Terwiel, "Muang Thai and the World: Changing Perspectives During the Third Reign."

4. See Suphaphan na Bangchang, "Wannakam lokkasat nai phutthasatsana therawat" [The literature on cosmology in Theravada Buddhism], for abstracts of texts in this tradition.

5. See full reference in the Bibliography.

6. Craig J. Reynolds, "Buddhist Cosmography in Thai History with Special Reference to Nineteenth-Century Culture Change," pp. 203–220.

7. B. J. Terwiel, "Muang Thai and the World," pp. 5–10, is an example.

8. Robert Heine-Geldern, *Conceptions of State and Kingship in Southeast Asia.*

9. See, for example, Lorraine Gesick, ed., *Centers, Symbols, and Hierarchies: Essays on the Classical States of Southeast Asia,* and Shelly Errington, *Meaning and Power in Southeast Asian Realm.*

10. Frank E. Reynolds, "Buddhism as Universal Religion and as Civic Religion," pp. 194–203. For more about the three strands of Buddhist knowledge see Reynolds and Reynolds, *Three Worlds,* pp. 11–22.

11. Charles F. Keyes, "Buddhist Pilgrimage Centers and the Twelve-Year Cycle," pp. 71–89.

12. Figure 1 is from "Northern Thai manuscript: Buddhist Manual," in the Shan/Northern Thai/Khmer Manuscript Collection, no. 28B, part of the John M. Echols Collection, Cornell University. The summary reads "Folding-book manuscript collection of miscellaneous and important Buddhist texts including 'How to construct a pagoda,' 'How to give a name to a new monk.' . . . Relating important Buddhist city states in India to the pagoda which became the center of the universe in Buddhist cosmology. The last is a portion in black and red and includes a map of Buddhist pilgrimage sites in India." It is fascinating that Joseph Schwartzberg is able to decode it—at least a convincing hypothetical decoding—as a record of a geography of pilgrimage. See David Woodward, ed., *History of Cartography,* vol. 2, pt. 2. Thanks to Professor Schwartzberg for introducing this manuscript to me and for discussing his findings with me. See also another study of the space of the pilgrimage in northeastern Thailand: James B. Pruess, "Merit-Seeking in Public," pp. 169–206.

13. H. L. Shorto, "The 32 Myos in the Medieval Mon Kingdom," pp. 572–591; and "The Dewatau Sotapan," pp. 127–141.

14. Shorto even proposed that the formula for the number, including the most superior shrine, was always $2^n + 1$; see "The 32 Myos," pp. 581–582.

15. David P. Chandler, "Maps for the Ancestors," pp. 170–187.

16. See Prungsri Vallibhotama et al., eds., *Sarupphon kansammana ruang traiphum phra ruang* [Summary of the seminar on Traiphum Phra Ruang], pp. 115–164, which includes many photographs of various temples.

17. For an extensive study of Thai paintings and various themes see Jean Boisselier, *Thai Painting*.

18. There are at least two extant copies of this Thonburi version of the pictorial Traiphum manuscript with many minor differences between them. One copy now belongs to the Berlin Museum. Parts of this copy have been published with short descriptions in Klaus Wenk, *Thailandische Miniaturmalereien nach einer Handschrift der indischen Kunstabteilung der staatlichen Museen Berlin*. The other copy is in the Vajiranana Room of the National Library in Bangkok, which possesses pictorial manuscripts of the Traiphum from earlier periods as well as Lao and Khmer versions.

19. Michael Wright, "Khonboran mong phumisat lok" [Ancient people perceived the world's geography], pp. 90–96.

20. Ibid., pp. 92–93.

21. Wright suggests that the accurate details of Ceylon may indicate that the author actually visited the island.

22. Boisselier, *Thai Painting*, pp. 80, 84, 200, 204.

23. Michael Vickery, "The Lion Prince and Related Remarks on Northern History," pp. 361–362; and Winai Pongsripian, "Traditional Thai Historiography and Its Nineteenth-Century Decline," pp. 69–82.

24. James B. Pruess, "Merit-Seeking in Public," p. 170.

25. Chandler, "Maps for the Ancestors," pp. 174–175.

26. A sketch of the entire map can be found in Sutthiwong Phongphaibun, *Rai-ngan kanwichai phutthasatsana thaep lumthalesap songkhla fangtawan-ok samai krung si-ayutthaya* [Research report on Buddhism along the eastern bank of Songkhla Lagoon in the Ayudhya period], in which the map is taken as a clue to the temples, land donations, and Buddhism in that region in the late Ayudhya period. The original manuscript is in the Vajiranana Room of the National Library, Bangkok.

27. Lorraine Gesick, "Reading Landscape," pp. 157–162.

28. For an elementary study of this map from the Berlin manuscript see Klaus Wenk, "Zu einer 'Landkarte' Sued- und Ostasiens." Michael Wright, "Phaenthi boran" [Ancient maps], is another study from the manuscript in Bangkok. There are differences in details of both maps (see note 18). Wenk, *Thailandische*, pp. 66–67, published only a portion of this map.

29. Terwiel, "Muang Thai and the World," p. 9.

30. Ibid., pp. 6–7.

31. See two examples of the Chinese coastal charts from the sixteenth and eighteenth centuries in J. V. Mills, "Chinese Coastal Maps," opposite p. 156; and Leo Bagrow, *History of Cartography*, pl. CIV.

32. Mills, "Chinese Coastal Maps," p. 151.

33. Paul Wheatley, *The Golden Khersonese*, chap. 1.

34. Royal Thai Survey Department, *Wiwatthanakan thang phaenthi nai prathetthai* [Development of mapping in Thailand], p. 5.

35. Victor Kennedy, "An Indigenous Early Nineteenth Century Map of Central and Northeast Thailand," pp. 315–348.

36. See the revised edition of *Traiphum Phra Ruang*, in which most of the numerical values (about the earth, seas, oceans, and so on) in chap. 9 are "examined and corrected." The revision is done according to certain mathematical formulas. Some of them are noted and explained in Reynolds and Reynolds, *Three Worlds*, but no explanation is given in the Thai revised edition.

37. For illustrations of the three worlds in Thai paintings see Reynolds and Reynolds, *Three Worlds*.

38. Frederick A. Neale, *Narrative of a Residence at the Capital of the Kingdom of Siam*, pp. 54–56. All the spellings are according to the original. The illustration is from p. 55.

Chapter Two: The Coming of a New Geography

1. Hong Lysa, *Thailand in the Nineteenth Century.*

2. Prince Dhaninivat, "The Inscriptions of Wat Phra Jetubon," in *Collected Articles*, pp. 21–22; *Nangnopphamat ru tamrap thao sichulalak* [Lady Nopphamat or a treatise of Thao Sichulalak], pp.1–3. The inscription was dated 1836; the date of the Nopphamat is uncertain—see the introduction of the book and see Nithi Aeusrivongse, *Pakkai lae bairua* [A quill and a sail], pp. 337–344. In *Phra Aphaimani*, perhaps the most popular literary work of the time, one of the main characters is a *farang* (Westerner) from "Lanka" (Sri Lanka or Ceylon).

3. B. J. Terwiel, "Muang Thai and the World," pp. 17–18.

4. Ibid., pp. 20–21; Dan B. Bradley, *Abstract of the Journal of Reverend Dan Beach Bradley, M.D.*, p. 26.

5. George H. Feltus, *Samuel Reynolds House of Siam*, p. 24.

6. Bradley, *Journal*, p. 28.

7. William Bradley, *Siam Then*, p. 49. For more details of this episode, see Caswell's letter in William Bradley, "Prince Mongkut and Jesse Caswell," p. 38.

8. *Bangkok Recorder*, vol. 1, nos. 21–22, Jan. 1866.

9. King Mongkut, *Phraratchahatthalekha phrabatsomdet phrachomklaochaoyuhua* [Royal correspondence of King Mongkut], p. 6.

10. Bradley, *Siam Then*, p. 102.

11. Sir John Bowring, *The Kingdom and People of Siam*, vol. 2, p. 144.

12. See one of Mongkut's letters to his American friend in which this matter was discussed at length in Mongkut, [*Royal Correspondence*], pp. 6–18.

13. Mom Rachothai, *Nirat london* [Poetry on the journey to London], p. 89.

14. Reynolds, "Buddhist Cosmography in Thai History," pp. 217–219.

15. See Craig Reynolds, "The Buddhist Monkhood in Nineteenth Century Thailand," chaps. 3–4, esp. pp. 79–96, for Mongkut's movement; see also Srisuporn Chuangsakul, "Khwamplianplaeng khong khanasong: suksa karani thammayuttikanikai (ph.s. 2368–2464)" [Development of the *sangha*: the case of the Thammayut sect (1825–1921)].

16. *Bangkok Recorder*, vol. 2, nos. 2, 9, 12 (17 Mar., 27 June, and 11 Aug. 1866).

17. Ibid., vol. 1, no. 21 (Jan. 1866), p. 211.

18. Thiphakorawong, *Nangsu sadaeng kitchanukit* [A book explaining various things]. In English see Henry Alabaster, *The Modern Buddhist*, which is an extensive report about Thiphakorawong's book, with remarks, discussion, and a large number of excerpts from *Kitchanukit*.

19. For a discussion of the book see Reynolds, "Buddhist Monkhood," pp. 129–132; and "Buddhist Cosmography," pp. 215–219. See also a summary of the book in Somjai Phairotthirarat, "The Historical Writing of Chao Phraya Thiphakorawong," chap. 3.

20. Thiphakorawong, *Kitchanukit*, pp. 245–249.

21. Ibid., pp. 83–107.

22. *Bangkok Recorder*, vol. 1, no. 2 (16 Mar. 1865), and vol. 2, no. 2 (17 Mar. 1866).

23. Thiphakorawong, *Kitchanukit*, p. 104.

24. Ibid., pp. 100–102.

25. Ibid., pp. 106–107.

26. Ibid., p. 1.

27. Damrong, *Khwamsongcham* [Recollections], p. 99.

28. Prayoon Uluchata [Phluluang], "Phrachomklao kap horasatthai" [King Mongkut and Thai astrology], pp. 43–51. For this particular issue and the controversy surrounding it see Nerida Cook, "A Tale of Two City Pillars: Mongkut and Thai Astrology on the Eve of Modernization," pp. 279–313.

29. Mongkut, *Phraboromrachathibai athikkamat athikkawan lae pakkhananawithi* [Royal explanations of the intercalated months and days and methods of calculating phases of the month], is a collection of Mongkut's writings on this topic. Or see Mongkut, *Prachum prakat ratchakan thi 4* [Collected proclamations of the fourth reign], vol. 4, pp. 120–141.

30. The Songkran proclamation is the first entry of every year in Mongkut, [*Collected Proclamations*].

31. Mongkut, [*Collected Proclamations*], vol. 3, pp. 272–273.

32. Ibid., vol. 2, pp. 96–97, 305.

33. Ibid., vol. 4, p. 25.

34. Ibid., vol. 2, p. 320.

35. See for example, *Bangkok Recorder*, vol. 1, no. 21, and Thiphakorawong, *Fourth Reign*, vol. 2, p. 160.

36. Mongkut, [*Collected Proclamations*], vol. 2, p. 199.

37. Ibid., vol. 4, pp. 24–25.

38. See, for example, ibid., vol. 4, p. 92.

39. Mongkut, [*Explanations of Intercalated Months and Days*], p. 2.

40. Mongkut, [*Collected Proclamations*], vol. 2, p. 313, and vol. 4, pp. 142–145, for example.

41. Ibid., vol. 4, pp. 117–120.

42. Fine Arts Department, comp., *Prachum chotmaihet ruang suriyupparakha nai ratchakan thi 4 lae ruang ratchakan thi 4 songprachuan lae sawankhot* [Collected documents on the solar eclipse in the fourth reign and on the illness and death of King Mongkut], p. 29. For more details and pictures of the 1868 full eclipse see Rawi Bhawilai, "Suriyupparakha 18 singhakhom 2411" [The eclipse on 18 August 1868], pp. 26–34; and Chaen Patchusanon, "Suriyupparakha temkhrat ph.s. 2411" [The full solar eclipse of 1868], pp. 124–141. The belt crossed Aden, India, and Borneo, where the Europeans had established observatory stations.

43. "Chotmaihet sadet wako" [Records on the royal visit to Wako], in *PP* 13/19, p. 16; and Thiphakorawong, *Fourth Reign*, vol. 2, p. 242. The other text more conventionally used by astrologers at that time was *Suriyayat*. The names of the Western texts were not given.

44. Damrong, [*Recollections*], pp. 36–37; see also *PP* 13/19, pp. (3)–(4) and *PP* 30/52, "Chotmaihet mua phrabatsomdet phrachomklao sawankhot" [Records on the death of King Mongkut], pp. 132–134.

45. See "Chotmaihet hon" [Records of astrologers], *PP* 8/8, p. 110.

46. But Mongkut preferred the *Saram* doctrine; see Mongkut, [*Explanations of Intercalated Months and Days*], pp. 72–73.

47. Ever since this event, Wako has been known only by name. Its exact location has

been forgotten and does not appear on any map. Recent attempts to rediscover it have ended in controversy; see Chaen, ["Full Solar Eclipse of 1868"].

48. Fine Arts Department, [Documents on the Solar Eclipse], p. 31.

49. Thiphakorawong, Fourth Reign, vol. 2, pp. 250–251.

50. Fine Arts Department, [Documents on the Solar Eclipse], pp. 31–33.

51. J. W. Van Dyke [Wandai], Phumanithet [Geography], preface. Although no romanized name of the author was given in the book, Rev. J. W. Van Dyke was a Presbyterian missionary in Siam between 1869 and 1886; see Thai Khadi Research Institute, "Mo bratle kap sangkhom thai" [Dr.Bradley and Thai society], app. 1, p. 4. There is no evidence whether he wrote in Thai or the book was a translation from his English original.

52. Warunee Osatharom, "Kansuksa nai sangkhomthai ph.s. 2411–2475" [Education in Thai society 1868–1932], pp. 67–85.

53. Ibid., p. 84.

54. W. G. Johnson, Phumisat sayam [Geography of Siam]. There is confusion over the date of the first publication of this book. The fifth printing of 1914 stated that Johnson wrote the book in English in 1900 but the translation was not finished in that year. (See preface by Phraya Methathibodi in the 1914 printing.) Johnson's own introduction to the first edition, as it appears in the fourth printing of 1907, was dated 1902. But I have found the 1900 edition: its title, many words, and spellings differ from later editions, but its content is virtually the same except for certain statistics which were updated in each printing.

55. Phraya Thepphasatsathit, Phumisat lem 1 [Geography book I], pp. 58–59.

56. Ibid., p. 34.

57. D. J. B. Pallegoix, Dictionarium linguage Thai sive Siamensis interpretatione Latina, Gallica et Anglica, pp. 523, 626; Pallegoix, Siamese French English Dictionary, p. 776; Dan Beach Bradley, Nangsu akkharaphithansap: Dictionary of the Siamese Language, pp. 412, 514; Khun Prasert-aksonnit et al., Photchananukrom lamdap lae plae sap thichai nai nangsu thai [Dictionary of vocabularies used in Thai literature], p. 282.

58. For example in Pallegoix, Siamese French English Dictionary (see note 57 above); and Samuel J. Smith, A Comprehensive Anglo-Siamese Dictionary, p. 671.

59. Van Dyke, Phumanithet, pp. 6–7.

60. The book proceeded by questions and answers. A number of questions on the same topic was called a mae, as in traditional Siamese literature. A "chapter" was marked by a group of mae in consecutive sequence; the sequence started afresh for each chapter.

61. Johnson, Phumisat sayam, pp. 59, 64, 67, and passim.

62. Ibid., p. 8.

63. Ibid., pp. 11–12.

64. In the 1914 publication, if not earlier, the map of Asia was not included, though it was still referred to on p. 11 of the book. Moreover, the map of Siam's boundaries was replaced by an up-to-date map of "the Kingdom of Siam" which showed more details of provincial administration and boundaries.

65. Thepphasatsathit, [Geography Book I] and [Geography Book II]. The author's name given here is the last official title conferred on him in his career. In earlier editions, therefore, the author's name may appear differently—for instance, as Khun Tharaphak-phathi.

66. Thepphasatsathit's [Geography Book I] was published thirty-six times from 1902

to 1958. The total number of copies was nearly three million. There is no exact record for [*Geography Book II*].

67. Abridged from Thepphasatsathit, [*Geography Book II*], pp. 50–75.

68. See A. Kolacny, "Cartographic Information," pp. 47–49; see also Arthur H. Robinson and Barbara B. Petchenik, *The Nature of Maps*.

69. For details see Robinson and Petchenik, *The Nature of Maps*, chap. 3, esp. pp. 30–32 and figs. 2.4–2.6; or see Kolacny, "Cartographic Information," p. 48. See also J. S. Keates, *Understanding Maps*, pp. 62–86.

70. The three methods given here are offered for the sake of the argument in this study only.

71. See Robinson and Petchenik, *The Nature of Maps*, pp. 61–66, for example.

72. Keates, *Understanding Maps*, p. 72.

73. Adisak Thongbun, "Wan witthayasat haeng chat kap phrabida haeng witthayasat thai" [National Science Day and the Father of Thai Science], pp. 3–4.

74. Prayoon Uluchata, ["King Mongkut and Thai Astrology"], p. 43.

75. Sulak Sivaraksa, "Chotmai chak wako" [A letter from Wako], pp. 36–41.

76. Prince Patriarch Wachirayanwarorot, *Thetsana phraratchaprawat phrabatsomdet phra paramentharamahamongkut phrachomklaochaoyuhua* [Sermon on the royal biography of King Mongkut], p. 40.

77. Prayoon Uluchata [Phluluang], *Horasat* [Astrology], introduction.

78. See the letter from Prince Thewawongwaropakan to Prince Damrong concerning the French surveyors in Chiraporn Sathapanawatthana, *Wikrittakan r.s. 112* [The 1893 crisis], p. 29; and see Prince Patriarch Wachirayanwarorot, *Pramuan phraniphon-prawattisat borankhadi* [Collected works—history], p. 117.

Chapter Three: Boundary

1. The use of the term "boundary" in this chapter is in fact applicable to modern boundaries but does not properly denote the indigenous practice of identifying the limits or extremities of a realm. For the sake of convenience, however, the term will be used in both senses throughout and the differences will be clarified as the discussion proceeds, especially in the last section of this chapter.

2. The quotations cited here and above are from *BP* 1, p. 54.

3. D. G. E. Hall, *Henry Burney: A Political Biography*, p. 73.

4. *BP* 1, pp. 60–61 and 85–86.

5. *BP* 1, pp. 154–155.

6. *BP* 1, pp. 122, 161; Hall, *Henry Burney*, p. 73.

7. *BP* 1, p. 122. All words including "nation," as well as the spelling, are according to the original.

8. *BP* 1, pp. 304–309.

9. See *BP* 1, p. 313, Article 4, and p. 377, Article 3. For Burney's proposal see *BP* 1, pp. 251–252.

10. *BP* 2/6, pp. 288–289.

11. The name of this river varies in *The Burney Papers*: Chan, Pak Chan, Pakchan. In Siamese records, the name of the river is given as Kra or Pakchan. The different names may refer to different sections of the river or to different but adjacent streams. All the names were used interchangeably; see, for example, *BP* 4/1, pp. 102–103, 139–142, 161. I will use "Pakchan" uniformly for convenience.

12. *BP* 4/1, pp. 82–85, 110.

13. *BP* 4/1, pp. 89, 94.

14. *BP* 4/1, pp. 86, 96.

15. *BP* 4/1, pp. 102–103, 109.

16. *BP* 4/1, pp. 118–119.

17. *BP* 4/1, pp. 131–132.

18. The quotation given here and the previous one come from *BP* 4/1, pp. 131–132.

19. *BP* 4/1, pp. 160 and 162 respectively. See the letter in full on pp. 156–162.

20. *BP* 4/1, pp. 198–199.

21. *BP* 4/1, pp. 122–125.

22. Thiphakorawong, *Third Reign*, vol. 2, pp. 104–106. See R. Renard, "The Delineation of the Kayah States Frontiers with Thailand: 1809–1894," p. 87, about this well-fortified township.

23. *BP* 4/1, pp. 153–155.

24. Walter F. Vella, *Siam Under Rama III 1824–1851*, p. 117.

25. Ibid., pp. 125, 129.

26. For more details see Vella, *Siam Under Rama III*, chap. 9; *PP* 34/62 and 35/62, "Thut farang samai krung rattanakosin" [Western envoys in the Bangkok period]; and Khachorn Sukhabhanij, *Khomun prawattisat samai bangkok* [Historical accounts of the Bangkok period], pp. 81–110 and 117–149. For the case of the American merchant, Robert Hunter, see Thiphakorawong, *Third Reign*, vol. 2, pp. 93–94, and *BP* 4/2, pp. 81–83, 92–94, 129–135, and 193–194.

27. The account given here and below is in *BP* 4/1, pp. 221–241, which is the correspondence among British authorities in 1847. They discovered the papers about the boundary in documents of Richardson's mission dating back to 1834. For the letter from the king of Chiangmai see pp. 227–229.

28. *BP* 4/1, pp. 242–263.

29. *BP* 3, pp. 142–143, 151–152, 155ff., the record dated 1829.

30. *BP* 3, pp. 161–164.

31. *BP* 3, pp. 192–193. This Malay unit of measurement is alternately mentioned as *rulong* or *orlong* in *The Burney Papers*. It is not a Siamese unit as stated in *BP* 3, p. 359.

32. *BP* 3, p. 193.

33. Ibid., p. 301; see the letter in full on pp. 300–304. See also a similar statement in another letter from Nakhon on pp. 359–361.

34. This was remarked by Mr. Ibbetson; see *BP* 3, pp. 294–295, 298–299.

35. *BP* 3, pp. 360–361.

36. See the letter in *BP* 4/1, pp. 140–142.

37. See the letter in full in *BP* 4/1, pp. 156–162. The word "jurisdiction" is from the original English translation of the Thai letter.

38. *BP* 4/1, pp. 163–169, 172.

39. *BP* 4/1, pp. 188–192.

40. Mongkut, *Phraratchahatthalekha phrabatsomdet phrachomklaochaoyuhua* [Royal correspondence of King Mongkut], pp. 352, 359; for more on this issue see pp. 351–363. See also Thiphakorawong, *Fourth Reign*, vol. 2, pp. 54–55, 67–71, 97–98; and Natthawut Sutthisongkhram, *Somdetchaophraya borommahasisuriyawong akkharamahasenabodi* [Sisuriyawong: the great minister], vol. 1, pp. 317–335.

41. See the full story in Nakhon Phannarong, "Kancheracha lae khotoklong rawang ratthaban sayam kap ratthaban angkrit kieokap huamuang chaidaen lannathai lae phama

samai phrabatsomdet phrachunlachomklaochaoyuhua raya ph.s. 2428–2438" [Negotiations and agreements between the Siamese and British governments concerning the frontier towns between Lanna and Burma in the reign of King Chulalongkorn during 1885–1895], pp. 106–120, 314–326.

42. Ibid., pp. 251–256.

43. Ibid., p. 341; the quotation is on p. 330 and the friendly path is on pp. 334–335; the letter in full is on pp. 329–341. The inquiry proceeded by questioning from British officials and responses by local chiefs. Bangkok officials acted more or less as interpreters. However, the records are in the standard Thai language.

44. Ibid., p. 341.

45. Richard Muir, *Modern Political Geography*, p. 119; my emphasis.

46. J. R. V. Prescott, *Boundaries and Frontiers*, p. 31.

47. Ibid., chap. 7; Muir, *Modern Political Geography*, chap. 6; and F. J. Monkhouse, *A Dictionary of Geography*, pp. 44, 132.

48. Prasert-aksonnit et al., [Dictionary of Vocabularies Used in Thai Literature], p. 557; see also pp. 386, 429.

49. Pallegoix, *Dictionarium linguage Thai*, p. 16.

50. Pallegoix, *Siamese French English Dictionary*, pp. 16 and 334.

51. Bradley, *Nangsu akkharaphithansap: Dictionary of the Siamese Language*, p. 84. The word "area" here is translated from *prathet*, which on p. 412 of this dictionary and in the context evidently means "inhabited areas, and fields or forests," not a nation.

52. *BP* 4/1, pp. 157–158.

53. See "Ruang muang nakhonchampasak" [A story of Champasak] in *PP* 44/70, pp. 173–193. For another example see "Phongsawadan Luang Phrabang" [Chronicle of Luang Phrabang] in *PP* 4/5, pp. 333, 336.

54. This fact is noted by Damrong, *Prachum phraniphon bettalet* [Collection of miscellaneous essays], pp. 26–29. But he did not think they were *khetdaen* markings because they were well "inside" the Siamese border, a point I will argue later.

55. Renard, "Delineation of the Kayah State Frontiers," pp. 81, 85.

56. Nakhon, "Negotiations and Agreements," p. 335.

57. ["Western Envoys in the Bangkok Period"] in *PP* 35/62, pp. 113, 148; my emphasis. In this source, the phrase was uttered by James Brooke. It is likely, however, that it was translated by the Siamese into the sense they understood.

58. ["Western Envoys in the Bangkok Period"] in *PP* 35/62, p. 149.

59. *BP* 3, p. 151, the letter dated 26 October 1829.

60. Ibid., p. 198.

61. The coexistence of these two indigenous kinds of boundary has been recognized only rarely in historical studies of the region. The exception is Moertono's study of old Java. But he mixed them together rather than distinguishing their different characteristics. See Soemarsaid Moertono, *State and Statecraft in Old Java*, pp. 114–115.

62. Robert L. Solomon, "Boundary Concepts and Practices in Southeast Asia," p. 15.

Chapter Four: Sovereignty

1. Victor Lieberman, *Burmese Administrative Cycles*, pp. 33–38.

2. O. W. Wolters, *History, Culture, and Region in Southeast Asian Perspectives*, pp. 16–17. See also Renee Hagesteijn, *Circles of Kings*. There are several other attempts to describe the power relations within a kingdom and among many kingdoms in the region

in a more systematic or even theoretical fashion. Among them, another well-known concept is Tambiah's galactic polity; see S. J. Tambiah, "The Galactic Polity: The Structure of Traditional Kingdoms in Southeast Asia," or his book *World Conqueror and World Renouncer,* chap. 4.

3. See a classic study of this historical theory of kingship in Tambiah, *World Conqueror and World Renouncer.* See also Sunait Chutintaranond, "Cakravatin: The Ideology of Traditional Warfare in Siam and Burma, 1548–1605."

4. For a history of Cambodia in relation to Siam and Vietnam before the nineteenth century see David Chandler, *History of Cambodia,* pp. 94–97, 113–116.

5. For more stories see Chandler, *History of Cambodia,* chap. 7, and Vella, *Siam Under Rama III,* chap. 7.

6. See "Phongsawadan khamen" [Chronicle of Cambodia], in *PP* 1/1, p. 295, and "Phongsawadan muang phratabong" [Chronicle of Battambang], in *PP* 12/16, p. 127. At that time the Cambodian king resided at Udong, while the Siamese troops were stationed at Battambang and the Vietnamese force was at Phnom Penh.

7. Chandler, *History of Cambodia,* p. 116.

8. From "Chotmaihet kieokap khamen lae yuan nai ratchakan thi 3, tonthi 1" [Accounts concerning Cambodia and Vietnam in the third reign, pt. 1], in *PP* 41/67, p. 235. The same statement with slight differences also appears in Chandler, *History of Cambodia,* p. 116; but Chandler quotes from a Vietnamese source.

9. Thiphakorawong, *Third Reign,* vol. 2, p. 107.

10. "Waduai hetkan muang khamen ton set songkhram thai yuan" [On the situation in Cambodia after the Siamese-Vietnamese war], in *PP* 31/56, p. 207; my emphasis.

11. Chandler, *History of Cambodia,* p. 133.

12. Ibid., p. 119.

13. R. Bonney, *Kedah 1771–1821,* pp. 18–22.

14. Ibid., p. 26.

15. Ibid., pp. 110–112; and see Kobkua Suwannathat-Pian, "The Dhonburi-Bangkok Political Ideology and Its Effects upon Thai-Malay Relations 1767–1851," pp. 95–106.

16. Lorraine Gesick, "Kingship and Political Integration in Traditional Siam 1767–1824," pp. 154–164; and Damrong's introduction to *Chotmai luang udomsombat* [Letters of Luang Udomsombat], p. 12.

17. See Kobkua, "Dhonburi-Bangkok Political Ideology," pp. 103–104; and Bonney, *Kedah 1771–1821.*

18. L. A. Mills, *British Malaya 1824–67,* pp. 150–153; see also [*Letters of Luang Udomsombat*], letters 9–15.

19. D. G. E. Hall, *Henry Burney: A Political Biography,* pp. 13, 28.

20. For the 1874 crisis in Bangkok see Noel Battye, "The Military, Government, and Society in Siam, 1868–1910," chap. 4. For another case in the late seventeenth century when King Narai of Ayudhya exploited his French connection to build up a French regiment to support his throne against his rival noblemen, see Nithi Aeusrivongse, *Kanmuang thai samai phra narai* [Thai politics in the reign of King Narai]. This incident is known as the 1688 Revolution; see Claude de Beze, *1688, Revolution in Siam,* and E. W. Hutchinson, *Adventures in Siam in the Seventeenth Century.*

21. Marcel Mauss, *The Gift: Forms and Functions of Exchange in Archaic Societies.*

22. Mary Elizabeth Berry's introduction to "Giving in Asia—A Symposium," p. 307.

23. This perception was held by the Siamese elite of the nineteenth century as well. See Mongkut, *Prachum prakat ratchakan thi 4* [Collected proclamations of the fourth reign], vol. 4, pp. 158–184; Damrong's introduction to *PP* 4/5, pp. 37–40. For modern scholars, the cost-profit interpretation appeared as early as 1936; see ["Western Envoys in the Bangkok Period"] in *PP* 34/62, note on p. 227. For more recent research in this light see Sarasin Viraphol, *Tribute and Profit: Sino-Siamese Trade 1652–1853*, and Suebsaeng Phrombun, "Sino-Siamese Tributary Relations, 1282–1853."

24. Mills, *British Malaya*, pp. 31–32.

25. Narathipphongpraphan, *Witthayawannakam* [A literature for knowledge], pp. 172–186. In explaining the new word, the author, an outstanding Thai philologist, consulted international law and used the British Empire as his model to define the meanings. Accordingly, the word *ananikhom* denotes exactly a "colony" in the modern sense, which is definitely not the notion of *prathetsarat*, or *muangkhun*, in premodern Siamese polity. But by equating the meanings of these terms since then, and given the demise of the premodern polity, the notion of *prathetsarat* has been displaced by the idea of a colony.

26. Wyatt, *Short History of Thailand*, pp. 158–161.

27. This is an assumption of Tej Bunnag, *Provincial Administration of Siam 1892–1915*. I discuss this matter later in Chapter 8 of the book.

28. Mills, *British Malaya*, p. 32.

29. Ibid., pp. 30–39.

30. *Crawfurd Papers*, pp. 38–39.

31. See James Low, "Retrospect of British Policy in the Strait of Malacca," in *BP* 5, pp.63–67; the word is from p. 65. This document specifically discusses the question of Kedah and the validity of the leases. It also refers to many other British authorities on this issue. See also Mills, *British Malaya*, p. 36.

32. *BP* 1, pp. 201, 215–216, 245–247, 257–258, 261, 299–301.

33. Mills, *British Malaya*, p. 156; Hall, *Henry Burney*, p. 155.

34. Hall, *Henry Burney*, pp. 282–283, 298, and 494–512. Here Burney explained his interpretation of the treaty against the argument by his rival British authorities at Penang.

35. See Article 12 of the Burney treaty. For more detail see Mills, *British Malaya*, pp. 150–153.

36. For the whole story see *BP* 2/6, pp. 1–35, 118–121. For an obviously pro-British view of the incident see Mills, *British Malaya*, pp. 140–162.

37. ["Western Envoys in Bangkok Period"] in *PP* 35/62, p. 152.

38. For the 1831 incident see *BP* 3, pp. 210–287; for the 1838 attempt see *BP* 3, pp. 477–530. [*Letters of Luang Udomsombat*] is a record of the 1838 incident in particular. See also Kobkua, "Dhonburi-Bangkok Political Ideology," pp. 104–105.

39. Bonney, *Kedah 1771–1821*, chap. 4.

40. Mongkut, *Phraratchahatthalekha phrabatsomdet phrachomklaochaoyuhua* [Royal correspondence of King Mongkut], pp. 65–66 and 640–641.

41. Ibid., pp. 633–640.

42. Bangkok, National Library, Manuscript Section, *Chotmaihet r. 4 ch.s. 1225* [Documents of the fourth reign 1863], no. 63, Admiral to the Phrakhlang, dated 5 October 1863.

43. Thiphakorawong, *Fourth Reign*, vol. 2, pp. 46–47.

44. Ibid., pp. 55–57.

45. Mongkut, [*Royal Correspondence*], pp. 115–116. The words "Siam" and "Viet-

nam" everywhere in this passage are translated from the words *thai* and *yuan* respectively in the original.

46. Mongkut, "Ruang phaendin khamen pen si phak" [The Cambodian realm partitioned into four parts], in *Prachum phraratchaniphon nai ratchakan thi 4 muat borankhadi* [Collected writings of King Mongkut: history section], pp. 91–93.

47. Milton Osborne and David K. Wyatt, "The Abridged Cambodian Chronicle," pp. 189–197.

48. "Phongsawadan muang saiburi" [Chronicle of Kedah], in *PP* 2/2, pp. 268–299; Sharom Ahmat, "Kedah-Siam Relations, 1821–1905," pp. 97–117.

49. Thamsook Numnonda, "Negotiations Regarding the Cession of Siamese Malay States 1907–1909," pp. 227–235.

50. Thiphakorawong, *Fourth Reign*, vol. 2, pp. 78–79, 118–119.

Chapter Five: Margin

1. See Surasakmontri, *Prawatkan khong chomphon chaophraya surasakmontri* [Autobiography of Field Marshal Chaophraya Surasakmontri], vol. 2, p. 622.

2. James McCarthy, *Surveying and Exploring in Siam*, p. 102, calls this tradition "Saesamfai," which means the same. See also [McCarthy], *An Englishman's Siamese Journal 1890–1893*, p. 186.

3. See "Phongsawadan chiangrung" and "Phongsawadan chiangkhaeng" [Chronicle of Chiang Rung and Chiang Khaeng respectively] in *PP* 9/9, for example.

4. See Chulalongkorn's letter to Prince Prachak in Natthawut Sutthisongkhram and Banchoed Inthuchanyong, *Phrachaoborommawongthoe kromluang prachaksinlapakhom* [Prince Prachaksinlapakhom], pp. 187–190.

5. Renard, "Delineation of the Kayah States," pp. 81–87.

6. "Phongsawadan muang lai" [Chronicle of Lai] in *PP* 9/9, p. 45. This chronicle was recorded by Siamese officials who interviewed Lai authorities in 1885.

7. Ibid., pp. 48–56.

8. Ibid., pp. 70–99; for Luang Phrabang and Lai, see pp. 85, 122.

9. "Phongsawadan muang thaeng" [Chronicle of Thaeng], in *PP* 9/9, was recorded on the same occasion as Lai's chronicle. It is not clear how long Thaeng had been Lai's tributary. Certainly Vietnam gave it to Lai after the latter drove the Ho away from Thaeng in the early 1870s (see pp. 50–52, 79–80). For the myth see pp. 103–113.

10. Damrong, "Chotmaihet kongthap prap ho" [Accounts of the force suppressing the Ho], in *PP* 14/24, pp. 232–234.

11. "Chotmaihet kieokap khamen lae yuan nai ratchakan thi 3" [Documents on Cambodia and Vietnam in the third reign], in *PP* 41/67, pp. 255–276.

12. "Tamnan muang phuan" [History of Phuan], in *PP* 44/70, pp. 114–130. For a detailed account of the tragedy of Phuan see Kennon Breazeale and Sanit Samuckkarn, *A Culture in Search of Survival: The Phuan of Thailand and Laos;* hereafter *Phuan*.

13. ["Documents on Cambodia and Vietnam"], in *PP* 41/67, p. 275. For a full account of Siam's depopulation of Phuan in 1827–1851 see Breazeale and Sanit, *Phuan*, chap. 1.

14. For the indigenous ideas of power and its candlelight power field see Benedict Anderson, "The Idea of Power in Javanese Culture," pp. 22–23.

15. Natthawut Sutthisongkhram, [*Prince Prachak*], p. 188.

16. This translation is taken from Winai Pongsripian, "Traditional Thai Historiog-

raphy," p. 392. The original Thai word for race here is *chat,* which can also be translated as "nation" (meaning birth, not a political unit).

17. This quotation in Thai is from Chiraporn Sathapanawatthana, *Wikrittakan r.s. 112* [The 1893 crisis], pp. 411–412; my translation. See the letter in full on pp. 405–421.

18. Damrong, *Khwamsongcham* [Recollections], pp. 246–247, 264.

19. Battye, "Military, Government, and Society in Siam," p. 121.

20. Damrong, [*Recollections*], p. 256.

21. In Thai see Surasakmontri, [*Autobiography*], especially vols. 2–4, which are accounts of the expeditions. In English see Breazeale and Sanit, *Phuan,* pp. 47–52 and passim in pt. 1; see also Andrew D. W. Forbes, "The Struggle for Hegemony in the Nineteenth Century Laos," pp. 81–88.

22. For an analysis of the sack of Luang Phrabang see Breazeale and Sanit, *Phuan,* p. 96, and Forbes, "Struggle for Hegemony," pp. 86–88.

23. See, for example, Battye, "Military, Government, and Society in Siam," p. 257.

24. Surasakmontri, [*Autobiography*], vol. 2, p. 499. In Thai, the phrase is *chatkan a- nakhet.* The word *chatkan* means manage, control, fix, tidy up; I use the verb "settle" here to convey the broad sense of the word.

25. Ibid., pp. 339–340.

26. Surasakmontri, [*Autobiography*], vol. 3, p. 13.

27. Ibid., p. 59.

28. Natthawut Sutthisongkhram, [*Prince Prachak*], pp. 190–191.

29. "Ruang kromluang prachaksinlapakhom sadet pai ratchakan na huamuang laophuan" [On Prince Prachak's mission to the Phuan region], in *PP* 46/74, pp. 195–198.

30. See Surasakmontri, [*Autobiography*], vol. 2, pp. 264, 389, and vol. 3, pp. 202– 203, 290, for example.

31. For the principal study in Thai, based on Thai documents, about the boundary disputes and resolutions on this front in particular see Nakhon Phannarong, "Kancheracha lae khotoklong rawang ratthaban sayam kap ratthaban angkrit kieokap huamuang chaidaen lannathai lae phama samai phrabatsomdet phrachunlachomklaochaoyuhua raya ph.s. 2428–2438" [Negotiations and agreements between the Siamese and British governments concerning the frontier towns between Lanna and Burma in the reign of King Chulalongkorn during 1885–1895]. In English, see Sao Saimuang Mangrai, *Shan States and the British Annexation,* chap. 10, which is based mostly on English documents.

32. Renard, "Delineation of Kayah States," p. 90; Sao Saimuang Mongrai, *Shan States,* p. 227; and Nakhon, ["Negotiations and Agreements"], pp. 314–326.

33. Renard, "Delineation of Kayah States," p. 90.

34. Sao Saimuang Mangrai, *Shan States,* pp. 229–231.

35. Ibid., p. 233.

36. Ibid., pp. 233–234; Renard, "Delineation of Kayah States," pp. 90–92; and Nakhon, ["Negotiations and Agreements"], pp. 208–213.

37. See Chandran Jeshuran, "The Anglo-French Declaration of January 1896 and the Independence of Siam," pp. 105–126.

38. Battye, "Military, Government, and Society in Siam," chap. 4.

39. Ibid., p. 315; Chandran Jeshuran, "The Anglo-French Declaration."

40. Chandran Jeshuran, "The Anglo-French Declaration," pp. 108–111.

41. Chaiyan Rajchagool, "The Social and State Formation in Siam 1855–1932," pp. 24–28.

42. Nakhon, ["Negotiations and Agreements"], pp. 210–211; Amphorn Tangseri, "Withesobai khong phrabatsomdet phrachunlachomklaochaoyuhua thimito maha-amnat yurop" [King Chulalongkorn's foreign policy toward the European powers], pp. 19–20.

43. Breazeale and Sanit, *Phuan,* p. 93.

44. Auguste Pavie, *Mission Pavie Indochine 1879–1895,* vol. 1, p. 194.

45. Ibid., vol. 6, pp. 111, 127, 135, 142.

46. Forbes, "Struggle for Hegemony," p. 88.

47. Pavie, *Mission Pavie,* vol. 6, p. 114.

48. Ibid., vol. 7, p. 270.

49. Surasakmontri, [*Autobiography*], vol. 4, pp. 154–172, especially pp. 155–159; see also Pavie, *Mission Pavie,* vol. 1, pp. 245–246, 288–289, 290, and Chiraporn, [*The 1893 Crisis*], pp. 61–66.

50. Orawan Nopdara, "Kanprapprung kanpokkhrong lae khwamkhatyaeng kap farangset nai monthon udon rawang ph.s. 2436–2453" [The reform of administration and conflicts with France in Udon Province during 1893–1910], p. 118.

51. See a firsthand account of the incident in Phra Narongwichit [Luan na Nakhon], *Chotmaihet r.s. 112* [Notes on the year 1893].

Chapter Six: Mapping

1. Larry Sternstein and John Black, "A Note on Three Polo Maps," pp. 347–349.

2. Paul Wheatley, *The Golden Khersonese,* pt. 2; R. H. Phillimore, "An Early Map of the Malay Peninsula," pp. 175–178; or Salwidhannidhes, "Study of Early Cartography in Thailand," pp. 81–89.

3. R. T. Fell, *Early Maps of South-East Asia,* pp. 71, 73.

4. For the history of cartography, basically European mapmaking, see Leo Bagrow, *History of Cartography.*

5. Fell, *Early Maps of South-East Asia,* pp. 72–75.

6. *Crawfurd Papers,* pp. 9, 11, 71–72. The map of the Chao Phraya channel provoked the court to protest to the British resident at Penang, because the map was regarded as dangerous to the security of the palace. See "Thut farang samai krung rattanakosin" [Western envoys in the Bangkok period], in *PP* 34/62, pp. 254–256.

7. *BP* 1, p. 58.

8. John Crawfurd, *Journal of an Embassy from the Governor-General of India to the Courts of Siam and Cochin China,* vol. 2, p. 199.

9. Edward Said, *Orientalism,* pp. 216–219.

10. Larry Sternstein, " 'Low' Maps of Siam," pp. 132–156; and "Low's Description of the Siamese Empire in 1824," pp. 9–34.

11. Sternstein, " 'Low' Maps of Siam," pp. 138–144; the quotation is from p. 138.

12. See the map in Sir John Bowring, *The Kingdom and People of Siam,* vol. 1.

13. Francis Garnier, *La Cochinchine francaise en 1864.*

14. Salmon, *Modern History or the Present State of All Nations,* vol. 1, which was written about 1724. The map of Southeast Asia in that book was drawn by a famous mapmaker, Herman Moll. For more examples of European-made maps of Siam before Garnier's "discovery" of the great bend of the Mekhong, see several travelers' accounts such as Simon de la Loubere, *The Kingdom of Siam;* John Crawfurd's *History of the Indian Archi-*

pelago (1820) and *A Descriptive Dictionary of the Indian Islands and Adjacent Countries* (1856); J. H. Moor, *Notices of the Indian Archipelago and Adjacent countries* (1837); F. A. Neale, *Narrative of a Residence at the Capital of the Kingdom of Siam* (1852). Sternstein also offers an excellent account of Captain Low's attempts in 1824 and 1830 to study the region's geography and produce the maps; for sketches of the maps see his " 'Low' Maps of Siam" and "Low's Description of the Siamese Empire in 1824."

15. See, for example, Crawfurd, *Journal of an Embassy*, vol. 2, pp. 214–215, and Bowring, *Kingdom and People of Siam*, vol. 1, pp. 1–4.

16. See ["Western Envoys in the Bangkok Period"] in *PP* 34/62, pp. 254–256.

17. *BP* 1, pp. 199–200.

18. Thiphakorawong, *Fourth Reign*, vol. 1, pp. 136–137, 140.

19. Bangkok, National Library, Manuscript Section, *Chotmaihet r. 4 ch.s. 1226–1230* [Documents of the fourth reign 1864–1868].

20. Sternstein, " 'Low' Maps of Siam," p. 145. Thiphakorawong, *Fourth Reign*, vol. 2, pp. 99–100, mentions the name in Thai as *"Doichok";* Sternstein is able to confirm that he was a Dutchman named Duysart (see n. 12 of his article).

21. Natthawut Sutthisongkhram, *Somdetchaophraya borommahasisuriyawong akkharamaha senabodi* [Sisuriyawong: the great minister], vol. 2, pp. 158–159.

22. Maha-ammattayathibodi (Seng), "Kamnoet kantham phaenthi nai prathetthai" [The birth of mapping in Thailand], pp. 1–2.

23. Ibid., pp. 2–3. For a brief biography of McCarthy see pp. 43–48.

24. For an example of the triangulation chart for Siam from the Indian Triangulation Eastern Frontier Series, see McCarthy, *Surveying and Exploring*, preceding chap. 1.

25. For more details of these projects see McCarthy, *Surveying and Exploring*.

26. Maha-ammattayathibodi, ["The birth of Mapping"], pp. 6, 14–15; and McCarthy, *Surveying and Exploring*, preface and pp. 1–3, 117.

27. [McCarthy], *An Englishman's Siamese Journal 1890–1893*, pp. 2–3. The publisher does not give the author's name, but it is stated on the first page that the book is an unabridged reprint of *Report of a Survey in Siam*, published anonymously in London and circulated in 1895. The content is almost identical with McCarthy, *Surveying and Exploring*, which was published later. Thus I retain the title of the reprint for the sake of reference while identifying the author as McCarthy.

28. See "The Royal Survey Department Siam: A Retrospect," p. 19.

29. Ibid., p. 20; Maha-ammattayathibodi, ["The Birth of Mapping"], pp. 5, 8; and "Phatthanakan dan kansuksa nai rongrian phaenthi" [The development of education in the mapping school], an article in Royal Thai Survey Department, *Thiraluk khroprop wansathapana 100 pi kromphaenthi thahan 2528* [Commemoration volume for the centenary of the foundation of the Royal Thai Survey Department 1985], p. 293. Yet all of these sources give very few details about the courses.

30. David Wyatt, *Politics of Reform in Thailand*, pp. 110, 115, n. 356, in which the name of the school appears as the "School of Royal Survey Department" but without any account of it. Warunee Osatharom, "Kansuksa nai sangkhomthai ph.s. 2411–2475" [Education in Thai society 1868–1932], one of the best studies on the history of modern education in Thailand, does not say a word about it either.

31. For a brief but helpful record of the history of the department see "Retrospect" (see note 28 above). The author of this document was probably Ronald W. Giblin, who headed the department during 1901–1909. The only writing about the history of the

department is the [*Commemoration Volume*], an official history whose information is, unfortunately, not helpful.

32. Tej Bunnag, *Provincial Administration of Siam 1892–1915,* pp. 1–2.

33. Examples of this system can be found in the case of those Lao towns which became the northeastern region of Thailand; see "Phongsawadan huamuang isan" [History of the northeastern towns] in *PP* 3/4, especially pp. 359–360, 363–364, and 394–395, for some explicit cases. See also Toem Wiphakphotchanakit, *Prawattisat isan* [History of the northeast]; and Orawan Nopdara, "Kanprapprung kanpokkhrong lae khwamkhatyaeng kap farangset nai monthon udon rawang ph.s. 2436–2453" [The reform of administration and conflicts with France in Udon Province during 1893–1910], pp. 118–122.

34. Orawan Nopdara, ["Reform in Udon Province"], pp. 127, 176–180.

35. ["History of the Northeastern Towns"], p. 370.

36. Chiraporn Sathapanawatthana, [The 1893 crisis], pp. 41–46, 67.

37. McCarthy, *Surveying and Exploring,* pp. 18–77. The dates of this mission given by Chiraporn, [*The 1893 Crisis*], pp. 44–45, are incorrect.

38. Surasakmontri, [*Autobiography*], vol. 2, p. 332.

39. Ibid., vol. 3, p. 234.

40. Battye, "Military, Government, and Society in Siam," pp. 319–350. He argues that the Siamese rulers at that time were men of a new generation. Educated in Western fashion, they were men of principle who sought to be treated equally with their European counterparts and refused to be intimidated. They had a firm conviction that the territories belonged to them since Siam was the immediate suzerain. So they prepared to fight for principle and territory. Despite his awareness of the ambiguous border, Chulalongkorn was resolved that he must reaffirm his dignity by all possible means including force. The strong will of these rather idealistic and impetuous young men in attempting to reform the traditional establishments rapidly, and to uphold the grandeur of their country in the international arena, was not, however, accompanied by commensurate strength. Siam was not well prepared militarily or politically. The Siamese army was in poor fighting shape. The infantry, stationed mainly in Bangkok with only "scattered units" in the outlying provinces, was in its infancy; the artillery as well as the cavalry were designed for ceremonies, not wars; the navy, whose officers were mostly Danes, was not prepared for war either. The army was in a transitional phase, moving from a traditional corvée force to a professional one, and the introduction of the latter was at that point largely for ceremonial purposes. Moreover, most of the fighting forces were war captives, ethnic peoples who had once fought against Siam but were defeated. The peasant masses still knew only the antique mode of warfare and weaponry and were ignorant of patriotic or anticolonial war. The conflict with France was over the retention of areas most of them had never heard of. In Battye's words, "from top to bottom, anachronism pervaded the military preparation of Siam against France" (p. 340).

41. McCarthy, *Surveying and Exploring,* pp. 72–73.

42. Henri Mouhot, *Travels in the Central Parts of Indo-China (Siam), Cambodia, and Laos.*

43. For an excellent account of this tragic expedition see Milton Osborne, *River Road to China: The Mekhong River Expedition 1866–1873.*

44. Surasakmontri, [*Autobiography*], vol. 2, p. 470.

45. Ibid., pp. 468–470; Pavie, *Mission Pavie,* vol. 1, pp. 199–200, 246; vol. 2, p. 101; vol. 6, p. 113; and Chiraporn, [*The 1893 Crisis*], pp. 28–29.

46. Pavie, *Mission Pavie*, vol. 6, p. 37.

47. See Surasakmontri, *[Autobiography]*, vol. 2, pp. 365–372, for the request and reply. The quoted statements are on pp. 372 and 365 respectively.

48. Quoted in Breazeale and Sanit, *Phuan*, p. 74.

49. Surasakmontri, *[Autobiography]*, vol. 4, pp. 154–155.

50. Pavie, *Mission Pavie*, vol. 7, p. 46, and vol.6, pp. 51–52.

51. Summarized from "Retrospect," pp. 20–23.

52. Pavie reported that Surasakmontri had McCarthy's map with him for the argument. For an unspecified reason, however, Surasakmontri did not unfold it. See Pavie, *Mission Pavie*, vol. 7, p. 67.

53. George N. Curzon, "The Siamese Boundary Question," pp. 34–55.

54. At the time I wrote my dissertation, I had not seen McCarthy's original map either. So I discussed at length why the 1985 reproduction is definitely not the 1887 map but one from 1899 or even later; see Thongchai Winichakul, "Siam Mapped." (Dissertation), pp. 297–308. For the information, and a reproduction of the map from the British Museum, thanks to Andrew Turton and Kennon Breazeale.

55. His map and address were published in *Proceedings of the Royal Geographic Society*, new series 10 (March 1888): 117–134; the map is facing p. 188.

56. Chiraporn, *[The 1893 Crisis]*, pp. 47–49; Pavie, *Mission Pavie*, vol. 1, p. 224.

57. Chiraporn, *[The 1893 Crisis]*, pp. 72, 77–81, 92–93, 119–128; Pavie, *Mission Pavie*, vol. 1, p. 325; vol. 2, pp. 86, 214.

58. For example, see Surasakmontri, *[Autobiography]*, vol. 2, p. 444. On one occasion in early 1886, Surasakmontri complained that the map made by the Survey Department was too small and too crude: "It can't be used for the movement of troops. It is merely an estimate map."

59. Breazeale and Sanit, *Phuan*, pp. 74, 89–92, 95–98, 116.

60. [McCarthy], *An Englishman's Siamese Journal*, is an account of his work during 1890–1893 in particular; see pp. 146–147 of that book or p. 175 of his *Surveying and Exploring* for the order from Bangkok giving details of the areas in which modern boundaries were to be worked out. A triangulation chart of this frontier is included in *Surveying and Exploring*, preceding chap. 1.

Chapter Seven: Geo-Body

1. "Retrospect," p. 23. Perhaps this is the original of the 1985 reproduction which claims to be McCarthy's 1887 map.

2. See map 8 accompanying the booklet [Development of mapping in Thailand] or fig. 6.18 of my dissertation, "Siam Mapped."

3. For details of the agreements of particular boundaries between Siam and British Burma, Siam and French Indochina, and Siam and British Malaya, see J. R. V. Prescott, *Map of Mainland Asia by Treaty*, pp. 382–408, 418–446, and *Frontiers of Asia and Southeast Asia*, pp. 54–59.

4. *[Development of Mapping in Thailand]*, pp. 8–9.

5. Robert Sack, *Human Territoriality*, p. 74.

6. Ben Anderson, *Imagined Communities*, pp. 131–132.

7. J. R. V. Prescott, *Boundaries and Frontiers*, chap. 1.

8. Thepphasatsathit, *Phumisat lem 1* [Geography book I], p. 95.

9. Salwidhannidhes, *Tamra phichika-phumisat* [A text on physical geography].

10. Clifford Geertz, "The Integrative Revolution," pp. 105–157.

11. Shelley Errington, "The Place of Regalia in Luwu," p. 228.

12. *Ramakian*, vol. 2, p. 73.

13. Khachorn Sukhabhanij, *Khomun prawattisat samai bangkok* [Historical accounts of the Bangkok period], p. 252.

14. Eiji Murashima, "The Origin of Modern Official State Ideology in Thailand," pp. 80–96; Kullada Kesboonchoo, "Official Nationalism Under King Chulalongkorn"; and "Official Nationalism Under King Vajiravudh," pp. 107–120. For the concept of official nationalism see Anderson, *Imagined Communities*, chap. 7.

15. It is interesting to note here that the word more commonly used is *prathetchat*. But the present king of Thailand, Bhumiphol, in many of his speeches, prefers the word *chatprathet*.

16. Pallegoix, *Dictionarium*, pp. 129, 175–176. See also Pallegoix, *Siamese French English Dictionary*, pp. 178, 192–193, respectively, which is virtually the same except that the last two entries are omitted.

17. Bradley, *Nangsu akkharaphithansap: Dictionary of the Siamese Language*, pp. 798, 806; my translation.

18. Prasert-aksonnit et al., *Photchananukrom lamdap lae plae sap thichai nai nangsu thai* [Dictionary of vocabularies used in Thai literature], pp. 579, 584; my translation.

19. Samuel J. Smith, *A Comprehensive Anglo-Siamese Dictionary*, p. 1028.

20. Ibid., p. 90; my translation.

21. Somdet Phra Wannarat, *Sangkhitiyawong* [Chronicle of the Buddhist councils], pp. 370, 381.

22. See *Phraratchaphongsawadan chabap phraratchahatthalekha* [The royal chronicle: Royal Autograph recension], vol. 1, p. 226; *Phraratchaphongsawadan krung si-ayutthaya chabap phan chanthanumat* [The royal chronicle of Ayudhya: Phan Chanthanumat recension], vol. 1 (*PP* 38/64), p. 174; *Phraratchaphongsawadan krung si-ayutthaya chabap chakkraphatdiphong (chat)* [The royal chronicle of Ayudhya: Chakkraphatdiphong (Chat) recension], vol. 1, p. 170; and *Phraratchaphongsawadan krung si-ayutthaya chabap phra phanarat* [The royal chronicle of Ayudhya: Phra Phanarat recension], p. 140.

23. Thawi Muktharakosa, *Phramahathiraratchao* [King Vajiravudh], p. 593.

24. David Morell and Chai-anan Samudavanija, *Political Conflict in Thailand*, pp. 244–246; John S. Girling, *Thailand: Society and Politics*, pp. 211–214.

Chapter Eight: Geo-Body and History

1. Chandran Jeshuran, "The Anglo-French Declaration of January 1896 and the Independence of Siam," pp. 108–111.

2. Battye, "Military, Government, and Society in Siam," p. 369.

3. Ibid., p. 376.

4. See the full poem with translation in James N. Mosel, "A Poetic Translation from the Siamese: Prince Damrong's Reply in Verse to Rama V," pp. 103–111.

5. Battye, "Military, Government, and Society in Siam," p. 396.

6. In the case of Thai history, a typical approach is that of Nithi Aeusrivongse, *Prawattisat rattanakosin nai phraratchaphongsawadan ayutthaya* [Bangkok's history in the royal chronicles of Ayudhya].

7. For the continuity/break of that time see David Wyatt, "The 'Subtle Revolution' of King Rama I of Siam," pp. 9–52; Nithi Aeusrivongse, *Pakkai lae bairua* [A quill and a sail], especially the article "Watthanatham kradumphi nai samai ton rattanakosin" [Bour-

geois culture in the early Bangkok period]; see also Klaus Wenk, *The Restoration of Thailand Under Rama I 1782–1809.* For the urgent need to relieve the tension see Craig Reynolds, "Religious Historical Writing and the Legitimation of the First Bangkok Reign," pp. 90–107.

8. Craig Reynolds, "The Plot of Thai History: Theory and Practice," pp. 318–325.

9. Rong Sayamanonda, *A History of Thailand,* pp. 135ff.

10. Khachorn Sukhabhanij, *Khomun prawattisat samai bangkok* [Historical accounts of the Bangkok period], pp. 240–244.

11. Among the best-known books in Thai are Chiraporn, [The 1893 crisis], and Suwit Thirasasawat, *Khwamsamphan thai-farangset r.s. 112–126: kansiadindaen fangkhwa maenamkhong* [Franco-Thai relations 1893–1907: the loss of the right bank of the Mekhong]. The same plot and story become conventional in school textbooks; for example, see Pharadi Mahakhan, *Prawattisat thai samaimai* [History of modern Thailand], pp. 164–165.

12. Wyatt, *A Short History,* pp. 201–208; the quotation is from p. 204.

13. Ibid., pp. 203–204, my emphasis; later in this chapter I will discuss how words can direct our point of view and create sentimental effects.

14. Khachorn Sukhabhanij, [*Historical Accounts of Bangkok Period*], p. 244.

15. Prince Damrong and Phraya Rajasena, *Thesaphiban* [The *thesaphiban* system of provincial administration], p. 7.

16. Tej Bunnag, *Provincial Administration of Siam 1892–1915,* p. v.

17. Ibid., pp. 17–19.

18. Ibid., p. 249.

19. Most research in this tradition is found in M.A. theses in various universities in Thailand. Examples are in Wutthichai Munlasin, ed., *Monthon thesaphiban: wikhroh priapthiap* [The *thesaphiban* provincial administration: comparative analysis].

20. Tej Bunnag, "Kanpokkhrong baep thesaphiban pen rabop patiwat ru wiwatthanakan" [Was the *thesaphiban* provincial administration a revolution or evolution?].

21. Tej Bunnag, *Provincial Administration,* p. 261; my emphasis. The passage is the final paragraph of the book.

22. Tej Bunnag, *Khabot r.s. 121* [The 1902 rebellions].

23. Khachorn Sukhabhanij, [*Historical Accounts of Bangkok Period*], pp. 232–233.

24. Edward Said, *Orientalism,* pp. 213–216; the quotation is on p. 213. For Lord Curzon's highly noted role in British colonialism see Chandran Jeshuran, *The Contest for Siam 1889–1902.*

25. Both Chiraporn, [*The 1893 Crisis*], and Suwit, [*Franco-Thai Relations*], utilize the article and map in their arguments as if they were anticolonial materials or statements in sympathy with Siam. Besides, when they refer to this map, Curzon's use of thick colored lines, which represent the approximation of boundary lines in different interpretations, are replaced by dots and dashes (·······-·). Perhaps the colored lines seem to them casual or unconvincing; the cartographic convention is necessary to make the map look scientific and academic.

26. As Ben Anderson has put it, the images of the Siamese monarchs tended to appear alongside other popular nationalist leaders of Siam's neighbors; see "Studies of the Thai State: The State of Thai Studies," p. 198.

27. See Thamrongsak Phetlert-anan, "Kanriakrong dindaen khun ph.s. 2483" [Demand for the return of territories in 1940], pp. 28–65.

28. Thamsook Numnonda, *Thailand and the Japanese Presence 1941–1945,* chap. 2.

29. Ibid; see Thak Chaloemtiarana, ed., *Thai Politics: Extracts and Documents 1932–1957*, chap. 2, for translations of various government documents on this matter.

30. E. Thadeus Flood, "The 1940 Franco-Thai Border Dispute and Phibuun Songkhraam's Commitment to Japan," pp. 304–325.

31. This map is taken from Thongbai Taengnoi, *Phaenthi phumisat prayok matthayom-suksa tonton lae tonplai* [Geographical atlas for junior and senior high school], p. 39. Sternstein translates the title of this map as "Evolution of the Boundary of Thailand" and gives the date of the original as 1940; see "A Catalogue of Maps of Thailand in the Museum of the Royal Thai Survey Department, Bangkok," p. 56. In fact, the earlier version of this map was produced in 1935 with significant differences from later ones; see the map in Thamrongsak, ["Demand for Return of Territories"], p. 54. But it is the 1940 version that became popular.

32. See Thamrongsak, ["Demand for Return of Territories"], pp. 51–62, and map pp. 54, 56; see also Phayont Thimcharoen, "Naewphromdaen rawang sayam kap indochin khong farangset" [The boundaries between Siam and French Indochina], p. 26.

33. See Minton Goldman, "Franco-British Rivalry over Siam," p. 226.

34. See Wyatt, *A Short History*, p. 207. See also D. G. E. Hall, *A History of South East Asia*, p. 729.

35. Sir Josiah Crosby, *Siam: The Crossroads*, pp. 113–114. Flood, "The 1940 Franco-Thai Border Dispute," tells a slightly different story: he says that Crosby was sympathetic to Siam's request but could not lend official sympathy to Siam because of American influence on British policy on this issue.

36. Konthi Supphamongkol, *Kanwithesobai khong thai* [Thai foreign policy], p. 24.

37. Ibid. For the role of this man, Vanit Pananonda, and the pro-Japanese faction in Phibuun's regime see Flood, "The 1940 Franco-Thai Border Dispute," pp. 312–313, 317, and 322–324, and Thamsook Numnonda, *Thailand and Japanese Presence*, pp. 115–116 and passim in chaps. 1 and 3. For the Japanese account of this man see Benjamin Batson and Shimizu Hajime, eds., *The Tragedy of Wanit*.

38. Royal Thai Survey Department, [Development of mapping in Thailand], pp. 13–14. Again, however, the illustrations are from Thongbai Taengnoi, [*Geographical Atlas*], pp. 27, 29, 31, 33, 35, 37, respectively, which are virtually the same as the 1935–1936 originals.

39. Larry Sternstein, "An Historical Atlas of Thailand," p. 7; Sternstein's emphasis, despite the term "an" in the title of his article. It should be noted that his study does not include the first map on my list. Thus there are only *five* maps in his study though officially it is a set of six.

40. But Sternstein's approach to these maps as "the physical condition and political situation of mainland Southeast Asia" leads him to put the title of each map in plural terms as "Kingdoms and Cities at the Time of . . ."

41. Royal Thai Survey Department, [*Development of Mapping*], p. 13, indicates that in the 1935 original it was called "the kingdom of Nongsae," believed to be the name of the capital of Nanchao. In Sternstein's articles, however, the map is specified as the kingdom in the reign of Ko-lo-feng, a Nanchao king, A.D. 748.

42. In the 1986 edition of Thongbai's atlas, p. 31, the date of this reign on the map is changed to B.E. [Buddhist Era] 1822–1843 (1279–1300) according to recent historical knowledge. But he does not update his text on p. 30 opposite the map.

43. Sternstein, "Historical Atlas," p. 20.

44. Somkiat Wanthana, "The Politics of Modern Thai Historiography," p. 341.

45. Sternstein makes this remark and suggests that because of this deficiency each map should be considered separately; see "Historical Atlas," p. 7. I will argue that the efficiency of the maps lies in their totality as a set, not as individual maps.

46. For his plays see Pra-onrat Buranamat, *Luang wichitwathakan kap lakhon prawattisat* [Luang Wichitwathakan and historical plays], especially chap. 4. The following description of Luang Wichit's plays comes mainly from this source. For his historical writings see Kobkua Suwannathat-phian, "Kankhian prawattisat baep chatniyom: phitcharana luang wichitwathakan" [Nationalist historiography: considering Luang Wichitwathakan], pp. 149–180; and Charnvit Kasetsiri, "Thai Historiography from Ancient Times to the Modern Period," pp. 156–170. For an excellent study of Luang Wichit's historical view see Somkiat Wanthana, *Politics of Historiography*, chap. 4. For some songs and their English translation see Thak Chaloemtiarana, ed., *Thai Politics*, pp. 317–322. Many songs have been deployed in military actions, either in peacetime or in a coup.

47. "Phra naresuan prakat itsaraphap" [King Naresuan declares independence], in Luang Wichitwathakan, *Wichitsan* [Selected works of Luang Wichitwathakan], vol. 1, p. 125.

48. None of the Thai chronicles mentions this attack. The Burmese chronicles do, but they say it was unsuccessful. Luang Wichit's play omits the details and outcome of the attack.

49. As Pra-onrat regards this episode as the climax of the play, she criticizes the author for not making the declaration of independence the climax (see [*Luang Wichit and Historical Plays*], p. 168). In my view, this episode is merely an additional miracle; the miraculous moment of declaration of independence is indeed the climax of the play.

50. Pra-onrat, [*Luang Wichit and Historical Plays*], pp. 171–178.

51. Ibid., pp. 207–212.

52. Ibid., pp. 79–80.

53. Edmund Leach, *Genesis as Myth and Other Essays*, p. 9.

54. King Chulalongkorn, "Samakhom supsuan khongboran nai prathetsayam" [The Antiquarian Society in Siam], pp. 45–46; the full text is on pp. 42–46.

55. Damrong, "Laksana kanpokkhrong prathetsayam tae boran" [The Siamese government in ancient times], p. 6.

56. This anachronistic historical perspective may also be true for other nations' pasts and heroes, such as Pagan in Anoratha's and Kyansittha's time, and Lan Sang in Saiyasettha's period.

57. Thongchai Winichakul, "Phurai nai prawattisat thai: karani phra mahathammaracha" [Villain in Thai history—the case of King Mahathammaracha of Ayudhya] pp. 173–196.

58. This phrase is the title of one of the most powerful and best-known works of modern Thai historical literature. First written by Damrong in 1917, the title as published in *PP*, pt. 6, was "Phongsawadan ruang rao rop phama" [Chronicle of our war with Burma]. Then in the 1920 reprint, the word *rao* (we) was changed to *Thai* (see *PP* 5/6, 6/6, 7/6). In later reprints it is known just as *Thai rop phama* [The Thai fought Burma]. The theme and the structuring of the past in this light were introduced in 1911 by Damrong as well; see *Sadaeng banyai phongsawadan sayam* [Lectures on Siam's history].

59. See Lorraine Gesick, *In the Land of Lady White Blood: Southern Thailand and the*

Meaning of History, an exciting ethnographic history, a journey into the domain of a local past which scientific, national history cannot suppress completely. I have also sketched the terrain in which another inquiry may be undertaken to explore the emergence of the new kind of past in a fashion similar as to geography in this book. See Thongchai Winichakul, "Siam Mapped," (Dissertation), pp. 333–338.

Conclusion: Geo-Body, History, and Nationhood

1. Edmund Leach, "The Frontiers of Burma," pp. 49–51.

2. [McCarthy], *An Englishman's Siamese Journal 1890–1893,* pp. 185–186; and *Surveying and Exploring,* pp. 101–102.

3. Chiraporn, [*The 1893 Crisis*], pp. 316–318.

4. Ibid., p. 318; see also Piyachat Pitawan, *Rabopphrai nai sangkhomthai ph.s. 2411–2453* [The Phrai system in Thai society 1868–1910], pp. 72, 75, 133–136.

5. Piyachat, [*The Phrai System*], pp. 145–156.

6. Toem Wiphakphotchanakit, *Prawattisat isan* [History of the northeast], vol. 2, p. 531. Toem did not specify the year of this order, though it is indirectly suggested that it was after 1899. Chiraporn, [*The 1893 Crisis*], p. 319, who quotes from Toem, suggests that it was ordered in the years immediately after the 1893 crisis. No primary source is mentioned in either study.

7. Thak Chaloemtiarana, ed., *Thai Politics,* pp. 246–247.

8. Charles F. Keyes, *Isan: Regionalism in Northeastern Thailand,* pp. 2–3, 60–61.

9. See David Streckfuss, "Creating 'The Thai': The Emergence of Indigenous Nationalism in Non-colonial Siam 1850–1980." A revised version is forthcoming by the Center for Southeast Asian Studies, University of Wisconsin-Madison.

10. This is believed to be a major problem of Thai historical scholarship even today; see Winai Pongsripian, ed., *Panha nai prawattisatthai* [Problems in Thai history], p. 3.

11. H. L. Shorto, "A Mon Genealogy of Kings," p. 64.

12. Khachorn Sukhabhanij, "Thanandon phrai" [The Phrai Status], pp. 69, 71. The essay was first published in 1960 and reprinted many times as a classic piece of Thai history. In fact, he gave the English title of this essay as "Freeman Status," with the explanation in the text why the *phrai* was not a serf but a free man. The Marxist narrative at which he aimed his critique was Jit Phoumisak, *Chomna sakdina thai nai patchuban,* first published in 1957; see Craig J. Reynolds, *Thai Radical Discourse: The Real Face of Thai Feudalism Today.*

13. Khachorn, "Thanandon phrai," p. 90.

14. From the introduction of the 1976 reprint of "Thanandon phrai."

15. Vella, *Chaiyo!,* pp. 29–31.

16. The whole quotation is taken from John S. Girling, *Thailand: Society and Politics,* p. 215, which is translated from *Sayamchotmaihet,* 2–8 December 1976.

17. Likhit Dhiravegin, "Nationalism and the State in Thailand."

18. Figure 20 comes from *Inside Asia* 7 (Feb.–Mar. 1986): 15; the photograph was taken by Conrad Taylor.

19. Charles F. Keyes, "The Case of the Purloined Lintel," pp. 261–292.

20. See Chawi-ngam Macharoen, *Thong thai* [Thai flags].

21. Chamun Amondarunarak [Chaem Sunthornwet], *Phraratchakaraniyakit samkhan nai phrabatsomdet phramongkutklaochaoyuhua* [The significant contributions of King Vajiravudh], vol. 6, pp. 8–30.

22. See the numerous documents about the annual celebration of the constitution in many provinces during 1935–1936 in the National Archives, Ministry of Interior *(Mo. Tho.)*, 2.2.13/2 and 2.2.13/7; 5.14/1 and 5.14/49. In one instance, it was placed on top of the replica of the mountain that traditionally represented Mount Meru.

23. Khru ngoen [pseud.], *Phlengthai tamnaiprawat* [Thai songs: historical background], pp. 1–22.

24. Fine Arts Department, comp., *Khamchichaeng ruang kanchai phleng kiattiyot lae kret khwamru ruang dontri thai* [Guideline for the use of honorable songs and miscellaneous knowledge of Thai music], pp. 1–2.

25. See Chawi-ngam, [*Thai Flags*], pp. 9–17, for a list of all acts and official regulations concerning the national flags including full details of the latest regulation revised in December 1976, shortly after the October massacre, "to increase awareness of the symbol of the country."

26. For this information, I am indebted to David Streckfuss who is currently doing research on the discourse of national security.

Glossary

BECAUSE this book involves the changing meanings of terms, the definitions given below include, if relevant, the present meaning, the literal meaning *(lit.),* and/or the traditional *(trad.)* use.

adharma	Evil, bad, villain
ana-	Power, authority
anachak	Kingdom; *lit.,* the royal power
anakhet	Territory, areas under control of a power, boundary; *lit.,* the limited domain of power
ananikhom	Colony
baht	*Trad.,* a traditional unit of measurement of time, equal to six minutes; 10 *baht* = 1 *mong* (hour)
banmuang	Country; *lit.,* village-town
Bunga mas (Malay)	Gold and silver tree, as a token of submission; *lit.,* golden tree
cakravatin (Sanskrit)	The Universal Monarch (in the Buddhist concept of kingship)
chaomuang	Ruler or governor of a town; *lit.,* lord of a town
chat	Nation, country; *lit.* and *trad.,* birth, commonality by birth, nature or characteristic by birth
chatprathet	Nation, country
Chomputhawip	The southern continent in the Hindu-Buddhist cosmology where human beings live
daen	Area, domain
Dawadung	The level of heaven in the Hindu-Buddhist cosmology where Sakka or Indra resides
dharma (Sanskrit)	Virtue, good
dindaen	Territory, area
ekkalak	Identity, common characteristic
ekkarat	Independence; *trad.,* the supreme king, second to none
farang	Westerners
hon	Astrologer
huamuang	Provincial towns; *trad.,* dependencies within the kingdom

203

itsaraphap	Independence; *trad.,* supreme power, supreme status, overlordship
khaek	Peoples of the Malay, South Asian (Indian, Pakistani, Bengali, Sri Lankan), and Middle Eastern (Arab, Persian, and others) ethnicities; Muslim
khanthasima	Territory, domain of power
khet	Limit of a domain or area, line, boundary
khetdaen	Boundary, limit, limited domain
khopkhanthasima	Limited territory, limited domain of power
khopkhet	Limit, boundary, line, limitation
khwampenthai	Thainess
krung	City, metropolis
Krungthep	Bangkok; *lit.,* city of angel or deity
lipda	A traditional unit of measurement for an angle, equal to one minute; 60 *philipda* = 1 *lipda,* 60 *lipda* = 1 *ongsa*
lok	Earth, world, globe
mong	A traditional unit of measurement of time, equal to one hour
muang	Town, city, country; a generic term for governed spatial units
muangkhun	Vassal, tributary township, dependency, now also meaning a colony
naga	The mythical water serpent living in the oceans or underworld
nat	Indigenous spirits or supernatural beings in Mon and Burmese culture
ongsa	A traditional unit of measurement for an angle, equal to a degree; 1 *ongsa* = 60 *lipda*
phaenthi	Map
phama	Burma, Burman, Burmese
philip (philipda)	A traditional unit of measurement for an angle, equal to one second; 60 *philipda* = 1 *lipda*
phongsawadan	Chronicle
phrai	Serf, serfdom, a kind of bondage in traditional Thai society
phum	Land, soil, world, space, domain
phumanithet	*Trad.,* geography; *lit.,* describing the land or world; no present use
phumisat	Geography (in all senses); *lit.,* science of the land or world
prathet	Nation, country; *trad.,* area, site; a generic term for any unspecified land with no indication of power or limit
prathetchat	Nation, country
prathetsarat	Tributary kingship and kingdom
samfaifa	Tributary under many overlords; *lit.,* under three skies (lords)
sangha (Pali)	The Buddhist order
Sayam	Siam
sima	The sanctuary stone marking a consecrated area
songfaifa	Tributary under many overlords; *lit.,* under two skies (lords)
Songkran	Thai New Year's Day in mid-April
suai	Tribute
sumsam	Careless

Suwannaphum	The name used in the past for the areas of mainland Southeast Asia today; *lit.*, golden land
tamkon farang	Tag along behind the Westerners
tamnan	Legend, myth, story about the past
then	Sham monk
thesaphiban	The name of the new provincial administrative systems in Siam from the 1890s onward; *lit.*, protection or control over territory
thewada	Deity, angel
Traiphum	The three-world cosmography; *lit.*, three worlds
Yuan	Vietnam, Vietnamese (a commonly used but not official term in Thai because it is pejorative)

Bibliography

Adisak Thongbun. "Wan witthayasat haeng chat kap phrabida haeng witthayasat thai" [National Science Day and the father of Thai science]. *Warasan ratchabanditsathan* [Journal of the Royal Institute] 9, no. 4 (July–Sept. 1984): 3–4.

Ahmat, Sharom. "Kedah-Siam Relations 1821–1905." *Journal of the Siam Society* 59, pt. 1 (Jan. 1971): 97–117.

Akin Rabibhadana. *The Organization of Thai Society in the Early Bangkok Period, 1782–1873.* Southeast Asia Program, Data Paper 74. Ithaca: Cornell University, 1969.

Alabaster, Henry. *The Modern Buddhist: Being the Views of a Siamese Minister of State on His Own and Other Religions.* London: Trubner & Co., 1870.

Alkire, William H. "Concepts of Order in Southeast Asia and Micronesia." *Comparative Studies in Society and History* 14 (1972): 484–493.

Amondarunarak, Chamun [Chaem Sunthornwet]. *Phraratchakaraniyakit samkhan nai phrabatsomdet phramongkutklaochaoyuhua* [The significant contributions of King Vajiravudh]. 8 vols. Bangkok: Khurusapha, 1968–1970.

Amphorn Tangseri. "Withesobai khong phrabatsomdet phrachunlachomklaochaoyuhua thimito maha-amnat yurop" [King Chulalongkorn's foreign policy toward the European powers]. M.A. thesis, Chulalongkorn University, 1980.

Anderson, Benedict. "The Idea of Power in Javanese Culture." In *Culture and Politics in Indonesia*, ed. Clair Holt. Ithaca: Cornell University Press, 1972.

———. Studies of the Thai State: The State of Thai Studies." In *The Study of Thailand: Analyses of Knowledge, Approaches, and Prospects in Anthropology, Art History, Economics, History and Political Science*, ed. Elizer B. Ayal. Papers in International Studies, Southeast Asian Series, no. 54. Athens: Ohio University, 1978.

———. *Imagined Communities: Reflections on the Origin and Spread of Nationalism.* 2nd ed. London: Verso, 1991.

Aphichat Thongyoo. *Watthanatham kap chumchon: thangluakmai khong nganphatthana* [Culture and local community: an alternative for development works]. Bangkok: Catholic Council for Development, 1984.

Ayusawa, Shintaro. "The Types of World Map Made in Japan's Age of National Isolation." *Imago Mundi* 10 (1953): 123–128.

Bagrow, Leo. *History of Cartography.* Revised by Robert A. Skelton. London: C. A. Watts & Co., 1964.

Barth, Fredrik, ed. *Ethnic Groups and Boundaries: The Social Organization of Cultural Difference.* Bergen: Universitetsforlaget; London: Allen & Unwin, 1969.

Batson, Benjamin, and Shimizu Hajime, eds. *The Tragedy of Wanit: A Japanese Account of Wartime Thai Politics.* Special Publication Series, no. 1. Singapore: Journal of Southeast Asian Studies, 1990.

Battye, Noel A. "The Military, Government, and Society in Siam, 1868–1910: Politics and Military Reform During the Reign of King Chulalongkorn." Ph.D. dissertation, Cornell University, 1974.

Beze, Claude de. *The 1688 Revolution in Siam.* Translated by E. W. Hutchinson. Hong Kong, 1968.

Boisselier, Jean. *Thai Painting.* Translated by Janet Seligman. Tokyo: Kodansha International, 1976.

Bonney, R. *Kedah 1771–1821: The Search for Security and Independence.* London: Oxford University Press, 1971.

Bowring, Sir John. *The Kingdom and People of Siam.* 2 vols. London, 1857. Reprint. Kuala Lumpur: Oxford University Press, 1969.

Bradley, Dan Beach. *Nangsu akkharaphithansap: Dictionary of the Siamese Language.* In Thai. Bangkok, 1873. Reprint. Bangkok: Khurusapha, 1971.

————. *Abstract of the Journal of Reverend Dan Beach Bradley, M.D., Medical Missionary in Siam 1835–1873.* Edited by George H. Feltus. Cleveland: Multigraph Department of the Pilgrim Church, 1936.

Bradley, William L. "Prince Mongkut and Jesse Caswell." *Journal of the Siam Society* 54, pt. 1 (Jan. 1966): 29–41.

————. *Siam Then: The Foreign Colony in Bangkok Before and After Anna.* Pasadena: William Carey Library, 1981.

Brailey, Nigel J. "Chiengmai and the Inception of an Administrative Centralization Policy in Siam." *South East Asian Studies* 11, no. 3 (Dec. 1973): 299–330 and no. 4 (Mar. 1974): 439–469.

Breazeale, Kennon, and Sanit Samuckkarn. *A Culture in Search of Survival: The Phuan of Thailand and Laos.* Monograph Series, no. 31. New Haven: Yale University Southeast Asia Studies, 1988.

Burghart, Richard. "The Formation of the Concept of Nation-State in Nepal." *Journal of Asian Studies* 44 (1984): 101–125.

The Burney Papers. 5 vols. in 6. Bangkok: Vajirana National Library, 1910–1914.

Chaen Patchusanon, Admiral. "Suriyupparakha temkhrat ph.s. 2411" [The full solar eclipse of 1868]. *Nawikkasat* 62, no. 11 (Nov. 1979): 124–141.

Chaiwat Satha-anan and Sombat Chanthornwong, eds. *Yumuangthai* [Living in Thailand]. Essays in honor of Professor Saneh Chamarik. Bangkok: Thammasat University Press, 1987.

Chaiyan Rajchagool. "The Social and State Formation in Siam 1855–1932." Ph.D. thesis, University of Manchester, 1984.

Chakkawanthipani. Bangkok: Fine Arts Department, 1980.

Chamroen Saengduangkhae. *Lokkathat chaothai phaktai thi prakot nai phlengklomdek* [The worldview of the Southern Thai as it appears in nursery rhymes]. Center for the

Promotion of Language and Culture of the Southern Thai Region. Songkhla: Sri Nakharinwirot University, 1978.

Chandler, David P. "Maps for the Ancestors: Sacralized Topography and Echoes of Angkor in Two Cambodian Texts." *Journal of the Siam Society* 64, pt. 2 (July 1976): 170–187.

———. *A History of Cambodia.* Westview Profiles. Nations of Contemporary Asia. Boulder: Westview Press, 1983.

Chandran Jeshuran. "The Anglo-French Declaration of January 1896 and the Independence of Siam." *Journal of the Siam Society* 28, pt. 2 (July 1970): 105–126.

———. *The Contest for Siam 1889–1902: A Study in Diplomatic Rivalry.* Kuala Lumpur: Penerbit Universiti Kebangsaan Malaysia, 1977.

Chariyawan Apornrat. "Panha khong ratthabanthai nai ratchasamai phrabatsomdet phrachunlachomklaochaoyuhua thikieokap khon-esia naibangkhap angkrit lae farangset" [Problems facing the Thai government in the reign of King Chulalongkorn concerning the Asian subjects of Britain and France]. M.A. (History) thesis, Chulalongkorn University, 1982.

Charnvit Kasetsiri. "Thai Historiography from Ancient Times to the Modern Period." In *Perceptions of the Past in Southeast Asia,* eds. Anthony Reid and David Marr. Asian Studies Association of Australia, Southeast Asia Publication Series, no. 4. Singapore: Heinemann Educational Books (Asia), 1979.

Charuwan Thammawat. *Lokkathat thangkanmuang chak wannakam isan* [Political perceptions from the literature of the northeast]. Publications of the Social Science Association of Thailand. Bangkok: Saengrungkanphim, 1980.

Chawi-ngam Macharoen. *Thongthai* [Thai flags]. Bangkok: Fine Arts Department, 1977.

Chirapha Phasitpratya. "Kansadetsawankhot khong phrabatsomdet phrachomklaochaoyuhua" [The death of King Mongkut]. *Warasanmanutsat* [Journal of Humanities] 2, no. 3 (July–Sept. 1971): 35–50.

Chiraporn Sathapanawatthana. *Wikrittakan r.s. 112* [The 1893 crisis]. Bangkok: Sri Nakharinwirot University (Prasanmit), 1980.

Chulalongkorn, King. "Samakhom supsuan khongboran nai prathetsayam" [The Antiquarian Society in Siam]. *Sinlapakorn* 12, no. 2 (July 1968): 42–46.

Commission for National Identity. *Ekkalak khong chat* [National identity]. Bangkok: Graphic Arts Publishing, 1983.

Cook, Nerida. "A Tale of Two City Pillars: Mongkut and Thai Astrology on the Eve of Modernization." In *Patterns and Illusions: Thai History and Thought,* eds. Gehan Wijeyewardene and E. C. Chapman. Canberra: the Richard Davis Fund and Department of Anthropology, Australian National University; Singapore: Institute of Southeast Asian Studies, 1992.

Crawfurd, John. *History of the Indian Archipelago.* 3 vols. Edinburgh, 1820.

———. *Journal of an Embassy from the Governor-General of India to the Courts of Siam and Cochin China.* 2 vols. 2nd ed. London, 1830. Oxford in Asia Historical Reprints. Kuala Lumpur: Oxford University Press, 1967.

———. *A Descriptive Dictionary of the Indian Islands and Adjacent Countries.* London, 1856. Oxford in Asia Historical Reprints. Kuala Lumpur: Oxford University Press, 1971.

The Crawfurd Papers. Bangkok: Vajiranana National Library, 1915. Oxford in Asia Historical Reprints. Kuala Lumpur: Oxford University Press, 1967.

Crosby, Sir Josiah. *Siam: The Crossroads.* London: Holis & Carter, ca. 1945.

Curzon, George N. "The Siamese Boundary Question." *Nineteenth Century* 28, no. 197 (July 1893): 34–55.

Damrong Rajanubhap, Prince. *Prachum phraniphon bettalet* [Collection of miscellaneous essays]. Bangkok: Khurusapha, 1961.

———. *Nithanborankhadi* [Historical anecdotes]. 13th printing. Bangkok: Bannakhan, 1966.

———. *Khwamsongcham* [Recollections]. Bangkok: Khlangwitthaya, 1974.

———. "Laksana kanpokkhrong prathetsayam tae boran" [The Siamese government in ancient times]. In *Prawattisat lae kanmuang* [History and politics]. A textbook for the general studies course Thai Civilization. Bangkok: Thammasat University, 1975.

———. *Sadaeng banyai phongsawadan sayam* [Lectures on Siam's history]. n.p., n.d.

Damrong Rajanubhap, Prince, and Rajasena, Phraya. *Thesaphiban* [The *thesaphiban* system of provincial administration]. Cremation volume for Phraya Atthakrawi-sunthorn (Sanguan Satarat). Bangkok: Fine Arts Department, 1960.

Dhaninivat, Prince. *Collected Articles by H. H. Prince Dhaninivat.* Bangkok: Siam Society, 1969.

East, W. Gordon, and Prescott, J. R. V. *Our Fragmented World: An Introduction to Political Geography.* New York: Macmillan, 1975.

Emmerson, Donald K. " 'Southeast Asia': What's in a Name." *Journal of Southeast Asian Studies* 15 (1984): 1–21.

Errington, Shelly. "The Place of Regalia in Luwu." In *Centers, Symbols, and Hierarchies,* ed. Lorraine Gesick. New Haven: Yale University, 1983.

———. *Meaning and Power in Southeast Asian Realm.* Princeton: Princeton University Press, 1989.

Fell, R. T. *Early Maps of South-East Asia.* Images of Asia Series. Singapore: Oxford University Press, 1988.

Feltus, George Haws. *Samuel Reynolds House of Siam, Pioneer Medical Missionary, 1847–1876.* New York: Revell, 1924. Translated into Thai anonymously as *Dr. renon hao mofarang samratchakan* [Dr. Reynolds House, a Western medical doctor in three reigns]. Bangkok: Christian Council of Thailand, Suriyaban, 1982.

Fine Arts Department, comp. *Prachum chotmaihet ruang suriyupparakha nai ratchakan thi 4 lae ruang ratchakan thi 4 songprachuan lae sawankhot* [Collected documents on the solar eclipse in the fourth reign and on the illness and death of King Mongkut]. Cremation volume for Luang Chamdoemphadetsuk. Bangkok, 1971.

———. *Khamchichaeng ruang kanchai phleng kiattiyot lae kret khwamru ruang dontri thai* [Guideline for the use of honorable songs and miscellaneous knowledge of Thai music]. Cremation volume for Sawang Phanthummasen. Bangkok, 1973.

Flood, E. Thadeus. "The 1940 Franco-Thai Border Dispute and Phibuun Songkhraam's Commitment to Japan." *Journal of Southeast Asian History* 10 (1969): 304–325.

Forbes, Andrew D. W. "The Struggle for Hegemony in the Nineteenth Century Laos: The Third Siamese Military Expedition to the Northeast (1885–1887)." In *Proceedings of the International Conference on Thai Studies, Australian National University, Canberra, 1987.* Vol. 3, pt. 1. Canberra, 1987.

Garnier, Francis. *La Cochinchine francaise en 1864.* Paris: Challamel aine, 1864.

Gawin Chutima. *The Rise and Fall of the Communist Party of Thailand (1973–1987).* Centre of South-East Asian Studies, Occasional Paper no. 12. Canterbury: University of Kent at Canterbury, 1990.

Geertz, Clifford. "The Integrative Revolution: Primordial Sentiments and Civil Politics in the New States." In *Old Societies and New States,* ed. Clifford Geertz. New York: Free Press, 1963.

Gesick, Lorraine. "Kingship and Political Integration in Traditional Siam 1767–1824." Ph.D. dissertation, Cornell University, 1976.

————, ed. *Centers, Symbols, and Hierarchies: Essays on the Classical States of Southeast Asia.* Southeast Asia Studies, Monograph Series, no. 26. New Haven: Yale University, 1983.

————. "Reading Landscape: Reflections on a Sacred Site in South Thailand." *Journal of the Siam Society* 73, pts. 1–2 (1985): 157–162.

————. *In the Land of Lady White Blood: Southern Thailand and the Meaning of History.* Ithaca: Cornell Southeast Asia Program, forthcoming.

Giddens, Anthony. *The Nation-State and Violence.* Contemporary Critique of Historical Materialism. Vol. 2. Cambridge, England: Polity Press, 1985.

Girling, John S. *Thailand: Society and Politics.* Ithaca: Cornell University Press, 1981.

"Giving in Asia—A Symposium." *Journal of Asian Studies* 46 (1987): 305–379.

Goldman, Minton F. "Franco-British Rivalry over Siam, 1896–1904." *Journal of Southeast Asian Studies* 3 (1972): 210–228.

Haas, Mary R. *Thai-English Student's Dictionary.* London: Oxford University Press, 1964.

Hagesteijn, Renee. *Circles of Kings: Political Dynamics in Early Continental Southeast Asia.* Dordrecht and Providence: Foris, 1989.

Hall, D. G. E., ed. *Historians of South East Asia.* London: Oxford University Press, 1961.

————. *Henry Burney: A Political Biography.* London: Oxford University Press, 1974.

————. *A History of South East Asia.* 4th ed. New York: St. Martin's Press, 1981.

Hall, Kenneth R., and Whitmore, John K., eds. *Explorations in Early Southeast Asia History: The Origins of Southeast Asian Statecraft.* Ann Arbor: Center for Southeast Asian Studies, University of Michigan, 1976.

Hawkes, Terrence. *Structuralism and Semiotics.* New Accent Series. London: Methuen, 1982.

Heine-Geldern, Robert. *Conceptions of State and Kingship in Southeast Asia.* Data Paper 18, Southeast Asia Program. Ithaca: Cornell University, 1956.

Hobart, Mark, and Taylor, Robert, eds. *Context, Meaning and Power in Southeast Asia.* Southeast Asia Program. Ithaca: Cornell University, 1986.

Hong Lysa. *Thailand in the Nineteenth Century: Evolution of the Economy and Society.* Singapore: Institute of Southeast Asian Studies, 1984.

Hutchinson, E. W. *Adventurers in Siam in the Seventeenth Century.* London, 1940.

Jackson, Peter. *Buddhism, Legitimation and Conflict: The Political Functions of Urban Thai Buddhism.* Singapore: Institute of Southeast Asian Studies, 1989.

[Johnson, W. G.] *Phumisat sayam (samrap rongrian thai)* [Geography of Siam (for Thai schools)]. Bangkok, 1900.

————. *Phumisat sayam (samrap chan prathom suksa)* [Geography of Siam (for primary schools)]. 4th ed. Bangkok: Department of Education, 1907.

Kanok Wongtra-ngan. *Khokhit chak krungsi-ayutthaya* [Lessons from the Ayudhya kingdom]. Office for the Promotion of National Identity, Secretariat Office of the Prime Minister. Bangkok, 1984.

Keates, J. S. *Understanding Maps.* New York: Wiley, 1982.

Kedourie, Elie. *Nationalism.* 3rd ed. London: Hutchinson, 1966.

Kennedy, Victor. "An Indigenous Early Nineteenth Century Map of Central and Northeast Thailand." In *In Memoriam Phya Anuman Rajadhon,* eds. Tej Bunnag and Michael Smithies. Bangkok: Siam Society, 1970.

Keyes, Charles F. *Isan: Regionalism in Northeastern Thailand.* Cornell Thailand Project Interim Report Series, no. 10. Southeast Asia Program, Data Paper 65. Ithaca: Cornell University, 1967.

―――. "Buddhist Pilgrimage Centers and the Twelve Year Cycle: Northern Thai Moral Orders in Space and Time." *History of Religion* 15 (1975): 71–89.

―――. "Political Crisis and Militant Buddhism in Contemporary Thailand." In *Religion and Legitimation of Power in Thailand, Laos and Burma,* ed. Bardwell L. Smith. Chambersburg, Pa.: Anima Books, 1978.

―――, ed. *Ethnic Adaptation and Identity: The Karen on the Thai Frontier with Burma.* Philadelphia: Institution of the Study of Human Issues, 1979.

―――. *Thailand: Buddhist Kingdom as Modern Nation-State.* Westview Profiles. Nations of Contemporary Asia. Boulder: Westview Press, 1987.

―――. "The Case of the Purloined Lintel: The Politics of a Khmer Shrine as a Thai National Heritage." In *National Identity and Its Defense: Thailand 1939–1984,* ed. Craig J. Reynolds. Monash Papers on Southeast Asia, no. 25. Melbourne: Aristoc Press, 1991.

Khachorn Sukhabhanij. "Thanandon phrai" [The Phrai status]. In *Prawattisat lae kanmuang* [History and politics]. A textbook for the general studies course Thai Civilization. Bangkok: Thammasat University Printing, 1975. Reprinted as a separate book with new introduction. Bangkok: Sri Nakharinwirot University (Prasanmit), 1976.

―――. *Khomun prawattisat samai bangkok* [Historical accounts of the Bangkok period]. Bangkok: Department of History, Sri Nakharinwirot University (Prasanmit), 1981.

Khaimuk Milinthalek et al. *Nangsu prachum phongsawadan: bannanithat lae datchani khonruang* [Abstracts of the Collected Chronicles with subject and title index]. Cremation volume for Nang Thepphusit (Mian Milinthalek). Bangkok: Fine Arts Department, 1977.

Khru ngoen [pseud.] *Phlengthai tamnaiprawat* [Thai songs: historical background]. Bangkok: Bannakit, 1981.

Kobkua Suwannathat-Pian. "Kankhian prawattisat baep chatniyom: phitcharana luang wichitwathakan" [Nationalist historiography: considering Luang Wichitwathakan]. *Warasanthammasat* [Journal of Thammasat University] 6, no. 1 (June–Sept. 1976): 149–180.

―――. "The Dhonburi-Bangkok Political Ideology and Its Effects upon Thai-Malay Relations 1767–1851." In *Proceedings of the International Conference on Thai Studies, Australian National University, Canberra, 1987.* Vol. 3, pt. 1. Canberra, 1987.

Kolacny, A. "Cartographic Information: A Fundamental Concept and Term in Modern Geography." *Cartographic Journal* 6, no. 1 (June 1969): 47–49.

Konthi Supphamongkol. *Kanwithesobai khong thai* [Thai foreign policy]. Bangkok: Thammasat University Press, 1984.

Kromkhotsanakan [Department of Public Relations]. *Khumu phonlamuang* [Handbook for citizens]. Bangkok: Aksonnit, 1936.

————. *Khetdaen khong rat* [The state's boundary]. Bangkok: Phanitsupphaphon Printing, 1940.

————. *Pramuan watthanatham haengchat* [A collection on national culture]. Bangkok, 1943.

Kullada Kesboonchoo. "Official Nationalism Under King Chulalongkorn." Paper presented at the International Conference on Thai Studies, Bangkok, August 1984.

————. "Official Nationalism Under King Vajiravudh." In *Proceedings of the International Conference on Thai Studies, Australian National University, Canberra, 1987*. Vol. 3, pt. 1. Canberra, 1987.

La Loubere, Simon de. *The Kingdom of Siam*. Oxford in Asia Historical Reprints. Kuala Lumpur: Oxford University Press, 1969.

Landes, David. *Revolution in Time: Clocks and the Making of the Modern World*. Cambridge: Harvard University Press, 1983.

La-o-thong Ammarinrat. "Kansongnakrian paisuksato tangprathet tangtae ph.s. 2411–2475" [Sponsorship of students studying abroad during 1868–1932]. M.A. thesis, Chulalongkorn University, 1979.

Leach, Edmund. *Political Systems of Highland Burma: A Study of Kachin Social Structure*. London School of Economics Monographs on Social Anthropology, no. 44. London, 1954. Reprint. London, 1970.

————. "The Frontiers of Burma." *Comparative Studies in Society and History* 3, no. 1 (Oct. 1960): 49–68.

————. *Genesis as Myth and Other Essays*. London: Jonathan Cape, 1969.

Lee Yong Leng. *The Razor's Edge: Boundaries and Boundary Disputes in Southeast Asia*. Research Notes and Discussion Papers, no. 15. Singapore: Institute of Southeast Asian Studies, 1980.

Lieberman, Victor. *Burmese Administrative Cycles: Anarchy and Conquest, c. 1580–1760*. Princeton: Princeton University Press, 1984.

Likhit Dhiravegin. "Nationalism and the State in Thailand." Paper for the Regional Workshop on Minorities in Buddhist Politics, Thai Studies Program, Chulalongkorn University, June 1985.

Lithai, King. *Traiphum phraruang* [Three worlds according to King Ruang]. Rev. ed. Bangkok: Fine Arts Department, 1983.

Lokkabanyat. Bangkok: Fine Arts Department, 1985.

Maha-ammattayathibodi (Seng), Phraya. *Kamnoet kromphaenthi* [Establishment of the Royal Survey Department]. Cremation volume for Phraya Maha-ammattayathibodi (Seng). Bangkok, 1956.

————. "Kamnoet kantham phaenthi nai prathetthai" [The birth of mapping in Thailand]. *Warasan phaenthi: chabap phiset* [Journal of Mapping: special issue]. Bangkok: Royal Survey Department, 1983.

Marr, David G., and Milner, A. C., eds. *Southeast Asia in the 9th to 14th Century*. Singapore: Institute of Southeast Asian Studies; Canberra: Research School of Pacific Studies, Australian National University, 1986.

Mauss, Marcel. *The Gift: Forms and Functions of Exchange in Archaic Societies*. New York: Norton Library, 1967.

McAleavy, Henry. *Black Flags in Vietnam*. London: Allen & Unwin, 1968.

McCarthy, James. "Siam." In *Proceedings of the Royal Geographic Society*. New Series 10 (Mar. 1888): 117–134.

———. *Surveying and Exploring in Siam*. London: John Murray, 1902.

[McCarthy, James] *An Englishman's Siamese Journal 1890–1893*. London, ca. 1895. Reprint. Bangkok: Siam Media International Books, n.d.

McFarland, George B. *Thai-English Dictionary*. Stanford: Stanford University Press, 1944.

McFarland, S. G. *An English-Siamese Dictionary*. Revised and enlarged by G. B. McFarland. Bangkok: American Presbyterian Mission Press, 1903.

Mills, J. V. "Chinese Coastal Maps." *Imago Mundi* 11 (1953): 151–168.

Mills, L. A. *British Malaya 1824–67*. Introduction by D. K. Bassett. London: Oxford University Press, 1966.

Moertono, Soemarsaid. *State and Statecraft in Old Java: A Study of the Later Mataram Period, 16th to 19th Century*. Monograph Series, no. 43. Modern Indonesia Project Publications. Ithaca: Cornell University, 1968.

Mom Rachothai. *Nirat london* [Poetry on the way to London]. Cremation volume for Chamnan Chipphiphop. Bangkok, 1962.

Mongkut, King. *Prachum prakat ratchakan thi 4* [Collected proclamations of the fourth reign]. 4 vols. Bangkok: Khurusapha, 1960–1961.

———. *Phraboromrachathibai athikkamat athikkawan lae pakkhananawithi* [Royal explanations of the intercalated months and days and methods of calculating phases of the month]. Bangkok: Mahamakut Royal College, 1968.

———. *Prachum phraratchaniphon nai ratchakan thi 4 muat borankhadi* [Collected writings of King Mongkut: history section]. Cremation volume for Phra Thammadilok. Bangkok, 1973.

———. *Phraratchahatthalekha phrabatsomdet phrachomklaochaoyuhua* [Royal correspondence of King Mongkut]. Bangkok: Mahamakut Royal College, 1978.

Monkhouse, F. J. *A Dictionary of Geography*. London: Edward Arnold, 1965.

Moor, J. H. *Notices of the Indian Archipelago and Adjacent Countries*. Singapore, 1837. Reprint. London: Frank Cass & Co., 1968.

Morell, David, and Chai-anan Samudavanija. *Political Conflict in Thailand: Reform, Reaction, Revolution*. Cambridge, Mass.: Oelgeschlager, Gunn & Hain, 1981.

Mosel, James N. "A Poetic Translation from the Siamese: Prince Damrong's Reply in Verse to Rama V." *Journal of the Siam Society* 47, pt. 1 (Jan. 1959): 103–111.

Mouhot, Henri. *Diary: Travels in the Central Parts of Indo-China (Siam), Cambodia, and Laos during 1858–1861*. 2 vols. London, 1864.

Muir, Richard. *Modern Political Geography*. London: Macmillan, 1975.

Murashima, Eiji. "The Origin of Modern Official State Ideology in Thailand." *Journal of Southeast Asian Studies* 19 (1988): 80–96.

Nakamura, Hiroshi "Old Chinese World Maps Preserved by the Koreans." *Imago Mundi* 4 (1947): 3–22.

Nakhon Phannarong. "Kancheracha lae khotoklong rawang ratthaban sayam kap ratthaban angkrit kieokap huamuang chaidaen lannathai lae phama samai phrabatsomdet phrachunlachomklaochaoyuhua raya ph.s. 2428–2438" [Negotiations and agreements between the Siamese and British governments concerning the frontier towns between Lanna and Burma in the reign of King Chulalongkorn during 1885–1895]. M.Ed. thesis, Education College (Prasanmit), 1973.

Nangnopphamat ru tamrap thao sichulalak [Lady Nopphamat or a treatise of Thao Sichulalak]. Cremation volume for Thompat Chatamara. Bangkok, 1963.

Narathipphongpraphan, Major General Prince. *Witthayawannakam* [A literature for knowledge]. Bangkok: Phraephitthaya, 1971.

Naritsaranuwattiwong, Prince. *Banthuk khwamru ruangtangtang* [Notes on diverse knowledge]. 5 vols. Bangkok: Social Science Association of Thailand, 1963.

Narongwichit, Phra [Luan na Nakhon]. *Chotmaihet r.s. 112* [Notes on the year 1893]. Cremation volume for Phra Aphirak-amphonsathan (Thuk Khemasunthon). Bangkok, 1940.

Natthawut Sutthisongkhram. *Somdetchaophraya borommahasisuriyawong akkharamahasenabodi* [Sisuriyawong: the great minister]. 2 vols. Bangkok: Phraephitthaya, 1973.

————. *Phraprawat lae ngansamkhan khong kromluang wongsathiratsanit* [A biography of Prince Wongsathiratsanit and his important contributions]. Bangkok: Rungruangsan, 1981.

Natthawut Sutthisongkhram and Banchoed Inthuchanyong. *Phrachaoborommawongthoe kromluang prachaksinlapakhom* [Prince Prachaksinlapakhom]. Bangkok: Watcharin Publishing, 1980.

Neale, Frederick A. *Narrative of a Residence at the Capital of the Kingdom of Siam.* London: Office of the National Illustrated Library, 1852.

Nithi Aeusrivongse. *Kanmuang thai samai phra narai* [Thai politics in the reign of King Narai]. Bangkok: Thai Khadi Research Institute, 1980.

————. *Prawattisat rattanakosin nai phraratchaphongsawadan ayutthaya* [Bangkok's history in the royal chronicles of Ayudhya]. Bangkok: Bannakit, 1984.

————. *Pakkai lae bairua* [A quill and a sail]. Bangkok: Ammarin Printing, 1984.

————. *Kanmuang thai samai phrachao krung thonburi* [Thai politics in the reign of King Taksin]. Bangkok: Sinlapawatthanatham Publishing, 1986.

————. "Nakhonsithammarat nai ratcha-anachak ayutthaya" [Nakhonsithammarat in the kingdom of Ayudhya]. In *Yumuangthai,* eds. Chaiwat Satha-anan and Sombat Chanthornwong. Bangkok, 1987.

Orawan Nopdara. "Kanprapprung kanpokkhrong lae khwamkhatyaeng kap farangset nai monthonudon rawang ph.s. 2436–2453" [The reform of administration and conflicts with France in Udon Province during 1893–1910]. M.Ed. thesis, Sri Nakharinwirot University (Prasanmit), 1977.

Osborne, Milton E. *River Road to China: The Mekhong River Expedition 1866–1873.* London: George Allen & Unwin, 1975.

Osborne, Milton, and Wyatt, David K. "The Abridged Cambodian Chronicle: A Thai Version of Cambodian History." *France-Asie* 22, no. 193 (1968): 189–197.

Pallegoix, D. J. B. *Dictionarium linguage Thai sive Siamensis interpretatione Latina, Gallica et Anglica.* (With the title in Thai: *Sappha-phachana phasathai.*) Paris, 1854.

————. *Siamese French English Dictionary.* (With the title in Thai: *Sariphot phasathai.*) Extended and revised from Pallegoix's *Dictionarium* by Reverend J. L. Vey. Bangkok: Printing Office of the Catholic Mission, 1896.

Panya Borisut. *Lokkathat khong khonthai wikhro chak wannakhadi khamson samai sukhothai* [The worldview of Thai people: an analysis of teaching literature from the Sukhothai period]. Bangkok: Odeon Store, 1980.

Pavie, Auguste. *Mission Pavie Indochine 1879–1895: geographie et voyages.* 7 vols. Paris: E. Leroux, 1900–1919.

Pharadi Mahakhan. *Prawattisat thai samaimai* [History of Modern Thailand]. Department of History, Sri Nakharinwirot University (Bangsaen). Bangkok: Sinlapabannakhan, 1983.

Phayon Thimcharoen. "Naewphromdaen rawang sayam kap indochin khong farangset" [The boundaries between Siam and French Indochina]. *Warasan phaenthi* [Journal of Mapping] 26, no. 3 (Jan.–Mar. 1984): 5–29 and no. 4 (Apr.–June 1984): 64–93.

Phillimore, R. H. "An Early Map of the Malay Peninsula." *Imago Mundi* 13 (1956): 175–178.

Photchananukrom chabap ratchabandityasathan [Thai dictionary: Royal Institute edition]. Bangkok, 1950.

Phraratchaphongsawadan chabap phraratchahatthalekha [The royal chronicle: Royal Autograph recension]. 2 vols. Bangkok: Khlangwitthaya, 1973.

Phraratchaphongsawadan krung si-ayutthaya chabap chakkraphatdiphong (chat) [The royal chronicle of Ayudhya: Chakkraphatdiphong (Chat) recension]. 2 vols. Bangkok: Khurusapha, 1961.

Phraratchaphongsawadan krung si-ayutthaya chabap phan chanthanumat [The royal chronicle of Ayudhya: Phan Chanthanumat recension]. 2 vols. *(PP* 38/64 and 39/64.) Bangkok: Khurusapha, 1969.

Phraratchaphongsawadan krung si-ayutthaya chabap phra phanarat [The royal chronicle of Ayudhya: Phra Phanarat recension]. Bangkok: Khlangwitthaya, 1971.

Phua phaendin thai [For the Thai land]. 3 vols. Office of General Information, Supreme Command of the Armed Force, Ministry of Defense, Bangkok, 1986–.

Piyachat Pitawan. *Rabopphrai nai sangkhomthai ph.s. 2411–2453* [The Phrai system in Thai society 1868–1910]. Bangkok: Thammasat University Press, 1983.

Pornpirom Iamtham. "Social Origin and the Development of the Communist Party of Thailand." Master of Development Studies dissertation, Institute of Social Studies, The Hague, 1982.

Pracha pasannathammo, Phra. "Than phuutthathat kap kanpatiwat watthanatham" [Buddhadasa Bhikku and cultural revolution]. *Pacharaysan* 10, no. 1 (1983): 51–81.

Prachum phongsawadan [Collected chronicles]. 50 vols. Khurusapha edition. Bangkok: Khurusapha, 1963–1970.

Pra-onrat Buranamat. *Luang wichitwathakan kap lakhon prawattisat* [Luang Wichitwathakan and historical plays]. Bangkok: Thammasat University Press, 1985.

Prasert-aksonnit, Khun [Phae Talalak] et al. *Photchananukrom lamdap lae plae sap thichai nai nangsu thai* [Dictionary of vocabularies used in Thai literature]. Bangkok: Department of Education, 1891.

Prayoon Uluchata [Phluluang]. "Phrachomklao kap horasat thai" [King Mongkut and Thai astrology]. *Sangkhomsatparithat* 6, no. 2 (Sept.–Nov. 1968): 43–51.

———. *Horasat* [Astrology]. Bangkok: Odeon Store, 1973.

Prescott, J. R. V. *Map of Mainland Asia by Treaty.* Carlton: Melbourne University Press, 1975.

———. *Frontiers of Asia and Southeast Asia.* Carlton: Melbourne University Press, 1977.

———. *Boundaries and Frontiers.* London: Croom Helm, 1978.

Pridi Bhanomyong. "Khwampenma khong chu 'prathetsayam' kap 'prathetthai'" [Historical background of the names "Siam" and "Thailand"]. In *Thai ru sayam* [Thailand or Siam], ed. Suphot Dantrakul. Nonthaburi (Thailand): Santitham, 1985.

Proceedings of the International Conference on Thai Studies, Australian National University, Canberra, 1987. 3 vols. Canberra: Australian National University, 1987.

Prudhisan Jumbala. "Interest and Pressure Groups." In *Government and Politics of Thailand,* ed. Somsakdi Xuto. Kuala Lumpur: Oxford University Press, 1987.

Pruess, James B. "Merit-Seeking in Public: Buddhist Pilgrimage in Northeastern Thailand." *Journal of the Siam Society* 64, pt. 1 (Jan. 1976): 169–206.

Prungsri Vallibhotama et al., eds. *Sarupphon kansammana ruang traiphum phra ruang* [Summary of the seminar on Traiphum Phra Ruang]. Published on the occasion of the celebration of the 700th year of Thai script. Bangkok: Fine Arts Department, 1983.

Rai-ngan kansammana ruang ekkalak khong chat kap kanphatthana [Report of the seminar on national identity and development]. Commission for National Identity, Office of the Prime Minister. Bangkok, 1985.

Ramakian. 2 vols. Bangkok: Khlangwitthaya, 1964.

Rawi Bhawilai. "Suriyupparakha 18 singhakhom 2411" [The eclipse on 18 August 1868]. *Sangkhomsatparithat* 6, no. 2 (Sept.–Nov. 1968): 26–34.

Reid, Anthony, and Marr, David, eds. *Perceptions of the Past in Southeast Asia.* Asian Studies Association of Australia, Southeast Asia Publication Series, no. 4. Singapore: Heinemann Educational Books (Asia), 1979.

Renard, Ronald D. "The Delineation of the Kayah States Frontiers with Thailand: 1809–1894." *Journal of Southeast Asian Studies* 18 (1987): 81–92.

Reynolds, Craig J. "The Buddhist Monkhood in Nineteenth Century Thailand." Ph.D. dissertation, Cornell University, 1973.

————. "Buddhist Cosmography in Thai History with Special Reference to Nineteenth-Century Culture Change." *Journal of Asian Studies* 35 (1976): 203–220.

————. "Religious Historical Writing and the Legitimation of the First Bangkok Reign." In *Perceptions of the Past in Southeast Asia,* eds. Anthony Reid and David Marr. Singapore: Heinemann Educational Books (Asia), 1979.

————. "The Plot of Thai History: Theory and Practice." In *Patterns and Illusions: Thai History and Thought,* eds. Gehan Wijeyewardene and E. C. Chapman. Canberra: the Richard Davis Fund and Department of Anthropology, Australian National University; Singapore: Institute of Southeast Asian Studies, 1992.

————. *Thai Radical Discourse: The Real Face of Thai Feudalism Today.* Ithaca: Cornell Southeast Asia Program, 1987.

Reynolds, Craig J. and Hong, Lysa. "Marxism in Thai Historical Studies." *Journal of Asian Studies* 43 (1983): 77–104.

Reynolds, Frank E. "Buddhism as Universal Religion and as Civic Religion: Some Observations on a Recent Tour of Buddhist Centers in Central Thailand." In *Religion and Legitimation of Power in Thailand, Laos and Burma,* ed. Bardwell L. Smith. Chambersburg, Pa.: Anima Books, 1978.

Reynolds, Frank E., and Reynolds, Mani B. *Three Worlds According to King Ruang: A Thai Buddhist Cosmology.* Berkeley: University of California Press, 1982.

Robinson, Arthur H., and Petchenik, Barbara B. *The Nature of Maps.* Chicago: University of Chicago Press, 1976.

Rong Sayamanonda. *A History of Thailand.* Bangkok: Thaiwatthanaphanit, 1977.

"Royal Survey Department Siam: A Retrospect." In [*Journal of Mapping: Special issue*]: 18–26.

Royal Thai Survey Department. *Wiwatthanakan thang phaenthi nai prathetthai* [Development of mapping in Thailand]. A booklet for the Ministry of Defense exhibition for the bicentenary of Bangkok. Bangkok, 1982.

————. *Warasan phaenthi: chabap phiset* [Journal of mapping: special issue] 24–25 (July 1981–June 1983).

————. *Thiraluk khroprop wansathapana 100 pi kromphaenthi thahan 2528* [Commemoration volume for the centenary of the foundation of the Royal Thai Survey Department 1985]. Bangkok, 1985.

Sack, Robert D. *Human Territoriality: Its Theory and History.* Cambridge, N.Y.: Cambridge University Press, 1986.

Said, Edward. *Orientalism.* London: Routledge & Kegan Paul, 1978.

Salwidhannidhes, Major Luang. *Tamra phichika-phumisat* [A text on physical geography]. Bangkok: Ministry of Defense, 1918.

Salwidhannidhes, Lt. Gen. Phraya. "Study of Early Cartography in Thailand." *Journal of the Siam Society* 50, pt. 2 (Dec. 1962): 81–89.

Sa-nga Luchaphatthanaphon, ed. *Wikrittakan ekkalakthai* [The crisis of Thai identity]. Bangkok: Pacharayasan, 1981.

Sangkhomsat chabap lokkathat chaolanna [Journal of social science: on the worldview of Lanna people] 6, no. 2 (Oct. 1983–Mar. 1984).

Sa-nguan Ankhong. *Singraek nai muangthai* [First things in Thailand]. 3 vols. Rev. ed. Bangkok: Phraephitthaya, 1971.

Santisuk Sophonsiri. "Ratthai kap chakkrawatniyom" [The Thai state and imperialism]. *Pacharayasan* 12, no. 2 (Mar.–Apr. 1985): 15–35.

Sao Saimuang Mangrai. *Shan States and the British Annexation.* Southeast Asia Program, Data Paper 57. Ithaca: Cornell University, 1965.

Saowapha Phaithayawat. "Lokkathat khong khonthai samai ton rattanakosin 2325–2416" [The worldview of Thai people in the early Bangkok period]. *Warasan prawattisat* [Journal of history] 7, no. 1 (Jan.–Apr. 1982): 1–41.

Sarasin Viraphol. *Tribute and Profit: Sino-Siamese Trade 1652–1853.* Cambridge, Mass.: Harvard University Press, 1977.

Sawan Suwannachot. *Prathetthai kap panha muang chanthaburi lae trat thi farangset yutkhrong rawangpi ph.s. 2436–2449* [Thailand and the problems of Chanthaburi and Trad under the French occupation of 1893–1906]. Bangkok: Teacher Training Department, 1976.

Seksan Prasertkul. Review of *Thailand: Society and Politics,* by John Girling. (In Thai.) *Aksonsat (Sinlapakorn University)* 6, nos. 1–2 (1983): 399–406.

Shorto, H. L. "A Mon Genealogy of Kings: Observation on Nidana Arambhakatha." In *Historians of South East Asia,* ed. D. G. E. Hall. Oxford: Oxford University Press, 1961.

————. "The 32 Myos in the Medieval Mon Kingdom." *Bulletin of the School of Oriental and African Studies* 26 (1963): 572–591.

————. "The Dewatau Sotapan: A Mon Prototype of the 37 Nats." *Bulletin of the School of Oriental and African Studies* 30 (1967): 127–141.

Sirilak Sakkriangkrai, ed. *Phraya suriyanuwat (koet bunnak) naksetthasat khonraek khong muangthai* [Phraya Suriyanuwat (Koed Bunnak): the first economist of Thailand]. Bangkok: Thaiwatthanaphanit, 1980.

Sit But-in. *Lokkathat chaothai lanna* [The worldview of Lanna Thai people]. Chiangmai: Chiangmai Book Center, 1980.

Smith, Bardwell L., ed. *Religion and Legitimation of Power in Thailand, Laos and Burma.* Chambersburg, Pa.: Anima Books, 1978.

Smith, Samuel J. *A Comprehensive Anglo-Siamese Dictionary.* (With the Thai title *Khamphi sappha-photchananuyok.*) Bangkok: Bangkholaem Press, 1899.

Solomon, Robert L. "Boundary Concepts and Practices in Southeast Asia." *World Politics* 23 (1970): 1–23.

Somjai Phairotthirarat. "The Historical Writings of Chao Phraya Thiphakorawong." Ph.D. dissertation, University of Northern Illinois, 1983.

Somkiat Wanthana. "Rat somburanayasit nai sayam 2435–2475" [The absolutist state in Siam 1892–1932]. Paper presented at the annual conference of the Social Science Association of Thailand, Bangkok, 1982.

―――. "The Politics of Modern Thai Historiography." Ph.D. dissertation, Monash University, 1986.

Somsakdi Xuto, ed. *Government and Politics of Thailand*. Kuala Lumpur: Oxford University Press, 1987.

Srisuporn Chuangsakul. "Khwamplianplaeng khong khanasong: suksa karani thammayuttikanikai (ph.s. 2368–2464)" [Development of the *sangha*: the case of the Thammayut sect (1825–1921)]. M.A. thesis, Chulalongkorn University, 1987.

Sternstein, Larry. "An Historical Atlas of Thailand." *Journal of the Siam Society* 52, pt. 1 (Apr. 1964): 7–20.

―――. "A Catalogue of Maps of Thailand in the Museum of the Royal Thai Survey Department, Bangkok." *Journal of the Siam Society* 56, pt. 1 (Jan. 1968): 47–99.

―――. *Portrait of Bangkok*. Bangkok: Bangkok Metropolitan Administration, 1982.

―――. " 'Low' Maps of Siam." *Journal of the Siam Society* 73, pt. 1 (1985): 132–156.

―――. "Low's Description of the Siamese Empire in 1824." *Journal of the Siam Society* 78, pt. 1 (1990): 9–34.

Sternstein, Larry, and Black, John. "A Note on Three Polo Maps." In *Felicitation Volumes of Southeast Asian Studies Presented to His Highness Prince Dhaninivat Kromamun Bidyalabh Bridhyakorn*. Vol. 2. Bangkok: Siam Society, 1965.

Streckfuss, David. "Creating 'The Thai': The Emergence of Indigenous Nationalism in Neo-colonial Siam 1850–1980." M.A. thesis, University of Wisconsin-Madison, 1987.

Suebsaeng Phrombun "Sino-Siamese Tributary Relations, 1282–1853." Ph.D. dissertation, University of Wisconsin-Madison, 1971.

Sulak Sivaraksa. "Chotmai chak wako" [A letter from Wako]. *Sangkhomsatparithat* 6, no. 2 (1968): 36–41.

―――. *Religion and Development*. Bangkok: Thai Inter-Religious Commission for Development, 1981.

―――. *Siam in Crisis*. 2nd ed. Bangkok: Thai Inter-Religious Commission for Development, 1990.

―――. *Seeds of Peace: A Buddhist Vision for Renewing Society*. Foreword by H.H. The Dalai Lama. Preface by Thich Nhat Hanh. Berkeley: Parallax Press, 1992.

Sumalee Weerawong, Lt. Comm., trans. "Muangthai plai samai ayutthaya" [Siam in the late Ayudhya period]. From *Modern History of the Present State of All Nations,* vol. 1 (by Salmon), ca. 1724. *Warasan phaenthi* [Journal of mapping] 27, no. 3 (Jan.–Mar. 1985): 99–111 and no. 4 (Apr.–June 1985): 60–70.

Sunait Chutintaranond. "Cakravatin: the Ideology of Traditional Warfare in Siam and Burma, 1548–1605." Ph.D. dissertation, Cornell University, 1990.

Suphaphan na Bangchang. "Wannakam lokkasat nai phutthasatsana therawat" [The literature on cosmology in Theravada Buddhism]. Paper presented at the conference on the Literature on Cosmology and the Proverbs of Phra Ruang, Graduate Program, Department of Thai Language, Chulalongkorn University, 1984.

Surasakmontri, Field Marshal Chaophraya. *Prawatkan khong chomphon chaophraya surasakmontri* [Autobiography of Field Marshal Chaophraya Surasakmontri]. 4 vols. Bangkok: Khurusapha, 1961.

Sutthiwong Phongphaibun, ed. *Lokkathat thai phaktai* [The worldview of the Southern Thai]. Songkhla: Sri Nakharinwirot University, 1978.

———. *Rai-ngan kanwichai phutthasatsana thaep lumthalesap songkhla fangtawan-ok samai krung si-ayutthaya* [Research report on Buddhism along the eastern bank of Songkhla Lagoon in the Ayudhya period]. Songkhla: Southern Thai Studies Institute, Sri Nakharinwirot University (Songkhla), 1980.

Suwit Thirasasawat. *Khwamsamphan thai-farangset r.s. 112–126: kansia dindaen fangkhwa maenamkhong* [Franco-Thai relations 1893–1907: loss of the right bank of the Mekhong]. Bangkok: Sri Nakharinwirot University (Prasanmit), 1980.

Swearer, Donald. "Sulak Sivaraksa's Buddhist Vision for Renewing Society." *Crossroads* 6, no. 2 (1991): 17–57.

Tambiah, S. J. "The Galactic Polity: The Structure of Traditional Kingdoms in Southeast Asia." *Annals of the New York Academy of Sciences* 293 (15 July 1977): 69–97.

———. *World Conqueror and World Renouncer.* Cambridge: Cambridge University Press, 1976.

Tej Bunnag. "Kanpokkhrong baep thesaphiban pen rabop patiwat ru wiwatthanakan" [Was the *thesaphiban* provincial administration a revolution or evolution?]. *Sangkhomsatparithat* 4, no. 3 (1966).

———. *Provincial Administration of Siam 1892–1915.* Kuala Lumpur: Oxford University Press, 1977.

———. *Khabot r.s. 121* [The 1902 rebellions]. Bangkok: Foundation for Textbook Projects in Social Science and Humanities, 1981.

Tej Bunnag and Smithies, Michael, eds. *In Memoriam Phya Anuman Rajadhon.* Bangkok: Siam Society, 1970.

Terwiel, B. J. "Muang Thai and the World: Changing Perspectives During the Third Reign." Paper presented at the seminar on Asia: A Sense of Place, Canberra, Australian National University, 1986.

Thai Khadi Research Institute. "Mo bratle kap sangkhom thai" [Dr. Bradley and Thai society]. Papers for the conference on Dr. Bradley. Bangkok: Thammasat University, 1985.

Thak Chaloemtiarana, ed. *Thai Politics: Extracts and Documents 1932–1957.* Bangkok: Social Science Association of Thailand, 1978.

Thamrongsak Phetlert-anan. "Kanriakrong dindaen khun ph.s. 2483" [Demand for the return of territories in 1940]. *Samutsangkhomsat* 12, nos. 3–4 (Feb.–July 1990): 28–65.

Thamsook Numnonda. "Negotiations Regarding the Cession of Siamese Malay States 1907–1909." *Journal of the Siam Society* 55, pt. 2 (July 1967): 227–235.

———. *Thailand and the Japanese Presence 1941–1945.* Singapore: Institute of Southeast Asian Studies, 1977.

Thawi Muktharakosa. *Phramahathiraratchao* [King Vajiravudh]. n.p., n.d.

Thepphasatsathit, Phraya. *Phumisat lem 1* [Geography book I]. Department of Education. Bangkok: Aksonnit Printing, 1902.

———. *Nangsu an phumisat lem 2* [Geography book II]. Department of Education. Bangkok: Aksonnit Printing, 1904.

Thiphakorawong, Chaophraya. *Phraratchaphongsawadan krung rattanakosin ratchakan thi 3* [Royal chronicle of the third reign of Bangkok]. 2 vols. Bangkok: Khurusapha, 1961.

———. *Phraratchaphongsawadan krung rattanakosin ratchakan thi 4* [Royal chronicle of the fourth reign of Bangkok]. 2 vols. Bangkok: Khurusapha, 1961.

———. *Nangsu sadaeng kitchanukit* [A book explaining various things]. Khurusapha edition. Bangkok: Khurusapha, 1971.

Thongbai Taengnoi. *Phaenthi phumisat prayok matthayomsuksa tonton lae tonplai* [Geographical atlas for junior and senior high school]. 23rd printing. Bangkok: Thaiwatthanaphanit, 1986.

Thongchai Winichakul. "Siam Mapped: A History of the Geo-body of Siam." In *Proceedings of the International Conference on Thai Studies, Australian National University, Canberra, 1987*. Vol. 1, Canberra: Australian National University, 1987.

———. "Siam Mapped: A History of the Geo-body of Siam." Ph.D. dissertation, University of Sydney, 1988.

———. "Phurai nai prawattisat thai: karani phra mahathammaracha" [Villain in Thai history—the case of King Mahathammaracha of Ayudhya. In *Thai Khadi Suksa*, eds. Kanchanee La-ongsri et al. Bangkok: Ammarin Printing, 1990.

Toem Wiphakphotchanakit. *Prawattisat isan* [History of the northeast]. 2 vols. Bangkok: Social Science Association of Thailand, 1970.

Traditional and Changing Thai World View. Southeast Asian Studies Program (Singapore) and Social Research Institute, Chulalongkorn University. Bangkok, 1985.

Turton, Andrew, et al. *Thailand: Roots of Conflict*. Nottingham: Spokeman, 1978.

———. "Limits of Ideological Domination and the Formation of Social Consciousness." In *History and Peasant Consciousness in South East Asia*, eds. Andrew Turton and Shigeharu Tanabe. Senri Ethnological Studies, no. 13. Osaka: National Museum of Ethnology, 1984.

Udomsombat, Luang. *Chotmai luang udomsombat* [Letters of Luang Udomsombat]. Preface by Prince Damrong. Cremation volume for Phra Rattanathatchamuni. Bangkok, 1962.

Uppakitsinlapasan, Phraya. *Chumnum niphon khong o.n.g.* [Collected writings of Phraya Uppakitsinlapasan]. Bangkok: Khurusapha, 1964.

Van Dyke, J. W. [Wandai]. *Phumanithet* [Geography]. Phetchaburi, 1874.

Vella, Walter F. *Siam Under Rama III 1824–1851*. New York: Association for Asian Studies, 1957.

———. *Chaiyo! King Vajiravudh and the Development of Thai Nationalism*. Honolulu: University of Hawaii Press, 1978.

Vickery, Michael. "A Note on the Date of the Traibhumikatha." *Journal of the Siam Society* 62, pt. 2 (July 1974): 275–284.

———. "The Lion Prince and Related Remarks on Northern History." *Journal of the Siam Society*. 64, pt. 1 (Jan. 1976): 326–377.

Wachirayanwarorot, Prince Patriarch. *Thetsana phraratchaprawat phrabatsomdet phra paramentharamahamongkut phrachomklaochaoyuhua* [Sermon on the royal biography of King Mongkut]. Cremation volume for Prince Thiwakonwongprawat. Bangkok, 1957.

———. *Pramuan phraniphon—prawattisat borankhadi* [Collected works—history]. Bangkok: Mahamakut Royal College, 1971.

Wannarat, Somdet Phra. *Sangkhitiyawong* [Chronicle of the Buddhist councils]. Trans-

lated by Phraya Pariyattithamthada (Phae Talalak). Cremation volume for Prince Pet-
chabun-intharachai. Bangkok, 1923.

Warunee Osatharom. "Kansuksa nai sangkhomthai ph.s. 2411–2475" [Education in
Thai society 1868–1932]. M.A. thesis, Chulalongkorn University, 1981.

Wenk, Klaus. *Thailandische Miniaturmalereien nach einer Handschrift der indischen Kunstabteilung der staatlichen Museen Berlin.* Wiesbaden: Franz Steiner, 1965.

———. "Zu einer 'Landkarte' Sued- und Ostasiens." In *Felicitation Volumes of Southeast
Asian Studies Presented to His Highness Prince Dhaninivat Kromamun Bidyalabh Bridhyakorn.* Vol. 1. Bangkok: Siam Society, 1965.

———. *The Restoration of Thailand Under Rama I 1782–1809.* Tucson: University of Ari-
zona Press, 1968.

Wheatley, Paul. *The Golden Khersonese: Studies in the Historical Geography of the Malay Peninsula Before A.D. 1500.* Kuala Lumpur: University of Malaya Press, 1961.

White, Hayden. *Metahistory: The Historical Imagination in Nineteenth Century Europe.* Baltimore: Johns Hopkins University Press, 1973.

———. *Tropics of Discourse.* Baltimore: Johns Hopkins University Press, 1978.

Wichitwathakan, Luang. *Wichitsan* [Selected works of Luang Wichitwathakan]. 5 vols.
Bangkok: Mongkol Printing, 1965–1966.

Winai Pongsripian. "Traditional Thai Historiography and Its Nineteenth Century
Decline." Ph.D. dissertation, University of Bristol, 1983.

———, ed. *Panha nai prawattisatthai* [Problems in Thai history]. Bulletin of the Commission for the Correction of Thai History, Office of the Prime Minister, vol. 1, no. 1.
Bangkok: Office of the Prime Minister Publishing House, 1987.

Wolters, O. W. *History, Culture, and Region in Southeast Asian Perspectives.* Singapore:
Institute of Southeast Asian Studies, 1982.

Woodward, David, ed. *History of Cartography.* Vol. 2. Chicago: University of Chicago
Press, forthcoming.

Wright, Michael. "Khonboran mong phumisat lok" [Ancient people perceived the
world's geography]. *Sinlapawatthanatham* [Arts and culture] 6, no. 3 (Jan. 1985):
90–96.

———. "Phaenthi boran" [Ancient maps]. *Sinlapawatthanatham* 7, no. 2 (Dec. 1985):
46–48.

Wutthichai Munlasin, ed. *Monthon thesaphiban: wikhroh priapthiap* [The *thesaphiban* provincial administration: comparative analysis]. Bangkok: Social Science Association of
Thailand, 1981.

Wyatt, David K. *Politics of Reform in Thailand: Education in the Reign of King Chulalongkorn.* New Haven: Yale University Press, 1969.

———. "The 'Subtle Revolution' of King Rama I of Siam." In *Moral Order and the
Question of Change: Essays on Southeast Asian Thought.* Southeast Asia Studies, Monograph Series, no. 24. New Haven: Yale University, 1982.

———. *A Short History of Thailand.* New Haven: Yale University Press, 1984.

Yuangrat Wedel. *The Thai Radicals and the Communist Party: Interaction of Ideology and
Nationalism in the Forest, 1975–1980.* Singapore: Maruzen Asia, 1983.

Yuyangthai [Living as Thai]. Radio and television scripts of the programs of the same
title. Bangkok: Project on the Dissemination of Thai Identity, Ministry of Education, 1978–1979; Bangkok: Commission for National Identity, Office of the Prime
Minister, 1981–.

Index

About the Author

As a prominent leader of the student movement in Thailand in the 1970s, Thongchai Winichakul was arrested and charged with being a communist, a rebel, and killing policemen in the massacre of student demonstrators at Thammasat University in 1976. The case was dropped in the amnesty of 1978. He has since turned to academic life. He received his B.A. in history from Thammasat University, Bangkok, in 1981, and his Ph.D. from the University of Sydney in 1988. He returned to teach at Thammasat for three years. He is currently assistant professor of Southeast Asian history at the University of Wisconsin in Madison. This is his first book.

Production Notes

Composition and paging were done on the
Quadex Composing System and typesetting
on the Compugraphic 8400 by the design
and production staff of University of
Hawaii Press.

The text typeface is Bembo and the
display typeface is Schneidler.

Offset presswork and binding were done by
The Maple-Vail Book Manufacturing Group.
Text paper is Glatfelter Offset Smooth,
basis 50.